PHILOSOPHY

FOR A TIME OF CRISIS

ADRIENNE KOCH is at present Associate Professor of History and Chairman of American Studies at the University of California, Berkeley. She received her B.A. from New York University, and her M.A. and Ph.D. from Columbia University, where her doctoral dissertation on "The Philosophy of Thomas Jefferson" was awarded the Woodbridge Prize in Philosophy. Miss Koch received two Guggenheim Fellowships in 1943 and 1944, and she later held grants from the Carnegie and Rockefeller foundations. Miss Koch was formerly Chairman of Humanities at New York University, Associate Professor of Philosophy at Tulane University, and Lecturer in American Political Theory at the New School for Social Research.

PHILOSOPHY FOR A TIME OF CRISIS was first published in 1959.

PHILOSOPHY
FOR A TIME OF CRISIS

An Interpretation with Key Writings
by Fifteen Great Modern Thinkers

ADRIENNE KOCH

A Dutton dep *Paperback*

NEW YORK

E. P. DUTTON & CO., INC.

ACKNOWLEDGMENTS AND COPYRIGHTS

It is always a thrill for a writer to acknowledge the various kinds of vital assistance given during the progress of a work, partly because such acknowledgments
recall the pleasures of shared experience and partly because they are made when
the toils of creation are done.

My first acknowledgments are to that group of critical and enthusiastic students who first joined me in this experiment in adult education, when a course
with this title and substance was first given at the Division of General Education,
New York University. However, one association cannot remain anonymous, and to
Dean Paul McGhee of that Division I am indebted for his deep humanity, his
faith in the matter and not simply the forms of adult education, and for his rich
friendship.

To my husband, Lawrence R. Kegan, I owe more than the normal uxorial
debt, for his criticisms entered so deeply into the work as to make it almost a
collaborative venture.

Finally, special thanks are due to the authors, publishers, and holders of copy-
rights mentioned below for their kind permission to reprint, by adaptation, the
selections presented:

COLUMBIA UNIVERSITY PRESS—"Naturalism and Democracy" by Sidney
Hook, from *Naturalism and the Human Spirit*, edited by Y. H. Krikorian, copyright 1944 by Columbia University Press, reprinted by permission of the publishers.

THE DIAL PRESS, INC.—"The Desirable and the Emotive in Dewey's Ethics" by Sidney Hook, from *John Dewey: Philosopher of Science and Freedom*, edited by Sidney Hook, copyright 1950 by The Dial Press, Inc. and used with their permission.

ESTATE OF ALBERT EINSTEIN—Selections from *Out of My Later Years* by Albert Einstein, published by Philosophical Library and Thames and Hudson Ltd., copyright 1956 by the Estate of Albert Einstein and used with their permission; selections from *The World As I See It* by Albert Einstein, published by Philosophical Library and Watts and Company, copyright 1958 by the Estate of Albert Einstein and used with their permission.

HARCOURT, BRACE AND COMPANY, INC.—Selections from *Two Cheers For Democracy*, copyright 1951 by E. M. Forster; reprinted by permission of Harcourt, Brace and Company, Inc. and Edward Arnold (Publishers) Ltd.

HARPER & BROTHERS—Selections from *The Eclipse of God* by Martin Buber, copyright 1952 by Harper & Brothers, reprinted by permission of the publishers; selections from *The God That Failed*, edited by Richard Crossman, copyright 1949 by Ignazio Silone, reprinted by permission of Harper & Brothers and Hamish Hamilton Ltd.

SIDNEY HOOK—Selections from *Heresy, Yes—Conspiracy, No*, by Sidney Hook, published by the John Day Company, copyright 1953 by Sidney Hook and used with his permission.

ALFRED A. KNOPF, INC.—Selections reprinted from *Alternative to Serfdom* by J. M. Clark, by permission of Alfred A. Knopf, Inc., copyright 1948 by The Regents of the University of Michigan.

THE LIBRARY OF LIVING PHILOSOPHERS, INC.—Selections from *The Philosophy of Bertrand Russell*, edited by Paul A. Schilpp, copyright 1946 by The Library of Living Philosophers, Inc. and reprinted with their permission; selections from "The Religion of the Spirit and the World's Need (Fragments of a Confession)" by Sarvepalli Radhakrishnan, from *The Philosophy of Sarvepalli Radhakrishnan*, edited by Paul A. Schilpp, copyright 1952 by The Library of Living Philosophers, Inc. and reprinted with their permission.

THE MACMILLAN COMPANY—Selections from *Paths In Utopia* by Martin Buber, published by The Macmillan Company, copyright 1949 by Martin Buber, reprinted by permission of The Macmillan Company and Routledge & Kegan Paul Ltd.

OXFORD UNIVERSITY PRESS, INC.—Selections from *Civilization on Trial* by Arnold J. Toynbee, copyright 1948 by Oxford University Press, Inc. and reprinted with their permission.

PARTISAN REVIEW—Selections from "Religion and the Intellectuals" by Sidney Hook, copyright March 1950 by *Partisan Review*, reprinted by permission of *Partisan Review* and Sidney Hook.

TABLE OF CONTENTS

PART FOUR: SELECTIONS FROM HUMANISTIC PHILOSOPHERS

PART FIVE: PHILOSOPHY FOR OUR TIME

INDEX

PART ONE
PHILOSOPHY AND OUR TIME

CHAPTER I

INTRODUCTION

If we consider the scope and complexity of the crisis that confronts modern man in the mid-twentieth century, we are compelled to believe that this is the most profound crisis in the history of civilization. Whether rightly or wrongly, people feel that this is a crisis of human existence, in which civilization may perish, and history itself may come to an end. Man, the fabulous artificer, having won secrets from the stars, may be flung on a rock to suffer the fate of Prometheus. But *may* is not *must*. Man's fate, however precarious, is not set, as in Greek tragedy—or as inevitable as historical materialism would have it. What our future will become depends at least in part on our understanding, our hopes, and our deeds.

We have thus moved from the individual's personal crisis to the universal crisis of all persons, a movement in both extension and depth. The root of man is involved; and when this happens he is compelled by his nature to appraise himself and his social world, critically yet not without sympathy. Man cannot meet this crisis on a purely economic level, as a matter involving the creation of the right economic arrangements; or on a purely political level, as a matter involving the organization of the right political arrangements; or, indeed, as a matter of private psychology, confined to the analysis of personal difficulties in living. All these and other basic matters are inextricably related in making effective explorations of what is right in any one of these major aspects of our existence. A necessary but by no means sufficient condition for meeting this crisis is to broaden our knowledge of the entire human scene and to deepen our self-knowledge. Such knowledge is an activity that engages the total person in a growing awareness of interpersonal ties.

This, after all, is the historic function of philosophy: to integrate, in its quest for truth, the findings of knowledge from whatever quarter; and, in its quest for a way of life, the values that give life meaning. Philosophy in this sense explores all pertinent knowledge in the spirit of free inquiry, with the end in view of establishing a way of life agreeable to reason and loyal to human excellence. It is not bound by vested property rights in conventional subject matters, nor is it the private preserve of professional philosophers. Furthermore, this philosophic activity is necessarily on-going, because of changes in our knowledge as well as in the conditions of our existence. One aspect of the present crisis is the accelerated rate of change in both, and that what appear to be shaken are the foundations themselves. If this is true, there is a special need for philosophical perspective in our time—for beliefs that enlighten temporary man and give direction to his existence. Thus, the very presence of the crisis calls for the most searching analysis on the part of our most gifted minds.

Knowing this, thoughtful men are not losing time. They have been challenged to explore the nature of the crisis and to search for ways to sustain and perhaps enrich life even in the face of our trials. It is from such men—deeply philosophical minds—that the selections in this book were made. These men cannot promise salvation in one outpouring of wisdom, or indeed at all. Nor are they interested in merely crying havoc, beguiled by that artistry whose passion is dire prediction. They are on man's side. To this extent, they are positive—they have beliefs and they care about the better of probable worlds. They are thus to be distinguished from those timid souls who are the "hollow men," cut off from reasonable hope. They are doing their best to help us see ahead, to view our accidents, engagements, and necessities in a pattern that takes account of the past and corrects the parochial and narrowly personal aspects of concern. Furthermore, being contemporaries, they have encountered the crisis in their own lives, and each one has responded by attempting to create an adequate integration and an effective faith.

The editor was guided by several principles in selecting the men. They are all men who have won enormous prestige in their own fields by hard work. For more than a generation, they have reflected deeply and imaginatively on the course of Western civilization while personally engaged in meeting the serious problems of a modern world undergoing great transformations. They have not been content to study and ponder in protective ivory towers, but have, in their various ways, felt called upon to communicate their vision and act as responsible political animals. In almost every case, they have had to cross professional fields and national boundaries, and have done so in a disciplined way to promote the cause of freedom. They form a group of influential and leading spokesmen for different philosophical perspectives as well as for different national-political perspectives. One reason for presenting this variety of viewpoints is to permit a richer insight and more critical examination of the philosophical alternatives open to us, a frank recognition that we are all engaged in a voyage of discovery, a real inquiry. The men are authentic because they themselves are generally aware of the depth and severity of the crisis which make it dishonest to pretend to cope with it definitively. They know that there is no short-run or all-out cure.

Therefore, in selecting the writings, primary emphasis falls on the individual perspectives, the specific angle of vision from which the writer views the social and moral landscape. Much more than this, of course, is present in their writings—by way of technical elaboration, factual underpinning, considerations of philosophic method. Admitting the value and merit of such substantial workmanship, there were two overriding reasons that confined the selections to the general theme of philosophy for a time of crisis. First, a single volume that could be read by those concerned with our present situation and not with technical matters was an explicit desideratum. Second, there is a felt universal need for vision, for an answer to nihilism, and some potential alternative to meaningless total destruction. From these points of view, with their urgent demands, the purely professional aspects of philosophic writing were either of incidental use or actual barriers to frustrate a decent impulse to seek some guide lines out of badly torn-up terrain. Only enough reference to these aspects was included to illuminate the individual perspective that was put forward. Toward this end, the editor searched the post-World War II writings of these thinkers to obtain thoughtful and representative formulations, and undertook to select and order the passages to assure that only pertinent and yet consecutive reflections would be presented in their own words and in brief compass.

The selections divide themselves naturally into three groups. The first group represents authors who are not professional philosophers, but who have thought seriously about their own fields and who, in confronting the crisis, have felt the necessity of going beyond those fields in a responsible way so as to achieve a sense of integration. Toynbee is a historian, but all civilizations, and therefore all the works of man, are his canvas. He gives us historical perspective. Einstein is the greatest physicist of our time. He presents us with the most authoritative interpretation of the role of science in modern life, and was a leading spokesman among the scientists in developing the political implications of nuclear physics. Silone is a philosophical novelist whose theme is the bearing of technical and totalitarian society on the fate and happiness of the human person. He was also the leader of the Italian Communist underground under Mussolini, and then broke with the Communist International. He knows the attractions of Communism, its tyrannies, and its great betrayal. Forster, another philosophical novelist, portrayed the meeting of the East and West in both its human and its ironic terms in his great work *A Passage to India*. Unlike Silone, he always remained deeply individualistic and found that art creates its own order. J. M. Clark is one of the leading American economists. He is an important theoretician of the mixed economy, and recognizes that the economist must break the narrow confines of his discipline to deal with social welfare. Erich Fromm is a psychoanalyst whose initial training was in sociology. He was probably the first psychoanalyst to try to join three disciplines: psychiatry, philosophy of values, and social-political analysis.

The second group of selections form a natural unity in their interpretation of the vital role played by religious belief in any civilization. The selections were so keyed as to present the views of a leading spokesman for each of the major religious traditions in our time. Maritain is probably the most influential Catholic philosopher. He is responsive to all the distinctive movements of our time, in politics and art, as well as in philosophy. Buber is the leading Hebrew philosopher today. He argues not only with the exacting tools of a professional philosopher, but also as a great scholar in the history of religions, and of Haesidic lore. Niebuhr is one of the leading spokesmen of the Protestant position, and views his protest as one not only against the social injustices of our time but also against the Church itself. Radhakrishnan has been a professor of comparative religions at Oxford and is one of the leading interpreters of the philosophies of the East. He served as India's Ambassador to the Soviet Union and is now the Vice President of India.

The third group are also professional philosophers but maintain the independence of philosophy from religion; they view philosophy as that activity in which man exercises his reason to give life meaning. Sartre is the leading French Existentialist. His literary work has brought Existentialism to the contemporary stage and to the paperback bookracks. Popper is an Austrian who took up residence in England, and is one of the leading representatives of scientific philosophy. Unlike many of his colleagues, he has tried to use his knowledge of scientific method to throw light on the history of Western political philosophy in order to establish the values of an open society. Russell is the grand old man of modern philosophy. He made the greatest contribution to modern logic. Withal, he has remained true to the liberal traditions of his grandfather, the Lord Russell of the Reform Acts of 1832, and has written extensively, influentially, and with great charm on the meaning of liberalism, Bolshevism, progressive education, marriage and morals, power and happiness. Hook is a professional philosopher and teacher who has continued the tradition of John Dewey in advancing naturalism and democracy by both logical analysis and the treatment of specific issues in contemporary education and contemporary society. Jaspers is probably the leading German philosopher today. He began as a psychiatrist and has mastered the materials of history, philosophy, and philosophical science in order to defend a new Humanism.

In this book of readings, then, philosophic men who have formulated comprehensive interpretations of the contemporary world are given the opportunity to present their understanding of the crisis of our time in terms of the alternatives that can claim to illuminate it. If Whitehead was right in asserting that "Mankind is now in one of its rare moods of shifting its outlook. The mere compulsion of tradition has lost its force," this book should provide food for thought, material from which reflective people can refashion their philosophy of the individual human person and of the values of our civilization.

In many respects, the views taken of the crisis on the part of the contributors are in agreement, but in other respects there are important and instructive differences among them. Occasionally, a writer assumes much about the nature of our times in the process of advancing his philosophy of life. The concluding part of this book will examine what emerges by way of significant variation in accounting for the crisis. Meanwhile, however, it is important to clarify the nature of the crisis which has been characterized as more profound than any other, and the role of philosophy as an interpretation and critique of civilization.

CHAPTER II

TOWARD AN UNDERSTANDING OF
THE PRESENT CRISIS

1. *"This Terrible Twentieth Century"*

In one indisputable sense, every human being is intimately familiar with times of crisis. When the Gautama Buddha left his sheltered palace grounds and encountered for the first time illness, old age, degrading poverty, and death, he confronted the original and enduring substance of personal crisis. The awareness of death alone suffices to instruct man in his tragic role as a guest visiting "My Host, the World." This fundamental limitation of the human condition makes the definition of man as a creature conscious of death at least as valid as the ancient definition of man as a rational animal. Such human anguish itself illuminates the craving for immortality which is evidenced in almost every culture and helps to explain the power of the world's religions.

When we talk of a "time of crisis," however, we mean something different from the individual crises that every man, each in his own time and for his own person, must encounter. For here we are dealing with cumulative changes—drastic and extensive— that take place in a public setting, creating a new and profoundly dangerous epoch in history. Historians, looking backward over the course of Western civilization, readily recognize periods of crisis in the career of man, indicated by upheavals in economic, social, and political organization that threatened long-established values and challenged the usual modes of control. And certainly each period of marked social and political change, by virtue of its bare newness and broad scope created transitional chaos, confusion, and frustration. Some of these crises in the past, like the Reformation with its religious wars, or the French Revolution with its Reign of Terror and Napoleonic sequel, were brutal times of trouble, marked by rampant violence and bloodshed. It is important to remember, however, that they were also times when the pains of adjustment and the price of suffering were not the sole elements in the social struggle. There was also confidence on the part of large groups in the promise of a better future for man, and there were operative designs to terminate the crisis and ease the way to a new order.

Unhappily, there have also been epochs in human history when civilizations were in process of disintegration, with no hope for the future to offset the pressures of immediate tragedy. In such periods of decline, there were widespread anxiety, dismaying insecurity, deepening isolation. In the climate of a declining civilization, even the more sensitive artists and prescient thinkers of the age despaired. Having no counsel to offer, they took refuge from the world in the sacred wood of private art or mystical religion, or contented themselves with expressing the futility of all human remedies. Gilbert Murray, in a study of declining phases of Hellenic civilization, summarized this mental outlook in a now familiar and inclusive phrase—"the failure of nerve." This phrase, in its broad significance, includes not only the disintegration of the Greek city-states but also the decline and fall of the Roman Empire. In that climate of slow dying, the degradation of intellect was evident in the spread of mysticism and asceticism and the obliteration of science. It is also significant that Rome became, in the late Empire, an undisguised despotism on Oriental lines—for it is generally agreed that the people had lost confidence in themselves and were ready to sacrifice every last vestige of their right to the illusory security which despotism affords.

Would that the fatal pessimistic outlook that destroys faith in the human person and in the creative solution of public problems were confined to these two undisputed instances of failure in Western civilization! But the symptoms of another failure of nerve can be detected in the contemporary world, and the climate of despair already encourages a callous readiness to dig the grave of Western civilization which will, it is judged, soon enough oblige by presenting its corpse. How has this mood come upon the people of the West?

Modern Western civilization spent its lusty infancy in the Renaissance and the Reformation, very sure of the dignity and the creativity of the concrete human person, and ready to put its faith in human knowledge and experience. Key factors that sustained this faith were the rise of modern science and of the nation-state. These factors, sometimes operating independently, sometimes in conflict, but most frequently conjoined, helped to undermine confidence in pre-existing Authority, whether that of Aristotle or of the Church. The vitality of this young humanistic outlook continued to prosper with the further advance of modern science and the nation-state, and as it developed it created liberating social conditions in the times decoratively called the "Age of Reason" of the eighteenth century, and the "Age of Progress and Industrialization" of the nineteenth. Yet all these promising developments consequent on the growth of larger-scale nation-states and technologies seemed to turn against the human person in the twentieth century. As "large-scale" became "larger" in the urban setting of daily life and the factory setting of daily work, there were a bewildering loss of community, a sharpening sense of alienation, and an assimilation of the human person to the mass man in a bureaucratic society.

Prophetic voices in the nineteenth century had been raised to proclaim the coming condition of modern man. Among these numerous voices were three that prove unforgettable: Marx, Kierkegaard, and Nietzsche. These three thinkers saw the onrushing developments with peculiar clarity, and exert a magnetic influence on the beliefs of our own day. The young Marx averred that "to be radical is to go to the root of the question. Now the

root of mankind is man." Marx saw the increasing disparity between the technological means which could provide increased
productivity and therefore freedom, on the one hand, and the
human condition of alienation which resulted from the social
relations of production and which remorselessly converted the
human person into a commodity, a thing. But as Marx's work
progressed, he became more and more concerned with the social
setting and seemed to forget the concrete human person. Not so
with Kierkegaard, who made the unique experience of the individual human being his central concern; and there he found fear
and trembling, the pride of the abstract intellect that could not
and would not deal with great subterranean human forces. He
charged that the life of man in an industrial society was essentially hostile to the Christian life. Appalled by the decline of real
religious faith, Kierkegaard tried to recapture authentic religious
belief in his own experience. Nietzsche also witnessed the decline
of Christianity, but his philosophy took a wholly different turn
from Kierkegaard's. He made the shattering pronouncement:
"God is dead." For religious faith, he transvalued values and put
the nation-state in its place; for the sheeplike worship of the past
he substituted the glorification of the superman and his power.

So arrestingly proclaimed, the theme of the dehumanization
of man found more spokesmen in the period after the First
World War. It is precisely this theme that we meet in Albert
Schweitzer's scholarly two-volume study *Civilization and Ethics*,
first published in 1923. "My subject is the tragedy of the Western
world-view. . . . Our civilization is going through a severe crisis.
. . . Most people think that the crisis is due to the war but they
are wrong. The war, with everything connected with it, is only a
phenomenon of the condition of uncivilization in which we find
ourselves." Our "uncivilization" he attributed to the disastrous
imbalance between our material and spiritual development.
Schweitzer further stated that the greatest danger inherent in ele-
vating material achievements over spiritual elements is that
"through the revolutions in the conditions of life men become in

greater numbers unfree, instead of free." Under modern conditions, human beings struggle for existence, they overwork, without finding time to collect and order their thoughts. Meanwhile, the dependence upon economic, social, and political organizations, of more and more gigantic scope, increases. "In every respect, our individual existence is depreciated. It is becoming ever more difficult to be a personality."

The charge that the contemporary world is suffering from a disastrous imbalance between its technological advance and its regard for the human person became a resounding chorus when the values of free society were threatened by the rise of totalitarianism and the world-wide depression. By the end of the Second World War, there was little disagreement that we were in the midst of a new era in the history of our civilization, an era of pervasive and devastating crisis that has united the peoples of the world, not in the spirit of amity dreamed of by philosophers of good will in every century, but by universal dread, by the common fate of living like Damocles in successive phases of a constant fear. The massing of problems, as the century progressed, encouraged the mood that proclaims the doom of Western civilization.

Gross testimony to document this judgment abounds in the titles of some prominent books published after World War II. In the warning of a group of distinguished scientists, it is one world or none. In the words of a leading historian, ours is a civilization on trial. Philosophers, educators, social scientists have all taken for their theme the decline of the West and the divided world. A brilliant French political analyst sees it as the century of total war. In this vein, Sir Winston Churchill summed up, at mid-century, his impression of the promising year 1900, and comments: "Little did we guess that what has been called the Century of the Common Man would witness as its outstanding feature more common men killing each other with greater facilities than any other five centuries together in the history of the

world. But we entered this terrible twentieth century with confidence."

This terrible twentieth century. Who will reflect on its course
and repudiate the phrase? Or deny that the confidence has gone?
Without vanity or the slightest shadow of complacency, our own
crisis must be considered as unique in the history of man, since
it is more general in its extent and more profound than any other
in the history of man. For it is a crisis of human existence. This
is the primary thread that appears in the fears arising from the
multitudinous forms of total destruction of the human person—
in the H-bomb, in the concentration camp, and genocide experiments, the mass emigrations occasioned by war. They are no less
felt in the destruction of the human community and finally in
the destruction of faith in mankind. It is a crisis of the human
person, of the relation of the person to nature, to his work, to
other people, to social organization.

The A-bombs dropped on Hiroshima and Nagasaki, together
with later developments in nuclear armaments, symbolize our
present plight by fusing all the critical elements of our situation
in a single shattering image. First of all, there is the fear of a war
which will lay whole cities low at one fell swoop, destroy human
life, and sear the entire surface of the earth. The new superweapons have created one world target of fear. Second, even if
total war should be avoided, there is the anxiety of the daily on-
slaught of cold war, unleashed by the rivalry of the two super-
powers who alone command the resources to stockpile as many
superweapons as possible, until deadlier ones can be developed.
The superweapons have thus intensified the split in the bipolar
world we live in. Third, the problems of the divided world, in
turn, have magnified the other critical political and economic
problems of our day, such as the issue of Western European unity
and the clamor of the vast peoples of Asia, Africa, and Latin
America for positions of industrial power and nationalistic prestige. Fourth, the increasing disparity between man's technical
control over nature and man's self-control and wisdom has

reached a new peak with the superweapons. And, finally, the crisis has a moral aspect. Can we ground our values in knowledge or are we left with individual, arbitrary faiths? If we cannot find reasonable grounds for our faith in man, then the faith backed by the most fanatical massing of power will alone survive—if anything does.

The thought that the crisis of our time is to be dated from the dawn of atomic bombs may meet objections arising from a confusion between the cause or causes and dating of something. There are critics who maintain that the present crisis began with the rise of totalitarianism in Europe; others who deny this and point to its roots in the post-Versailles economic and social troubles; still others who argue that Versailles could not have been different since the ground was already set in the aggressive nationalisms and imperialistic conflicts of modern states. Quite a differently oriented group of analysts would contend that all of these attempts to seek a starting point for the crises are really shortsighted—that one must go back to the technological revolution that produced the machines upon which man grew increasingly dependent, and less human forthwith. But, of course, the technological revolution itself was but the application of modern science in that epoch which is often used to date the emergence of the modern world.

It should already be apparent that in this retrospective assignment of the crisis to a supposed cause or causes, there is involved an almost infinite regress. The way out of this embarrassing intellectual muddle is to establish a cut-off point by the use of a pragmatic criterion of relevance to the problem at hand. A crisis, as the dictionary indicates, is a turning point in the development of a disease when a change takes place which is decisive for recovery or death. It is a state of affairs in which a decisive change for better or worse is imminent. That the period prior to World War II, with its world-wide depression, Nazi and Fascist aggressions, and Communist international conspiracy, was an era of radical, drastic change on many levels hardly needs comment.

But it is precisely the intervening lesson provided by World War II, so sinister in its final phase when the atomic bomb was dropped over Hiroshima and Nagasaki, that sets the stage for the crisis of our own time.

The end of World War II gives us a key, for it marks off an era of history, a turning point in man's career when a cluster of overwhelming issues are posed for the continued existence of Western civilization and the world itself. Three issues, over and above the existence of superweapons, converge to give a special character to the present crisis: the threat of Soviet and Chinese Communism; the challenge of the underdeveloped countries in Asia, Africa, and Latin America; and the fate of freedom in the West. All three issues have their own momentum; and any one of them would create a crisis for modern Western civilization; but their combined momentum, joined with the developments in military technology, threatens the whole life of man and gives a unique urgency to the crisis of our time. Therefore, in order to reach a better understanding of the nature and scope of the present crisis, I propose to consider each of these issues briefly in turn.

2. *The Threat of Communism*

"A spectre is haunting Europe—the spectre of Communism." With these well-known opening words, the *Communist Manifesto* of 1848 proclaimed the coming doom of capitalism through an apocalyptic revolution that would free the downtrodden of the earth and establish a universal classless society. Today, one century later, Communism is no longer a specter: it is one of the two pre-eminent world powers; it controls the manpower and physical resources of a large part of the world; and it constitutes a military force of a scope never before achieved in history, which ruthlessly threatens not only Europe but the remainder of the non-Communist world. Three historical leaps account for this transformation. The First World War liquidated the old Austro-Hungarian Empire, weakened Germany, and enabled the Bolshevik Party to take power in Russia, forging, in rapid time, a new, totalitarian society. The Second World War liquidated the military prowess of Germany and Japan and the colonial possessions of Great Britain, France, and the Netherlands, and enabled the Russian and Chinese Communist parties to take power in Eastern Europe and China. The present phase of Communism's rise to world power results from the amalgam of Marxist theory, the Leninist Party, the Stalinist Five Year Plans for forced industrialization, all now mobilized under conditions of nuclear, automated, and rocket technology. It is important to analyze the Communist ingredients of this megaton brew because there is a recurrent, widespread, and understandable feeling in the West that the Communist threat can be made to disappear only if we accept their protestations of and need for peaceful coexistence, and abandon a policy of mutual terror.

This brings us then to the cluster of beliefs and convictions by which the self-disciplined Communist rulers shape their deeds. Literally thousands of volumes have been devoted to the exploration of their theory and all it portends by way of political action. Only the barest and most essential features can, in this brief space, be indicated. Part of the theory is a legacy from Marx. Another part is a development conditioned by Russian tsarist rule, and the necessity of so designing revolutionary work that it could go forward to the seizure of power in the name of the proletariat—largely Lenin's work. After the Bolshevik Revolution, a continuous elaboration of doctrine took place, adapted to the exigencies of maintaining and expanding power for the Soviet state. This was largely the work of Stalin. There have been later developments of doctrine, both by way of elaboration and of modification, associated with the experience of the Chinese Communists, and formulated by Mao Tse-tung. More recently, Khrushchev has introduced certain changes to take account of the new military technology and the new world situation. Although there have been drastic alterations in the original Marxist formulation, there remains a basic core of theory which promotes the large design of Communist world strategy by providing the rulers of Communist society a continuing source of assurance and a flexible guide to action. The theory apparently still serves to give history a push toward their inevitable triumph. It is for this reason that the theory continues to be considered so essential in every phase of Communist education and is employed so seriously in every debate on a new program and turn in policy.

Fundamental in the theory of historical materialism is Marx's attempt to square theory with history and action. In a sweeping fashion, historical materialism claims to explain the entire course of history in terms of a few simple laws of motion. All history is the history of class struggle—and a class is defined in terms of the role it plays in relation to the dominant means of production. Thus, to understand social change one must not make a false sentimental turn and look to the "superstructure"—the moral ideals, or laws, or religious beliefs, for example—but to the basic economic and property relationships that determine the next turn of events. Even a paramount political reality like the state must be properly interpreted as only the executive arm (the law and the army) which defends the property rights of the owning class. The most simple and distinctive property relationship is between those who do and those who do not own the means of production—the haves, and the have-nots. As technology changes, economic difficulties are created within the division of labor. These are the goads that exacerbate and accelerate the class struggle. But also, the established legal property relations become fetters on advancing technology; and these fetters are broken by the upsurge of the formerly oppressed class that is given historical support by the advance in technology. No class will commit suicide, however. Therefore the only way by which the previously oppressed class can take over the means of production from the owning class is by violent political means, or revolution.

This apparent account of the past is fortified by what appears to be prediction of the present. In capitalist society, the worker and the intellectual, man in general, is "alienated" from himself. He either sells his labor as a commodity, or his thoughts, or his professional services; or, on the other hand, being a "capitalist," he makes use of others as tools for selfish private benefit—the polar process of exploiting and being exploited draining off human energy from truly human concerns to impersonal, abstract money relationships. The Marxist theory of the laws of motion of capitalist society also claims to have predicted the recurrent crises that have come to be associated with the business cycle, and a general crisis of capitalism associated with the decline in the rate of profit which could be only temporarily offset by state intervention on behalf of large-scale capital. Finally, the climax in the history of capitalism was seen to be a dénouement of world wars and colonial revolts. Advanced capitalism tries to escape its internal contradictions by seeking and exploiting colonial areas as bases for raw materials, cheap labor, and finished-goods markets, and this transforms the national to an international class struggle. But since the area of the earth is limited and the appetites of capitalism are unlimited, capitalist competition must result in imperialist world war. Also, over the same period, the capitalist exploitation of backward areas must set in motion the same class struggle that it generated within the capitalist states, with the consequence that national resistance joins with the class consciousness of the colonial masses to revolt against the foreign capitalist exploiters. This situation accelerates the road to proletarian revolution and further intensifies the contradictions of capitalism because the existence of the Communist state cuts off markets and sources of supply—the larger the state, the larger the cutoff—and serves as a symbol of the possibility and promise of revolutionary upheaval. Therefore, the theory claims that the capitalist states must seek to destroy the Communist states or be destroyed in turn. This is summed up in Lenin's classic warning: "So long as capitalism and socialism exist, we cannot live in peace."

However strong the materialist dogma is with respect to the past and in some apparently successful predictions of the present, the whole moral and promissory force implicit in this groundwork culminates in its applications to the future. Here the lofty vista opens up a realm so brilliantly bathed in light that countless sacrifices and victims, any and every means to the Messianic end, are overlooked. For the Marxist sees in the development of large-scale capital the creation of technological tools that can now be made to yield "enough" for everybody, provided the capitalistic fetters are pried off. The magic key here is to socialize large-scale means of production, and convert the system of production for profit to one of production for use. This is the dream of Socialist theory, a dream that crossbred Soviet Communist theory still invokes. But the dream has a purchase price, the high price of revolution—for only thus can the working class take over power from the capitalists, and through a transition phase, the dictatorship of the proletariat. Even the dream had its pseudoscientific value for those who took power in the name of the Soviets—for the Soviet Union is supposedly the promised land of Socialism, the real outcome of scientific Socialism. One final comment concerns the ideal of an eventual classless society, where freedom will exist for all, and the administration over things will have replaced the old exploitative administration over persons. *Until* the enemies are deposed, either from within or from without, merciless terror must be applied to all who would subvert the Socialist fatherland.

Any close reading of this theory of historical materialism, when seen in the light of Communist actions and power, should help to establish the claim that the Communist threat is a major factor in the crisis of our time. It is an operative element in the crisis because it is essentially a theory of how to provoke protracted and general world crisis that is accepted by a militant party of true believers as the unquestionable truth in explaining all theory and guiding all action. Here is a theory that appears to be all-embracing, both over time, space, and the activities of man, and subject to confirmation, like any other scientific theory. There are many students of history who are attracted and persuaded by its simplicity and broad generalizations as it applies to the past. There are many who are attracted by its apparent success in predicting such matters as the business cycle, the growth of capitalist monopoly, and the period of world wars and colonial revolts in the present. Finally, there are those who, like the rulers of Russia and Communist China, are persuaded that a theory which can account for the past and predict the present can be employed to direct the course of the future. And they are given apparently objective grounds for confidence in its validity because of their remarkable successes.

This theory, with its alleged scientific status, constitutes a real threat because it is employed as a tool, not by political parties in the normal Western sense, but by monolithic, centralized and disciplined Communist parties which form the established governments of Russia and Communist China and wield a monopoly of political, economic, and spiritual power over one billion people. These uniquely powerful parties are the realization of the Leninist conception of the party which emerged as a result of an extensive period of political activity. In fact, the Leninist type of party forms, together with the Marxist theory of protracted conflict, the unchanging core of Communist theory and practice. Therefore, we must also analyze, however briefly, the role and reality of the Leninist Party, since it is the fundamental, distinctive, social reality of both Russia and Communist China, and one of the great realities of our deeply divided world. This kind of party may help account for the fact that only 240,000 Russian Communist Party members could seize, secure, and rapidly expand their power until they have become the rulers of one of the two strongest states in the world, capable of threatening the other powers with rocket attacks; and for the fact that only 20,000 Chinese Communist Party members could move from the countryside to the rule of 650 million people who have become the strongest power in Asia.

The initial and decisive phase in the development of this conception of the revolutionary party was, as we have suggested, the work of Lenin. It began with his polemics against Russian So-

cialists at the turn of the century. His essential contribution at
this stage was the formulation of the need for a strong conspiratorial group that would function as a kind of political army. He
felt that the workers would tend to be satisfied with the everyday
struggle for improved living conditions characterized by trade
unionism and could only develop a revolutionary consciousness
if radical intellectuals made them aware of their historic mission.
Furthermore, given the difficulties of political action under
tsarism when revolutionary parties were generally outlawed, he
urged the necessity for professional revolutionaries who would
devote their whole lives to the fight against tsarism and would
form a Central Committee of the Party, a sort of general staff to
an underground political army. The next stage was set by the
World War and the collapse of tsarism in 1917. Lenin returned
to Russia to lead his party to power, first, by exploiting the growing discontent of the workers, soldiers, and peasants, and then,
by tortuous intrigue, forcefully overthrowing the democratically
constituted Provisional Government. The October Revolution
began with the dissolution of the Constituent Assembly, the first
Russian Assembly which had been elected shortly before the
October Revolution by free and universal suffrage. The reasons
for this fateful move were that the leaders of the Communist
Party could not control an assembly with a non-Communist
majority; and, as Lenin declared, "It is naïve to wait for a formal
majority for the Bolshevists. No revolution does that." The final
stage in the establishment of the monolithic party followed hard
on the period of civil war and "war Communism" with the re-
pression of all other political parties and all means for independent political criticism, together with the creation of the Cheka,
the secret-police instrument of Communist terror to ferret out
and squash any opposition from the masses. In Central Russia,
peasant revolts against the seizure of food were crushed. As a result of worker unrest in Petrograd, a group of influential Communists formed a Workers' Opposition to demand the end of
worker-militarization and the institution of factory self-manage-

ment: they were crushed. The sailors of the Kronstadt naval base who led Lenin to power in 1917, but who now demanded democratic freedoms, were also crushed. When the expected German Revolution failed to materialize, Lenin judged it essential to gain new strength at home and, accordingly, he advanced a new program at the Tenth Congress of the Communist Party in 1921. Here he proclaimed the New Economic Policy which allowed free trade in the villages and limited free enterprise in the cities, and provided new decrees prohibiting the formation of party groups and agitation against the program of the Central Committee.

In this Leninist phase many of the original Marxist theoretical notions about the origin and course of the Socialist Revolution were abandoned. For Marx held that the inexorable forces of the social relations of production themselves create a proper Socialist consciousness in the workers and lead them to organize the revolt against capitalism; that capitalism would be overthrown only at its highest point of development; and that the workers who are the overwhelming majority of the population would establish workers' democracy to govern their own relations, but a proletarian dictatorship to defend the revolution against the capitalist elements who have been expropriated. All these original Marxist notions were discarded by Lenin when they came up against the hard realities of the moment. The Russian Communist Party was not the architect but rather the scavenger of a revolution against tsarism which had been carried out by others. It is sometimes forgotten that the Russian workers formed less than 10 per cent of the population, and were generally not attracted to the Russian Communist Party. Nor did the Revolution take place in a country with the economic preconditions of capitalist maturity, such as Marx had designated, but in one where agriculture was predominant. And after October, the dictatorship was not in fact a dictatorship of even the small segment of workers, but a dictatorship of the Party over the people, and increasingly a dictatorship of the Central Committee over the membership. This right of the Party, as the self-appointed guardian of workers' rights, to substitute its certain knowledge and resolute will for the illusions and hesitations of the workers constitute the foundations of Leninism.

The second decisive phase in the development of the Party covers the thirty years of Stalin's reign and deepened the process Lenin began. When Stalin became the General Secretary of the Party in 1922, he used this post to appoint his own men to positions of importance in order to assure his majority at Party congresses, and thus bring the Party machine and the Central Committee itself under his control. At first, he joined with Kamenev and Zinoviev to keep Trotsky from assuming Lenin's role and thereby reduced Trotsky's influence. Next, he joined with Bukharin, Rykov, and Tomsky to turn against his former allies, and reduced their influence; and by 1927 he had them expelled from the Party. In 1928 he turned against his later allies, and in 1929 announced that all decisions of the Politburo would be unanimous. He also proclaimed the First Five-Year Plan, which undertook the forced collectivization of agriculture and the accelerated industrialization of the economy. Every form of compulsion was used to carry out the plan, with the result that millions of people died and other millions were sent to concentration camps in the uninhabited regions of northern Europe and Asiatic Russia, camps that were run by the GPU, the successor of the Cheka, for the exploitation of forced labor. Millions of livestock were killed by starving peasants, and Russian agriculture suffered a setback which has left it the weakest sector of the economy. Still another result was the development of heavy and strategic industries, to the neglect of consumer-goods production and housing construction, keeping the mass of the people near the margin of subsistence. The program repelled so many Communist Party members that Stalin felt impelled to institute the great bloody purges and public trials against the old Party leaders, other Party members, army generals, and important officials. The terror of the purge ruthlessly established Stalin's absolute control over the

Party, and the Party's total control over the state, the people, and all aspects of Russian society. This establishment of the totalitarian state was justified by the necessity of accomplishing the accelerated industrialization of a backward economy to impose the basic economic conditions of Socialist construction. Such was the nature of Stalin's program of "Socialism in one country."

The next decisive phase in the determination of the Party is exemplified by Stalin's foreign policies. Since the Marxist theory emphatically reiterates that the logic of capitalism will drive the capitalist powers to war with Socialism, it was essential to strengthen and expand the power of the totalitarian state, both to defend the Socialist fatherland and to advance the ultimate victory of Communism over the world. Stalin's foreign policy initially emphasized the passive defensive aspects of the strategy, during the entire period from his rise to power in 1922 to Hitler's rise to power in 1933. Confronted with the growing power of Nazi Germany, Stalin's foreign policy shifted to collective security to win support against the threat of Hitler among the Western powers within the League of Nations. The existence of this real enemy, joined with the enmity of Japan, also made it possible further to justify and intensify the privations, suppressions, and cruelties of his program of accelerated industrialization and enforced collectivization. But when Munich appeared to appease Hitler, Stalin again shifted his foreign policy and negotiated the nonaggression pact with Germany to exploit Hitler's aggression for the defense and expansion of the totalitarian Russian state. The pact seemed to provide two advantages: defense, by its promise of Soviet neutrality, thus permitting Nazi aggression against Poland without a war on two fronts; and expansion, by the promise of the partition of Poland and the division of eastern Europe into spheres of influence. Apparently, Stalin believed that his deal with Hitler would be maintained, and thus was utterly surprised and unprepared for the German attack on the Soviet Union. By the summer of 1941, the Red Army had suffered more terrible disasters than those which crushed the tsar's army; and by the end of 1941 the German officers were able to see the suburbs of Moscow through their field glasses. With the assistance of the Western "capitalist" powers, Russia survived the ordeal of war, pushed back the German army from the gates of Stalingrad, and appeared as the "savior of civilization from Hitlerite barbarism."

Stalin did not hesitate to capitalize on the immense prestige built up during the war in order to drive forward the Communist objectives. Guided by the theory that further conflict was inevitable, and that the expansion of productive power was essential for the victory of Communism, he took advantage of the political blindness of the West, the war weariness and unrest in the world, and the extended position of the Red Army at the end of the war, to establish Communist power over eastern and central Europe and in the Balkans, and to demand a voice in the settlement of affairs in Germany, Manchuria, and other areas of the world. This deep-seated hostility against former allies is strikingly exemplified by the postwar disagreements over the division of Europe which was arranged at Yalta and Teheran. For Stalin, there could be no friendly governments except those run by the Communist Party and no sphere of influence but absolute Communist control. From 1945 the Communist rulers consolidated their territorial gains in eastern Europe and drove their forces outward until they were stopped in Greece, Berlin, Yugoslavia, and Korea. The historical and political logic of the Russian régime now made the United States the leading imperialist enemy of the Socialist camp, because the United States prevented that complete sweep of Communist influence over Europe and Asia which was Stalin's initial postwar hope.

Given this perspective of Communist theory and practice, we can better appraise the meaning of the current policies of the Communist leaders and their significance as a major factor in the world crisis. Since Stalin's death, a number of changes have been made which represent more flexible tactics under new conditions rather than any basic change in the goals of Communism.

For example, Stalin's view that there would be a deep economic crisis in the major capitalist countries after the war no longer exercises the same urgency in planning their actions. Both the higher level of economic development within the Soviet Union and the existence of a skilled labor force that has been brought up and educated under a régime that has become one of the two great world powers permit a relaxation of tensions internally. Where Stalin was opposed, Khrushchev could now propose the decentralization of industry and the devolution of regional authorities, as well as an increase in the level of consumer goods, in response to the pressures for greater personal security on the part of the Party, the army, the state bureaucracy, and industrial management. One reason for this set of actions was undoubtedly associated with the problems and difficulties of succession. Khrushchev, while advocating the new policies, continued to use his post of Secretary of the Party to strengthen his control in the Party congresses and in the Central Committee, using one group against another, and then turning against his former supporters. Thus, for example, he obtained General Zhukov's support by relaxing controls over the army, and then, once he had removed Malenkov, turned on Zhukov and strengthened the Party's control over the army. And even when he attacked Stalin in his special report to the Twentieth Congress, he was careful to condemn the personal crimes of Stalin while reaffirming the sacred position of the Party leadership as the sole repository of the Marxist faith: "Lenin resolutely stood against every attempt at belittling or weakening the directing role of the party in the structure of the Soviet state. He worked out Bolshevik principles of party direction and norms of party life, stressing that the guiding principle of party leadership is its collegiality. Already during the pre-Revolutionary years, Lenin called the Central Committee of the party a collective of leaders and the guardian and interpreter of party principles." The tumultuous ovation accorded Khrushchev's speech in which the new Secretary of the Communist Party attacked Stalin was itself evidence of the continued power of the Leninist role of the Party. For, although he removed Stalin from his pedestal and although most of those present had been accustomed to praising the dead leader as a secular god when he was alive, no one dared to protest the characterization of him as a monster.

This new flexibility of tactics is also manifest in Russia's foreign policy today. One all-important objective factor in this connection is the existence of an allied Communist Party in China. Where Stalin could permit no fraternal association of Communist parties, but required absolute control by the Russian Communist Party, the new leaders have seen the advantage, if not the necessity, of reaching an alliance with the Chinese Communist leaders because of their power and long-range influence in Asia. This is the significance of the debates on the "paths to socialism" and Khrushchev's willingness to accept the possibility of a "peaceful and parliamentary path to socialism," but only so long as the "political leadership of the working class and its advance detachment is the indispensable and decisive factor for all forms of transition to socialism." This doctrine, together with the prestige of Communist China as a symbol of anticolonial revolt, is being employed to take advantage of the serious unrest in the underdeveloped areas of the world. The other all-important factor is the fact of Russia's overwhelming power with the development of thermonuclear and rocket weapons. This development permitted the Communist leaders to advance the doctrine of mutual terror, thereby attempting to weaken the joint defensive pacts between the United States and its allies. This situation was exploited as "the spirit of Geneva," after which the Communist leaders felt secure in preventing genuine discussions on the unification of Germany and in shipping Czech arms to Egypt, an episode which led to the Suez crisis. It was at this time that the Russian leaders threatened to use their weapons against the allies and then actually turned the Red Army against the Hungarian workers' revolution.

It should now be clear that whatever changes have been made

by the Russian Communist leaders have not altered their strategic program. In this connection it is useful to recall a remark Khrushchev made at a Kremlin banquet in honor of the East German Communist leaders. He ridiculed those in the West who have been saying "something has changed" since the summit conference at Geneva—because the Soviet leaders are now smiling. "But if anyone believes that our smiles involve abandonment of the teachings of Marx, Engels and Lenin, he deceives himself poorly. Those who wait for that must wait until a shrimp learns to whistle."

The full meaning of this saying can be grasped by examining more closely the official long report given by Khrushchev as the Secretary of the Communist Party at its Twentieth Congress in February, 1956. Because it is little known in the West, and because it is associated with the strategy of "peaceful co-existence," it is best to rely on his own language. He began with an analysis of the objective factors characterizing the international situation today. He pointed to the tremendous strides made by the Soviet economy and contrasted them with the "still greater enrichment of the monopolies, more intensive exploitation and . . . lowering of . . . living standards . . . sharpening of the competitive struggle among capitalist states, maturing of new economic crises and upheavals." In order to overcome the increasing crises, capitalist powers have resorted to the time-honored expedient of forming aggressive military alliances to restore their position by military measures. "We know from history that, when planning a redivision of the world, the imperialist powers have always lined up military blocs. Today the 'anti-Communism' slogan is again being used . . . to cover up one's power claims for world domination." But the existence and power of Communist Russia and Communist China is a new dynamic factor in history and must give the capitalist rulers pause. "The whole course of international relations in recent years shows that great popular forces have risen to fight for the preservation of peace. The ruling imperialist circles cannot ignore this. Their more far-sighted representatives are beginning to admit that the 'positions of strength' policy . . . has failed. . . . These public figures still do not venture to state that capitalism will find its grave in another world . . . but they are already obliged to admit openly that the socialist camp is invincible." It is this situation which promotes conditions favorable to peaceful co-existence. "Our enemies depict us Leninists as advocates of violence always and everywhere. True, we recognize the need for the revolutionary transformations of capitalist society into socialist society. It is this that distinguishes the revolutionary Marxists from the reformists. . . . There is no doubt that in a number of capitalist countries violent overthrow of the dictatorship of the bourgeoisie . . . is inevitable. But the forms of social revolution vary. . . . The greater or lesser intensity which the struggle may assume, the use or non-use of violence in the transition to socialism depend on the resistance of the exploiters. . . . Of course, in those countries where capitalism is still strong, where it possesses a tremendous military and police machine, serious resistance by reactionary forces is inevitable. There the transition to socialism will take place under conditions of sharp class, revolutionary struggle."

This fundamental Communist policy is also advocated by the leaders of the Chinese Communist Party. Probably the best statement of it appears in Mao Tse-tung's work *On the Protracted War*. Its importance stems not only from Mao's pre-eminence as the leader of the Communist revolution in Asia, but also from his role as a political symbol of the more general revolution against three centuries of Western domination and condescension, a revolution which receives impetus from the success of the Chinese revolution. "This war is not only the banner of China's liberation, but is pregnant with significance for world revolution. We will lead the Chinese revolution to its completion and also exert a far-reaching influence on the revolution in the East as well as in the whole world." For two decades he waited in the countryside of China and in the mountains of Yenan without being deflected from his goal of total power in China. Stoical endurance and nerveless waiting, guided by a revolutionary strategy that can take advantage of the shifts and gusts of fortune, are preconditions for victory. They are summarized in three formulas of Mao's. First, Marxist doctrine serves as a telescope or microscope which permits the Communist revolutionary to distinguish the essential from the irrelevant in the subjective assessment of objective factors. Second, "in order to win victory, we must try our best to seal the eyes and ears of the enemy, making him blind and deaf." And third, "Enemy advances, we retreat; enemy halts, we harass; enemy waits, we attack; enemy retreats, we pursue." The classic Socratic injunction of "Know thyself" is transformed into the Communist injunction: "Know your enemy and know yourself, and you can fight a hundred battles without disaster."

The conclusion drawn from the situation of protracted struggle is that peace is only a form of struggle, a continuation of the conflict, but by other means; that permanent peace can be achieved only by abolishing the class struggle consequent upon the establishment of a Communist world; and that any Communist move, however warlike, is just and advances the cause of peace, while any capitalist move, however conciliatory, is stupid or unjust because it advances the ends of war. "We aim at peace not only in one country, but throughout the world, and we not only aim at temporary peace but at permanent peace. In order to achieve this objective we must wage a life-and-death war, we must be prepared to sacrifice anything." For "war, this monster of mutual slaughter among mankind, will be finally eliminated through the process of human society. But there is only one way of eliminating it, namely, to oppose war by means of war, to oppose counter-revolutionary war by means of revolutionary war."

In accord with this strategic doctrine, and the lessons learned from the Leninist Party and the Stalinist Five-Year Plans, Mao and other Chinese leaders have proceeded to bring the various segments of a semifeudal, semicolonial, and sprawling economy under the absolute direction of the planning authorities. Since the program was undertaken at a level of development even below that of Russia in 1900 and is being pushed on a scale far vaster than that which Stalin had to encompass in 1928, the human cost in lives is likely to be considerably higher than in the original model. Strong political compulsions are employed to industrialize heavy industry at the expense of collectivized agriculture, with the result that the sluggish agricultural development requires a consumption level close to subsistence for a rapidly growing population estimated to be 650 million people. As early as 1953, Mao proclaimed the beginning of the transition to Socialism and the "peaceful transformation" of the bourgeois class. This doctrine, which had never appeared in Communist ideology hitherto, was developed to accommodate the fact that in Asia, where the economies are backward, the peasants numerous and workers few, and the elements of the bourgeois class limited, weak, and often opposed to the foreign capitalists who control their raw materials, it is feasible to "educate" the bourgeois class to co-operate with the Party in building Socialism.

These internal policies confirm and strengthen the external policies of the régime. The primary objective of the Chinese Communist leader in these times is to establish a strong and unified China, not only to consolidate Communist control over his own vast country but also to expand Communist influence in Southeast Asia. As in the case of Moscow, the United States becomes the target for Peking's most vitriolic attacks, because it is viewed as the leading "imperialist" power and the most formidable obstacle to the realization of its international goals. Communist China will not forget that the United States gave support to modern Japan and South Korea, and aid to those countries in Southeast Asia from Burma to the Philippines where Communist China sees its own long-term influence at stake. But as Mao's theory of protracted war so clearly established, the Chinese Communist leaders are not men in a hurry, and can wait for opportunities to arise in which to extend their control in the gigantic area of interest to them, an area stirring with unrest, rich in natural resources, with impoverished and discontented populations whose resentment is conveniently directed against three centuries of Western influence, with the United States as the symbol of that kind of power today. The position of the Chinese Communist leaders as bona fide Asians, as well as Communists, who are in control of an Asian power of international proportions, in the mid-twentieth century, provides a solid foundation for the Sino-Soviet alliance in the present world crisis.

3. *The Challenge of the Underdeveloped Areas*

The Communist revolution cuts across and aggravates a revolution that is now taking place in the underdeveloped areas of the world. These areas comprise peoples of almost all of Asia, Africa, and Latin America. They cover roughly two-thirds of the world's population. They pose a challenge to the West because of their great poverty, their seething nationalism, their vast and vastly accelerating population, and their desire to leap into the industrial accomplishments of the twentieth century. The manner in which they solve these issues or encounter failure will greatly affect the future of freedom in the world.

The first aspect of this transformation of non-Western societies has been characterized as a "revolution of rising expectations." These societies are very poor, and their people no longer feel the necessity of accepting either the curse or tradition of their poverty. One index of their poverty is the extremely low per capita income, averaging less than $150 per annum, an average that conceals a wide variation with an estimated low of around $50 per annum for the two countries that lead in population, China and India. This poverty is a chronic situation, associated with a predominantly archaic agricultural economy. It is accompanied by an extremely low level of food consumption at or very near the physiological limit and resulting in hunger and "the hidden hunger," malnutrition. It entails a life expectancy about half that of the Western world, a life of low energy and frequent disease. The encounter with the West made these people aware of the disparity between the two standards of life and of the technical possibilities that might be used to raise their standards

The encounter with the West also supplied the momentum for the revolution of nationalism. The very concept of the nation state and the politics of self-determination were Western prod ucts. But what is more, the areas embrace the entire traditiona colonial world that has come to resent almost any dependence on what they stigmatize as "Western imperialism." This hostilit is deep-seated, due partly to the disruption of previous values attitudes, and modes of life consequent on Western impact, an partly to the actual subservience and subordination enforced by colonial policies. The peasants were alienated by the introduction of commercial agriculture, by monoculture, by increased tenancy sharehold status, indebtedness, and land subdivision—with th accompanying disruptions of traditional family patterns and th village polity. The workers in the cities were largely uprootec peasants, who lost the security of their old communities withoul finding any security in their new ones. The growing middl classes, having been educated in Western ideals, increasingly resented both their colonial status and their quasi-feudal tradi tional societies. And the old ruling classes naturally were dis turbed by the changes in the *status quo*. This transformation o' colonies into nations occurred on a large scale and reached nev proportions after World War II.

At the same time, the rate of population growth in these area: has reached or will reach such tremendous proportions as to con stitute a substantial obstacle to the eradication of their poverty These countries can be divided into two groups with respect t population growth: those with accelerating rates of populatior growth at the present time, and those with high growth potential This population revolution arises from the fact that all of thes areas have had and continue to have high birth rates, and th demarcation between the two groups relates to the death rate. In the first case, the death rate has fallen, largely because of im proved medical and public health conditions, which were intro duced by the West at low cost. In the other case, the death rate

still balances the high birth rate, but present medical and public
health procedures will result in lower mortality. Thus, in the case
of Latin American countries the crude birth rate has remained
at around 40 per thousand, while the death rate has fallen to 17
per thousand, resulting in a population growth of around 2.5 per
cent per year. With the further decline in the mortality rate to
the Western average of close to 10 per thousand, the rate of
growth will rise to 3 per cent. Similar conditions exist in Egypt,
Ceylon, and Algeria. On the other hand, birth rates in Asia and
Africa average around 40 to 45, while death rates average around
30, but with the decline in the latter, and particularly with the
decline in the rate of infant mortalities, these countries will grow
at the explosive rates of close to 2 or 3 per cent. This decline in
mortality rates is expected partly as a result of the almost complete control of malaria, which has been responsible for a great
portion of the deaths in these areas.

This explosive population growth has overwhelming significance for these countries and for the West. The population of
these areas accounts for two-thirds of the present world population of 2.7 billion people. It appears most probable that their
proportion will increase, and by 1975 may equal the present
world population and account for 70 per cent of the projected
world population at that time. If this eventuates, it may increase
the disparity in living standards between them and the West and
thereby the political, social, and economic tensions in the world
as a whole.

It is in this context of poverty, nationalism, and population
growth that we can come to understand their plans for accelerated industrialization. The governments of these areas believe that industrialization is the only means to higher living
standards and to national independence and prestige. They want
to apply Western techniques in a hurry but with no feeling of
solidarity with the West. Moreover, because of the lack of private
incentives, native entrepreneurial and technical skills, and urgent
political pressures, they are disposed to give central governments

a leading role in directing economic development. And in view of the need to provide and expand social overhead services, such as education, public utilities, public health, and in many cases transportation and communication facilities, government investment will play a large role. But the rate of population growth will create severe problems, if it does not pose a real obstacle to the achievement of their economic goals. It is this situation that provides opportunities for Communism and a challenge to the West.

India and China today dramatically illustrate this set of issues. Both countries began under their present governments after World War II in revolt against the West. Both governments have vast populations, that of China around 650 million people, that of India around 400 million people. By 1975 the population of China is projected at 900 million; India 565 million. Both began as predominantly agricultural and poor economies, with incomes of around $50 per capita in the early 1950's. The leaders of both countries vigorously sponsored economic plans. However, in the case of China the plan is designed to maximize the development of heavy industry and to collectivize agriculture without increasing the resources for agriculture as a whole and the living standards of the people as a whole. In the case of India, the plan calls for improving the position of agriculture and the rural areas and the living standards of the people, while developing power, steel, and other industrial sectors, as well as consumer goods. In China the plan is designed and controlled entirely by the leaders of the Party, without public discussion, and with direct government implementation in all spheres. In India, the plan and the drafts of the plan are publicized and the central government shares responsibility with private industry and the regional states in carrying it out. The model for the Chinese plan is obviously Soviet Russia. Nehru, after a visit to China, said that the objective of the Indian plan was not to "sacrifice democratic institutions at the altar of economic progress. . . . In the long run, economic prosperity based on a denial of human freedom and dignity could not carry a country far." This contrast between the objectives and programs of the two leading Asian nations in the world is of far-reaching importance in the crisis of our time.

4. *The Fate of Freedom in the West*

It is against this setting of the challenges that arise from the underdeveloped countries and Communism that we must come to understand the crisis of the West itself. Modern technology increasingly requires a world which can only be precariously divided—and there is no turning back, no reversibility on the development of knowledge and technology. They are cumulative. There are voices, and often persuasive and influential voices, that blame all our evils on the pride of materialistic or scientific man and who call for a halt or restriction on the scientific and technological developments. Even if such voices should succeed in promoting measures to this effect in the West, they will be faced by powers in the Soviet Union and the East who have embraced or are embracing the view that technological development is strategic and primary, whether for state power or for human development. If the West is to be saved, we must recognize this development, and advance our own, rather than restrict it or turn our backs on it.

There is a modern theme that forms a counterpoint to the theme just noted—one that sees all truth and value only in the advance of science and technology and that views all problems concerning human ends, or discussion of human values, as echoes of a pre-scientific age. They would turn their backs on problems of human ends, and see all problems as problems of means-ends, or instrumentalities which never break any chain that terminates in intrinsic or inherent values or simply human ends. This view holds that science and technology are all, and the rest is relative to subjective or group attitudes. On this view, all evil springs from an unscientific view of human and spiritual problems; evil, because not based on acceptance of what science alone can give us, knowledge of means and means-ends relations, but never human ends. It is this view which lends support to the conception of politics as only and simply an affair of power, where the greatest sustainable resources and might can effect right. It supports the rejection of democratic philosophy as a philosphy concerned only with a given, perhaps privileged, group, but not as something that best conforms to human nature, since ultimately human nature has few, if any, invariants, and is wholly malleable. There are not human ends, only vastly more powerful and large-scale means. All of this is reflected in the crisis of values. A society can function as a community only where there are common shared values. This kind of community does not exist today, and there is even more dispute about values than ever before in the history of man. Part of this arises from the paradoxical association of science with destruction, of certitude with unprovability, of freedom with security. The "rational" arguments for frankly mystical faiths are on the increase, when rationality itself appears to have lost its reason.

This crisis, therefore, can be viewed as one of trying to reconcile and balance technological development, based on free and unrestricted scientific inquiry, with human and spiritual development, based on the integrity of the human person and the necessities and obligations of human communities. Technological development is made to promote and not to pervert personal and community development, recognizing that the world is more and more our community with the present scale of technology.

This issue, in its broadest form, has many facets, which appear in various fields. There is the crisis of democracy—which is the problem of whether industrial society can serve to promote and advance human and social development and sustain itself. This partly involves despair about the use of vast power in the hands of those who achieve it. The state is called upon more and more to sustain, if not to promote and advance, human welfare, until it acquires more and more power to maintain itself, in the form of the group who initially has this power to wield against all criticism, if need be. There is the related challenge in attempting to balance high levels of employment without inflation in a capitalistic industrial society. Can we have both full employment and stability, or must we sacrifice one for the other? Third, there is the challenge to the West in the problem of organizing itself on a loose collaborative basis so that it can co-operate in common efforts, including the defense against Communism and the support of democratic economic development in the underdeveloped countries. Of course, these problems are exceedingly complex, and there is no easy solution. Perhaps most serious of all is the feeling that there just is no solution, with the consequent loss of direction, the lack of a clear future course, and the destruction of hope and the creation of anxiety.

This set of developments completes the process begun with the growth of modern science and of the nation-state in the Renaissance. In one sense, the great issue before contemporary man is whether both of these can be utilized for freedom or for its destruction? It is dramatized by the bipolar position of the United States and the Soviet Union, which Alexis de Tocqueville foresaw almost a century and a quarter ago in his *Democracy in America:*

There are at the present time two great nations in the world, which started from different points, but seem to tend towards the same end. I allude to the Russians and the Americans. Both of them have grown up unnoticed; and whilst the attention of mankind was directed elsewhere, they have suddenly placed themselves in the front rank among the nations, and the world learned their existence and their greatness at almost the same time.

All other nations seem to have nearly reached their natural limits, and they have only to maintain their power; but these are still in the act of growth. All the others have stopped, or continue to advance with extreme difficulty; these alone are proceeding with ease and celerity along a path to which no limit can be perceived. The American struggles against the obstacles which nature opposes to him; the adversaries of the Russian are men. The former combats the wilderness and savage life; the latter, civilization with all its arms. The conquests of the American are therefore gained by the ploughshare; those of the Russian by the sword. The Anglo-American relies upon personal interest to accomplish his ends, and gives free scope to the unguided strength and common sense of the people; the Russian centres all the authority of society in a single arm. The principal instrument of the former is freedom; of the latter, servitude. Their starting-point is different, and their courses are not the same; yet each of them seems marked out by the will of Heaven to sway the destinies of half the globe.

It is true that the present bipolar division of world power and the challenge of the underdeveloped areas have thrust the United States, most unwillingly and certainly most unprepared, into a position of world leadership. There are formidable dangers in trying to assume this role, and perhaps even greater ones in trying to shed it, for the future of Western civilization. It is therefore most important that we reflect on the present position of the United States in the world crisis, a concern which is also natural, since this book is written by an American and is primarily addressed to American readers.

The United States, finding itself in the unexpected and unintended role of world leadership, responded to the Soviet challenge with a variety of means that were wholly new to its career. It worked patiently and against great obstacles to help reconstruct the economies of European countries, devastated and bankrupt from the toll of World War II. When the Marshall Plan began to bear fruit, the bold new program of Point IV began to take hold in the judgment of the rulers and common people in backward areas, inclining them to the view that the United States stood for technical assistance, for economic betterment, rather than merely for bigger and more merciless production goals for itself, at any price. Naturally, there were setbacks and disappointments in both programs, but they were two affirmative responses to the crisis of our time. At the same time, the United States began the long-range policy of giving military support to areas threatened by potential Soviet aggression. One phase of climax was reached in Korea, where the United States threw in its military manpower and best equipment (short of atomic weapons) to check the Communist-led North Koreans in their attempted engulfment of the entire peninsula. It was supported in this action by other United Nations troops and wings, and that support was far more significant than the purely physical aid it rendered. It gave solidarity to the concept of an association of free nations working together to stop the aggression the Kremlin inspired and controlled. The role of the United States, a nation unused to widespread intervention or responsibility, in securing political, economic, and military support from those who also understood and felt threatened by the aggressive policies of the Soviet Union and its Iron and Bamboo Curtain satellites, should not be underestimated.

However, the United States is not at all sure that it has the forces of history on its side; nor has it the secular religion that guarantees it is destined to see cosmic victory for its interests and free society. So it has come to pass that the ideals advanced by the United States in the exercise of its power do not appear to the world at large to be as positive as those insistently urged by Soviet policy—and apparently are not as revolutionary. Anti-Communists should try not to blink the fact that the ideals of democratic capitalism, in the eyes of many underprivileged millions, are not accounted a success. This judgment has at least two aspects: intellectuals and "opinion makers" outside America are not nearly so convinced of our cultural and social worth as we are; and the recent history of other democracies in Europe particularly, and with some stretching of the term in Latin America too, raises awkward questions for everyone about the ability of democratic countries to withstand the onslaughts of depression, inflation, or even dictatorial government. Therefore, the philosophy of democracy, even when it is shorn of the widely unpopular accompanying term "capitalism," is not generally believed to be as dynamic or as human as Communism declares itself to be.

The internal political picture in the United States hardly helps in this already uneven struggle. Hasty and rash pronouncements that issue as policy one day to be repudiated the next by the same branch of government or one of its rivals, ultimatums delivered to our allies forcing "time schedules" on them for compliance with the plans that have been made, sincerely enough, for the welfare of all, congressional dissension and debate publicly sermonizing countries that "fail" to live up to what we, in comparative prosperity and ease, consider they must do—all injure our prestige for leadership. Very serious questions are further excited by our rough-and-tumble methods of combating Communist subversion. The first few years of the 1950's may well be viewed by European historians as the sapping and mining of American liberty and pragmatic common sense. The need to adopt security measures to safeguard military power is not forthwith a blank check for investigating committees, loyalty boards, and security agents to employ whatever irresponsible techniques of exposure they choose, often injuring the innocent and stupidly well-meaning as decisively as those who have really carried treason to the heart of democratic safety. And there are the shameless spectacles of Little Rock, the denial of equal political, social, and economic rights to negroes. Elements like these in the domestic arena of politics are magnified, for a variety of reasons, by European and Asian critics into a chronic disease from which they pretend they must, in self-protection, measure their distance. And, as constantly in the history of the American Republic, the old complaint against American culture as crude and "materialistic" not only lingers on but acquires fresh force from every misstep. The accumulation of vast new power, in any event, would have made our policies suspect. The widespread influence of successful "ad men" and the lack of real thought on the part of our propagandists open our democratic philosophy to attack as no more than a manufactured ideological "ism" designed to further American self-interest.

We in the United States may feel strongly that our way of

life will advance freedom and that the Soviet way will destroy and enslave man. A simple corollary then appears to us to be that all countries that have accepted the ways of freedom, or that yearn for it, should join with us in protecting ourselves against Communist aggression. We willingly grant that it is possible to have very different political and economic internal policies (witness Marshall aid to Great Britain during the Labor Party's administration) and still join in service of a minimum common cause. Cherishing such a policy, however, involves economic burdens for all participants and some limitations on sovereignty. These we feel should be borne against the infinitely worse alternative of eventual slavery. Others, however, question the wisdom or the necessity of such policies. One basic factor behind such questioning, that gives neutralism a new lease of life no matter what local engagements the Soviet Union precipitates, rests on the ground that neither bipolar power is likely to use the total weapons they are stockpiling at such heavy cost. The argument is prevalent that both nations, good or evil as their intentions may be, are fully cognizant that there is no longer such a thing as a "knockout blow"; that swift retaliation is almost certain; and that the consequences would be such as to destroy both antagonists, as well as all others on the sidelines, whether manned by effective armies or not armed at all. This belief is given upport by the agreement of the military analysts, public officials, opinion makers, and even tried military leaders themselves.

If we too are entitled to foster some such faith (and blunders, plus impassioned requirements to make good on threats, plus human lapses of reason and sense can never be left out of the general account), where do we stand? A century of protracted cold war with local military engagements is the best that realistic optimism can offer us. Terrible as this may be, the alternative of total war makes its desirable. The long haul, in addition to being who knows how long, will be a thorny road to travel. The East will continue to view the issue before the world as colonialism and freedom from domination by the white master race. European unity will doubtless remain an objective in the face of innumerable flare-ups and corrosive antagonisms. The United States can hardly gain security from loud words about massive retaliation, especially in view of the fact that the East already looks upon us as the first to have used or tested the atomic and hydrogen bombs, and in their area. The political crisis, therefore, can be expected to deepen, instead of being "solved," for it is like a hydra-headed monster—no sooner is one issue successfully mastered, than a cluster of others rise up to torment the tired. The Communist countries, from their point of view, need only wait for new crises and political and diplomatic troubles to sharpen within the free world.

Peaceful co-existence in the long cold war that may lie ahead is anything but Utopian; great efforts will be repaid by small rewards, but they must be pursued to the end of hope. In this war the totalitarian state enjoys the advantage of being free to pursue its objectives consistently, without criticism from any part of the people. The nontotalitarian states must answer this challenge by creating equal strength and unity of purpose, to defend their way of life against Communist assaults, and without strangling that freedom which is their glory. The pressures and difficulties inherent in this enterprise, and the sacrifice of cherished national goals that will be the price of unity of purpose with other free nations, are precisely what the Communists will be waiting to exploit. Both strength and unity are so difficult to achieve within the context of freedom that one or both may fail.

Thus, we need for the future a kind of intelligence, good will, and patience which we can not claim to have achieved in the recent past. Some Americans have little tolerance for the prospect of cultivating such difficult arts toward potential allies in the free world; they will have to bear in mind the consequences of threatening them, or turning our backs upon them. In a world where we must live with one another and with our self-declared Communist destroyers, only the criminally stupid or insane would invite an unnecessary risk. Our greatest hope must be to avert to-

tal war, and to join our own efforts with the changes wrought by
time to help time change *them* more surely than they us.

In exercising its role of leadership, therefore, the United States
will have to keep at least three things in mind. First, we are not
engaged in a popularity contest or an ideological conflict between
socialism and capitalism, but in a long hard struggle for both our
own and others' freedom to pursue our different ways of life, without imposition or dictation from outside. If we are not universally
loved or even substantially appreciated when we think we deserve it, there are reasons for our impaired popularity. We must
not forget that we were fortunate to start with an Anglo-Saxon
political tradition on a new continent with immense land and
natural resources, and that we were given ample time to experiment with the uninhibited exercise of self-interest under a world
order maintained for over a century by the British navy and
system of balance of power. To others, our goals do not inspire
either confidence or enthusiasm because they appear to be almost
wholly materialistic. Our professions do not appear to them to
square with the facts of a very mixed economy with substantial
government support and with a substantial dose of continued
economic protectionism. And for the much-vaunted picture of
a free man in a free society, they tend to see the tremendous
pressures toward conformity in our society. Forces like enter-
tainment for the masses; production for the masses; advertising
for the masses; uniform education for the masses influence the
whole of culture, and the residual personality of the people on
whom they are put to work. The more acute the crisis becomes,
the more insistent appear the pressures to conform.

Secondly, it is likely that the role of the state in all societies
will increase. We find ourselves in the undesirable position of
despising totalitarianism, where the state takes over all aspects of
life, depriving the life of the person, the family, the group of its
freedom. But the technological commitments of modern states,
however, tend to Big Government in every country, regardless of

its political philosophy; and this development will challenge us and all democratic governments to reconsider the relation of the individual to the state in the new setting, in order to preserve essential areas of freedom. We are no longer able to conceive of democratic government as solely concerned with negative restraints, but must endow it with responsibility for providing enlightened economic aids to its working population. That government is not best which governs least in the contemporary world, but which provides real opportunities for high standards of living and still preserves political freedom. Paradoxically, the growth of Big Government, which is viewed with alarm, is taken by some as prelude merely to a world state. For it is claimed that only world government can effectively prevent world war under the conditions of the new weapons. Those who fear the loss of individual freedom as a reflex of the growth of one's own government would have a problem of an entirely new weight if the national will or "sovereignty" were to be reduced in scale to fit into a global state.

And third, leadership for the ends we champion cannot be exercised effectively without moral vision and a serious long-term commitment to workable ideas and ideals of freedom. Others see us as deeply materialistic, satisfied to produce more and better automobiles and television sets for motives of personal self-interest, or more advanced weapons and interplanetary projectiles for motives of political self-interest. It is not that we should reject such motives, especially since they are also what others would like to have satisfied themselves, and in large part others find it possible to criticize us for their lack of such means. But we must also come to recognize that our history and our tradition do present ideas and ideals which are distinctively American and which, if we choose to advance them, may serve as operating models in helping us to realize the great idea—that man can make his own history so that he will be free to realize his best nature. It is not enough to have merely an emotional attachment to the

American way of life; we must also have knowledge of our own past and current world problems, as well as vision and perseverance to carry on a continuing revolution which is civilization-wide, to institute realistic arrangements for self-management in human affairs, to promote equal opportunity, and to maintain the innate dignity of man. And here we can learn to advance a characteristically American trait, to carry on "the great experiment" which De Tocqueville described: "In that land, the great experiment of the attempt to construct society upon a new basis was to be made by civilized man; and it was there, for the first time, that theories hitherto unknown, or deemed impracticable, were to exhibit a spectacle for which the world had not been prepared by the history of the past."

This vision animated the philosopher-statesmen who played a strategic role in the founding of the American Republic, not simply as an abstract theory but as a continuing revolution that could, if truly adhered to, serve as a model of a free humanity. In Madison's terms, "Our country, if it does justice to itself, will be the officina-Libertatis [workshop of Liberty], to the Civilized World, and do more than any other for the uncivilized." Here technology and freedom become technology for freedom, and are conjoined to make "the great experiment" a "workshop of liberty." And, similarly, Jefferson wrote: "It is indeed an animating thought, that while we are securing the rights of ourselves and our posterity, we are pointing out the way to struggling nations, who wish like us to emerge from their tyrannies also. Heaven help their struggles, and lead them, as it has done us, triumphantly through them." Here is a confession of faith that recognizes the practical means to promote the common ends of a struggling humanity, a philosophy that can serve to guide men in meeting the crisis of their times. Can such a philosophy inform the work of men and statesmen today? Can it re-establish faith in an order of nature and value in man and his powers of reason? Are freedom and the life of reason values, and if so are they possible in such an age? Can such a philosophy give meaning and hope to man's endeavors while at the same time recognizing the real features of the crisis itself? Have we learned anything new out of our anxiety, of the situation of engagement with evil and total power?

CHAPTER III

THE PERSPECTIVE OF PHILOSOPHY

1. *The Role of Philosophy*

The crisis of our time is real and palpable. It cannot be eradicated by exhortation and verbal crusade. Since this is so, what does philosophy have to do with it? The purpose of this chapter is to answer that question. It will be essential to understand what meaning to attach to the term "philosophy" before one can claim that philosophy has any relevance to the troubled climate of our times.

One reason for the skepticism about philosophy in a time of crisis is that there is a widespread view that philosophy is, at best, something very special and largely irrelevant to the concerns of living. This view is held, not simply by the proverbial man in the street, but by a great number of professional philosophers in the academies of Great Britain and the United States. These men are preoccupied with the formal techniques of philosophical analysis in order to dissect and clarify bits of scientific or ordinary language. They are sometimes more concerned about the proper forms of statements and the "meaninglessness" of almost all prior philosophical thought than about what they themselves have to offer by way of clarification or content. And as this movement has grown in depth and questions were raised about the nature of philosophical analysis itself, more and more of their work has turned into an analysis of "analysis."

There are, of course, other more traditional views as to the nature of philosophy. George Santayana once wrote of his own philosophy: "In the past or in the future, my language and my borrowed knowledge would have been different, but under whatever sky I had been born, since it is the same sky, I should have had the same philosophy." For Santayana, philosophy is worth cultivating because it is an effort to uncover enduring truths that illuminate the human enterprise, and is not manufactured for, or dispensable in, any crisis. Marx, on the other hand, conceived this view as prejudiced speculation and too far removed from the things and men of this world. He was preoccupied with crisis, and urged a revolution in philosophy to take account of it. "Until now philosophers have only interpreted the world; the point is to change it." Although the philosophical analysts believe that both these contrasting views of philosophy are wrong, they probably divide much of the academic world today not yet captivated by philosophical analysis.

Finally, there is the view of philosophy as a profession of faith and deep personal commitment. Boethius, in prison under sentence of death, invoked the consolation of philosophy. Condorcet, imprisoned by the tyranny of a group who believed fanatically that they were the destined leaders of revolutionary humanity, worked steadily on his impassioned defense of the progress of the human mind. The greatest of them all, Socrates, symbol of the philosophical man in the Western world, refused to accept the offer to escape from prison and from death by poison rather than to forsake the philosophy by which he had lived.

In this book, the conjunction of "philosophy" with "a time of crisis" is intended to refer to an integrated enterprise involving critical and sustained reflection on issues of grave importance to modern man. This view of philosophy comes close to its philological meaning as the love of wisdom, and to its historical significance as the free range of human reason. The philosopher, as such, first appeared in Western history around 2,500 years ago in Greece, when man broke with previous mythical thought by daring to think independently for himself about any phase of human experience. Thus, all histories of Western philosophy start with Thales and the speculations of the Milesian school about the universe. Here we see cosmogony replacing myth, individual thinkers replacing priestly corporations, and rational inquiry replacing elaborate ritual. And once this process of daring speculation began, it did not stop there.

If philosophy began in wonder about the universe, it reached a new height with the quest for self-knowledge in the classic figure of Socrates. His mission was the care of the soul, a virtuous activity by which he fought against ignorance, self-satisfaction, and complacency. For he held that the unexamined life, the uncriticized life is not worthy of man. By engaging young Athenians in this independent critical inquiry, Socrates did in fact undermine the morality of social constraint and of unquestioning obedience to authority and custom. As a result, the political leaders of Athens were concerned, whether during the rule of the thirty tyrants or under the democratic régime. In the first case he was summoned by Critias, who was his former pupil and then the supreme tyrant of Athens, and ordered to stop teaching, with the concealed threat of death for disobedience; in the latter case, he was tried and condemned to death by a democratic jury. It is now generally agreed that the prosecution did not want to make a martyr of Socrates, but wanted to exile him. This Socrates would not accede to, giving the following grounds:

I shall never give up philosophizing and urging you and making my point clear to everyone I meet, saying what I always say: "My good sir, you are an Athenian, a citizen of the city which is greatest and most noted for its wisdom and power; are you not then ashamed to be worrying about your money and how to increase it, and about your reputation, and about your honor, instead of worrying about the knowledge of good and truth and how to improve your soul?" And if anyone contradicts me and says that he does not worry about his soul, I shall not let him off at once and go away, but question him and examine him and refute him; and, if I think that he does not possess virtue, but simply says he does, I shall reproach him for underestimating what is most valuable, and prizing what is unimportant.

. . .

I shall do this to everyone I meet, young and old, stranger and citizen
—but particularly to you citizens of Athens because you are nearer to
me in blood, for this you must realize is God's command to me; and
I think that no greater good has ever happened to you than this my
service to God. For all that I do is go round and persuade young and
old among you not to give so much attention to your bodies and your
monies as to the perfection of your souls.

It is not hard to see why Socrates is esteemed as one of the great
moral heroes of mankind, a secular saint who lived and died for
his faith in man and in the supremacy of human reason.

In this origin and early development of Western philosophy,
we can see three components that persist in the great tradition of
philosophy from Plato and Aristotle through Whitehead and
Dewey, and therefore help us to identify its role. First, philosophy
involves a conscious examination of beliefs. We all have beliefs.
We become more mature, more expert at appraising the validity
and effectiveness of our beliefs to the extent that we become
more conscious of them and their consequences. Reason, as the
objective rehearsal of our beliefs, is an essential human activity.
In philosophy, thought is characteristically disciplined by both
reason and experience: reason, to control the relationships of
thoughts to other thought; experience, to direct what might be
taken for granted, or considered stable in the course of inquiry.
It engages in this activity by satisfying its own standards of
knowledge and consistency, and not some outside authority,
since even the acceptance of authority involves personal choice
and should be grounded. This component of philosophic inquiry
accounts for the repeated emphasis on such matters as method,
logic, and epistemology.

A second aspect of philosophy in its classic sense is the integration of beliefs which have been critically appraised. The emphasis
here is on integration as distinct from specialization, on the perspective of a thinker who sees all knowledge and all events not
simply as special fields or as a chaotic, accidental heap but as

subject matter for inquiry, by the use of one's own powers of reasoning. It does not involve the construction of a closed, consistent system, since this is an impossible task. There is a difference between integration and fixity in human knowledge as in human behavior; between being systematic and having a fixed system; between a unifying perspective and a unified doctrine. Socrates, for example, undeniably had a unifying perspective but not a system in the technical sense. Where such a system is constructed, the aesthetic component of design plays a great role, as in Plato. The integrative element in philosophy refers to habits of mind and broad perspectives which serve as orienting attitudes. We can achieve such a unifying perspective only by relating what we know about all kinds of matters. And since there are always gaps in our knowledge and experience, integration requires that we move beyond what we know by suggesting connections. In this activity, we recognize that all knowledge does not proceed simply from what is somehow given in experience, but requires imaginative constructions which we hope ultimately to ground in some way in experience. The philosophic mind recognizes that there is reliable knowledge, but no fixed boundaries in knowledge, partly because of the always unfinished character of what is known and partly because no part of nature itself has a fixed boundary or even a fixed existence. Consequently, a ceaseless work goes on of probing the foundations of knowledge and establishing connections among different areas of knowledge. This work marks off the philosophic mind, of whatever professional training, from the professional scientist working with established means within the existing division of intellectual labor. Aristotle, Aquinas, Spinoza, Kant, and Hegel are classic examplars of this aspect of philosophy.

The third element in the conception of philosophy which is now under discussion is a central concern with the root values of man and society. The philosophic enterprise conjoins an inquiry into knowledge and values in order to enhance the quality of life. We are all more or less engaged in this activity of valuation. The philosopher is simply more critical and enlightened in this quest. It is partly for this reason that Socrates, Plato, and Aristotle, though ancient Greeks, are still read—and what is more, are enjoyed and admired today. The persistent examination of man in nature and society accounts for the continuous development of ethical and political theory in the great tradition.

Thus, what gives vitality and nobility to classic philosophy is above all the commitment to achieve disciplined, integrative thoughts on all the issues important to man. The sustained cultivation of reason and the life of reason joins the great philosophers in a common enterprise and makes them the intellectual and moral leaders of our civilization.

2. *The Relevance of Philosophy*

Now what has philosophy, conceived in this way, to do with the present crisis? We have seen that the crisis can be characterized as a turning point in the history of Western civilization where the values of the concrete human person, his integrity, his freedom to think and act and write, are not only subject to increasing restraints, but his very existence is threatened. This characterization high-lights the crisis in values. The classic conception of philosophy obviously has great relevance for this issue, since it analyzed the key concepts of ethics and elaborated the ideals and values which move much of Western civilization. The philosophers of Greece developed the values of reason, self-knowledge, and culture. The philosophers of the Renaissance gave us a new vision of reason and the human person. The philosophers of the Enlightenment affirmed a new set of social and political ideals expressed in the theory of government by consent and in the person's rights to "life, liberty, and the pursuit of happiness."

Second, we have taken account of the pervasiveness and scope of the political conflicts in our time. To understand the conflicts between Communist and non-Communist, and between non-Western and Western societies, we must at the very least describe and appraise political programs and objectives relating to forms of organization and modes of power as these may affect the individual citizen, the relations within a state, and the external relations among such states within the entire world. At the immediate level, these are tactical and strategic matters, which are traditionally the business of politicians—but today politics is too important a matter to leave to politicians. At another stage of analysis, there are the data and patterns of disinterested political inquiry. Political philosophy meets an urgent need which neither raw politics nor behaviorial analysis can fulfill. For the great political philosophers were concerned with relating political behavior and organization to the ends of man. They were preoccupied with three main tasks: the analysis of the key concepts of politics; the elaboration of a general theory of the fundamental relations among men that require forms of political organization; and the evaluation of different political agencies in terms of ethical standards. The significance of their work lies in the fact that all the major political conceptions and almost all the political programs of contemporary societies, whether liberal or totalitarian, were molded by their thought. One need only recall such names as Hobbes, Locke, Rousseau, Marx, and Nietzsche to realize the great influence of past political philosophy on the contemporary scene.

Third, the crisis may also be viewed as a crisis of science and technology. For one thing, there is the attack on reason and science itself from many quarters; for another, there is the attack on values by some of the avowed high priests of the scientific attitude; and lastly there is the impact of military and industrial technology, the things in the saddle which increasingly ride man. This set of problems turns up in personal life, as skepticism about the grounds of knowledge or faith; in theory, as the unbridgeable gap between the world of science and the realm of values; and in social life, as the terrifying disproportion between man and technics. All these issues continue to have a deep, unsettling effect on the lives and beliefs of men all over a world which has been unified, not by any shared purposes or common ideals, but by the universal and ever accelerating sweep of modern technology. Philosophers have certainly made it their business to analyze the grounds of knowledge and the role of belief; and with the rise of modern science, have turned their attention increasingly to the issues raised by the crisis of science and technology. It is sufficient to refer to the English empiricist tradition, the American pragmatist tradition, and the current philosophy of science to realize the pertinence of philosophy in this area.

Finally, the crisis is total in its impact on the human person, and the multiple issues raised by it are interrelated and can only be dealt with by crossing professional boundaries. This is already indicated by a crisis of values, of politics, of science and technology. These issues were chosen for purposes of illustration, but many others are involved. For example, an appraisal of United States foreign policy must take account not only of the American character and American resources but also of Soviet imperialism, new military technologies, and the revolutionary aspirations and demographic growth of the peoples in the underdeveloped areas. This requires a broad integrative point of view as well as some control over diverse empirical materials. And it gives new point and fresh urgency to a critical examination of democratic political theory in general and American political theory in particular. Only political theory that accepts and attempts to deal with these problems in a responsible way can hope to throw some light on the conditions and prospects of freedom in our time. And we must go beyond political procedures and examine democratic ways of life as a structure of attitudes and controlling objectives.

The total aspect of the crisis emphasizes the necessity for the integrative attitude essential to the philosophic enterprise. This attitude is probably present more in philosophy than in any other professional activity. For the normal professional specialist guards against any intrusions by others and hesitates to make any excursions himself into other areas. The end of this movement has been characterized as knowing more and more about less and less until we know absolutely everything about nothing. Of course, it is possible to attack the generalist for the reverse movement, for knowing less and less about more and more until he knows absolutely nothing about everything. But where we must deal with a set of major problems of human existence today, we simply cannot avoid a responsible and disciplined consideration of materials belonging to different fields. And it is apparent that almost no professional group, as a group, outside the philosophers in the classic tradition, have made it their business to cultivate the integrative attitude.

On this view, even the history of philosophy can serve to illumine our present plight. We can learn what the great minds of the past have thought about the world and man. This is a humbling process, for although we have learned to control and make many things, we have not gained much in wisdom. We are still confronted with the problems of the nature of the world and knowledge, the nature of the good society and the good life, and while in the modern world television melodramas and space projectiles may give us new sensations and new powers, these only raise more urgently the old question, "for what good?" What we learn, then, from the history of philosophy is what the acknowledged heroes of the mind have thought about great issues—and that should give us greater scope in controlling our own knowledge and values. A comparison of what we think we know and value today with the thought and values of the great philosophers should make it possible for us to revalue our own ideals and make our presuppositions more explicit.

Civilization and culture are cumulative growths. The cultivated mind and the civilized man do not exist in isolation, but only develop through a process of sharing experience and conversing with other cultivated minds and civilized beings. There is a unity of man which is best exemplified by the unity of his efforts in explaining the world and himself. This is implicit in many of the great works of art as it is in the self-corrective inquiry that characterizes the great scientists and moralists. If the object of education be in part offering man alternative visions from which he may gauge the ways and values of the good life, there can be no question that the history of philosophy is an essential component of a continued education.

Properly approached, past philosophy should preserve us from "the Gothic habit of mind" that Jefferson despised, at the same time that it should permit us to be more than instinctive modernists. In regard to the worship of looking backward, we must distinguish between viewing the history of philosophy as the Great Books that contain all permanent knowledge and as man's continuous endeavor to learn about the world and himself. It is clear that truth is not wholly consecrated in the Great Books. For one thing, there is too much opposition for it all to be true. This makes it necessary to engage in a conscious selection on the basis of the best established knowledge of our time. Truth does not exist by authority of the past, but is only established by continuous criticism and testing that must be a perpetual contemporary activity. For another thing, though we may know more than our predecessors, it is important to know this. Truth is never absolutely established, but what we learn from a critical examination of the history of science, as well as of philosophy, is that certain methods and procedures are more successful than others in giving us warranted conclusions. Therefore knowing what our predecessors have thought and the basis for their thinking so, as well as the basis for their thought being either correct or incorrect today, will make us more consciously modern.

3. *The Relevance of Contemporary Philosophy*

The contemporary situation in philosophy is one that is most fateful for our civilization in a way that previous philosophers have not had to meet. For we are made aware, most threateningly and informatively, both subjectively and objectively, that our world will survive and be worth survival only if it can solve the problems that require essentially human co-operation for common human goals. What we need is a two-pronged drive to assimilate the heritage of the past and to cope with the terrible issues of the present. Clearly, if we can learn something from the history of philosophy, we should learn more from those contemporary philosophical minds who have been dealing with the problems of our time and reworking the classic tradition to meet the needs of contemporary man as part of a lifelong and full-time commitment. For our time requires a re-examination of those general, directive, leading, over-all conceptions that can throw light in the darkness that surrounds us, that can provide hope that is more than faith in a fool's paradise, and that can move us to positive action to form and reform ourselves, and thereby our history.

Responsible philosophers today not only respond to our existential situation. There are certain new developments which permit them to have more relevance for us than past philosophers. These developments relate to the novel materials and methods that can be employed in philosophic construction in our time. Unlike any other civilization, our historical knowledge embraces the history of all previous civilizations, the life of primitive societies, and the activities of people in every region and condition of the world. This historical knowledge presents a concrete opportunity, that never existed before, to learn what is needed to integrate mankind in the light of its history. Further, we have started on the tracks of advanced knowledge of man himself, in the light of anthropological materials, the results of depth psychology, and the design of thinking machines. For the first time it appears feasible to look toward the tentative construction of a theory of the total personality. And finally our knowledge of various aspects of nature, from the creation of energies that flow from the sun to the creation of elementary bits of living matter, constitutes a novel element in our philosophic heritage. Our growth in methods of inquiry, joined to our knowledge of nature and man, and our experience of social change may ultimately permit the disciplined and comprehensive construction of philosophies for meeting issues of human import.

In the meantime, we must work with what philosophy we

have, of a much less ambitious, more informal, though still controlled, character, to help us examine and appraise some of the real options open to us. The readings collected in this book are designed to serve this end. They represent significant statements of some of the leading thinkers in the Western world who have tried to appraise the problems of modern man and frame a philosophy adequate for survival or, better yet, for the enhancement and enrichment of life. Their thoughtful, imaginative, and authoritative exploration of alternatives should help us to find our own bearings and rethink our own values. The selections were made with the guiding principle that a philosophy of personal and political freedom is still more dynamic and meaningful for modern man than any other. All the writers are for freedom. This principle of selection accounts for the exclusion of representatives of two most important movements in contemporary philosophy—that of Communism and logical analysis. The reason for excluding them is that their theoretical position claims that values cannot be defended on any intelligent grounds, but simply reflect ideological class prejudices or emotive personal preferences.

In addition, certain other criteria were employed in selecting the men and their writings. Above all, content was the real guide line of the entire operation. How good were the ideas? Within this broad setting, the qualities of communication and authenticity were important. These ruled out any fancy steppers or journalistic middlemen in the philosophical world. On the first ground, readable meaning rather than Descartes's degree of clarity was the desideratum. Nontechnical and informal language were a necessity so that intelligent and serious readers who may not be specialized could find something of value here. On the second ground, the selections were mined from the sources of inspiration, fruitful ideas, profound scholarship, significant and original philosophical perspective. Each of the authors has won prestige the hard way and is the kind of writer the intelligent and sensitive modern reader should be acquainted with, or fail to experience some of the good in our culture.

The final guide was variety, not that of a hodgepodge character, or to show the international brotherhood or to pep up the appetites of jaded readers. What was wanted was the widest possible range of significant statement and vision, so that something like the intellectual landscape could be viewed. Variety was used as a guiding principle and not as a mechnical gauge counting nations. There are in fact Englishmen, Germans, Italian, Indian, and American (both native and nationalized) contributors. But the test was the point of view, *sometimes* distinctively colored with a national culture.

Here is a goodly group of men who make philosophy come alive. For they present it, not as schema of dead and dry categories, but as integrated and informed vision that goes beyond what is given and known by the application of special and professional skills and knowledge to arrive at a positive faith—a faith that will enhance the dignity and possibilities of modern man, of those aspects of the human person which ennoble nature.

PART TWO
SELECTIONS FROM PHILOSOPHICAL WRITERS

CHAPTER IV

ARNOLD J. TOYNBEE (1889–   )

Arnold J. Toynbee, perhaps the only contemporary historian who has won world-wide interest and acclaim, has recently retired from his post as Research Professor of International History at the University of London and Director of Studies at the Royal Institute of International Affairs. His multivolumed *A Study of History* combines an extraordinary depth of historical learning with what seems to be boundless imagination of both a mythological and terminological bent. It has been called "the most provocative work of historical theory written in England since Karl Marx's *Capital*." It would be too much to expect a work of such vast historical scope to be "popular" in the sense of being thoroughly read and digested; but a fair sample of its revolutionary perspective has been made familiar to the general reader through the medium of mass-circulation magazines and Sunday supplements and through the public lecture platform.

Toynbee's main theme is that history can be understood only by considering civilizations as the real units of history, and not through the conventional approach confined to the career of a given nation. He finds that twenty-one such civilizations have existed in the past six thousand years, that all have decayed or perished with the exception of Western civilization (that is, Latin-Christian civilization, sprung from the Hellenic in its Roman phase), but that this last survivor is well advanced in its "Time of Troubles," so that no one can vouch for its future prospects. Nevertheless, Toynbee's frequent appeal to the rhythm of "challenge and response," which makes itself felt over the entire field of action, attempts to emphasize the factor of human creativity, and to cast into the limbo of outworn beliefs "the iron law of fate," whether that law is taken to be determinism of a racial or environmental or economic form. Should the unknown capacities

73

for human creativity be guided and liberated by the "gentle" way of religious transfiguration, Western civilization might save itself, essentially by giving itself up to that Society which is the goal of civilizations: a conversion of the soul "from the World, the Flesh, and the Devil, to the Kingdom of Heaven."

Born in London in 1889, Arnold J. Toynbee received a thorough education in the classics at Balliol College, Oxford, and flourished in the prevailing climate of security that people felt was real in the early part of this century, entertaining the nice delusion, as Toynbee himself describes it, that "history had happened to others." The First World War was the first catastrophe to explode this jolly innocence, just as the years of peace that mounted steadily toward the Second World War constituted proof of a disintegration of Western civilization. Toynbee now believes that a third world war would be likely to be fatal to the human race, and draws the moral that in this "eleventh hour" we must meet the challenge of a radically unified physical globe by a radically unified world religion.

Readers of the following selection from Toynbee's essays, whether or not they find themselves agreeing with his main themes or any detail in his interpretation, will quickly concede that Toynbee's writing meets the ideal defined by Lord Acton: "That which is distinct from the combined history of all countries, and is not a burden on the memory but an illumination of the soul."

AN HISTORIAN'S VIEW OF
THE CRISIS OF MODERN CIVILIZATION
—
ARNOLD J. TOYNBEE

1. *Are We Doomed?*

Does history repeat itself? In our Western world in the eighteenth and nineteenth centuries, this question used to be debated as an academic exercise. The spell of well-being which our civilization was enjoying at the time had dazzled our grandfathers into the quaint pharisaical notion that they were "not as other men are"; they had come to believe that our Western society was exempt from the possibility of falling into those mistakes and mishaps that have been the ruin of certain other civilizations whose history, from beginning to end, is an open book. To us, in our generation, the old question has rather suddenly taken on a new and very practical significance. We have awakened to the truth (how, one wonders, could we ever have been blind to it?) that Western man and his works are no more invulnerable than the now extinct civilizations of the Aztecs and the Incas, the Sumerians and the Hittites. So to-day, with some anxiety, we are searching the scriptures of the past to find out whether they contain a lesson that we can decipher. Does history give us any information about our own prospects? And, if it does, what is the burden of it? [1] *

A survey of the historical landscape in the light of our existing knowledge shows that, up to date, history has repeated itself about twenty times in producing human societies of the species to which our Western society belongs, and it also shows that, with the possible exception of our own, all these representatives of the species of society called civilizations are already dead or moribund. Moreover, when we study the histories of these dead and moribund civilizations in detail, and compare them with one another, we find indications of what looks like a recurring pattern in the process of their breakdowns, declines, and falls. We are naturally asking ourselves to-day whether this particular chapter of history is bound to repeat itself in our case. Is that pattern of decline and fall in store for us in our turn, as a doom from which no civilization can hope to escape? In the writer's opinion, the answer to this question is emphatically in the negative. The effort to create a new manifestation of life—be it a new species of mollusc or a new species of human society—seldom or never succeeds at the first attempt. Creation is not so easy an enterprise as that. It wins its ultimate successes through a process of trial and error;

* See *Sources* at the end of the chapter.

and accordingly the failure of previous experiments, so far from dooming subsequent experiments to fail in their turn in the same way, actually offers them their opportunity of achieving success through the wisdom that can be gained from suffering. Of course a series of previous failures does not guarantee success to the next comer, any more than it condemns him to be a failure in his turn. There is nothing to prevent our Western civilization from following historical precedent, if it chooses, by committing social suicide. But we are not doomed to make history repeat itself; it is open to us, through our own efforts, to give history, in our case, some new and unprecedented turn. As human beings, we are endowed with this freedom of choice, and we cannot shuffle off our responsibility upon the shoulders of God or nature. We must shoulder it ourselves. It is up to us.[2]

2. *The Present International Situation*

What is the issue that is arousing this anxiety to-day all over the world: among the Americans, the Canadians, ourselves, our European neighbours, and the Russians . . . I shall give you my own personal view, which is, as you will see, a controversial one. My personal belief is that this formidable issue is a political issue, not an economic one, and I further believe that it is not the question whether the world is going to be unified politically in the near future. I believe—and this is, I suppose, my most controversial assertion, but I am simply stating what I do sincerely think—I believe it is a foregone conclusion that the world is in any event going to be unified politically in the near future. (If you consider just two things, the degree of our present interdependence and the deadliness of our present weapons, and put these two considerations together, I do not see how you can arrive at any other conclusion.) I think the big and really formidable political issue to-day is, not *whether* the world is soon going to be unified politically, but in which of two alternative possible ways this rapid unification is going to come about.

There is the old-fashioned and unpleasantly familiar way of

continual rounds of wars going on to a bitter end at which one surviving great power "knocks out" its last remaining competitor and imposes peace on the world by conquest. This is the way in which the Graeco-Roman world was forcibly united by Rome in the last century B.C., and the Far Eastern world in the third century B.C. by the Roman-minded principality of Ts'in. And then there is the new experiment in a co-operative government of the world—no, not quite a new one, because there were abortive attempts at finding a co-operative way out of the troubles that were actually brought to an end by the forcible imposition of the *Pax Romana* and the *Pax Sinica*; but our own pursuit, in our own lifetime, of this happier solution has been so much more resolute and so much more self-conscious that we may perhaps fairly regard it as a new departure. Our first attempt at it was the League of Nations; our second attempt is the United Nations organization. It is evident that we are engaged here on a very difficult political pioneering enterprise over largely unknown ground. If this enterprise did succeed—even if only just so far as to save us from a repetition of "the knock-out blow"—it might open out quite new prospects for mankind: prospects that we have never sighted before during these last five or six thousand years that have seen us making a number of attempts at civilization.

After greeting this gleam of hope on our horizon we should be sinking into a fool's paradise if we did not also take note of the length and the roughness of the road that lies between our goal and the point at which we stand to-day. We are not likely to succeed in averting "the knock-out blow" unless we take due account of the circumstances that unfortunately tell in favour of it.

The first of these adverse circumstances, with which we have to contend, is the fact that, within the span of a single lifetime, the number of great powers of the highest material calibre—if we measure this calibre in terms of sheer war potential—has dwindled from eight to two. To-day, in the arena of naked power politics, the United States and the Soviet Union face one another alone. One more world war, and there might be only a solitary great power left to give the world its political unity by the old-fashioned method of the conqueror imposing his fiat.

This startlingly rapid fall in the number of great powers of the highest material calibre has been due to a sudden jump in the material scale of life, which has dwarfed powers of the dimensions of Great Britain and France by comparison with powers of the dimensions of the Soviet Union and the United States. Such sudden jumps have occurred before in history. Between five and four hundred years ago, powers of the dimensions of Venice and Florence were similarly dwarfed by the sudden emergence of powers of the dimensions of England and France.

This dwarfing of the European powers by the United States and the Soviet Union would have happened, no doubt, in any case in course of time. It is, I should say, an inevitable ultimate consequence of the recent opening-up of the vast spaces of North America and Russia, and of the still more recent development of their resources by the application there, on a massive scale, of technical methods partly invented in the laboratories of Western Europe. But the time taken by this inevitable process might have been as much as a hundred years if it had not been telescoped into a third or a quarter of that span by the cumulative effect of two world wars. If the change had not been thus accelerated, it would have been a gradual process that might have allowed all parties time to adjust themselves to it more or less painlessly. As a result of its having been speeded up by the two wars, it has been a revolutionary process which has put all parties in a quandary.[3]

3. *War and Class in Our Civilization*

Through these triumphs of clockwork the Western middle class has produced three undesigned results—unprecedented in history—whose cumulative impetus has set Juggernaut's car rolling on again with a vengeance. Our Western "know-how" has unified the whole world in the literal sense of the whole habitable and traversable surface of the globe; and it has inflamed the institutions of War and Class, which are the two congenital diseases of civilization, into utterly fatal maladies. This trio of unintentional achievements presents us with a challenge that is formidable indeed.

War and Class have been with us ever since the first civilizations emerged above the level of primitive human life some five or six thousand years ago, and they have always been serious complaints. Of the twenty or so civilizations known to modern Western historians, all except our own appear to be dead or moribund, and, when we diagnose each case, *in extremis* or *post mortem*, we invariably find that the cause of death has been either War or Class or some combination of the two. To date, these two plagues have been deadly enough, in partnership, to kill off nineteen out of twenty representatives of this recently evolved species of human society; but, up to now, the deadliness of these scourges has had a saving limit. While they have been able to destroy individual specimens, they have failed to destroy the species itself. Civilizations have come and gone, but Civilization (with a big "C") has succeeded, each time, in re-incarnating itself in fresh examplars of the type; for, immense though the social ravages of War and Class have been, they have not ever yet been all-embracing. When they have shattered the top strata of a society, they have usually failed to prevent the underlying strata from surviving, more or less intact, and clothing themselves with spring flowers on exposure to the light and air. And when one society has collapsed in one quarter of the world it has not, in the past, necessarily dragged down others with it. When the early civilization of China broke down in the seventh century B.C., this did not prevent the contemporary Greek civilization, at the other end of the Old World, from continuing to rise towards its zenith. And when the Graeco-Roman civilization finally died of the twin diseases of War and Class in the course of the fifth, sixth, and seventh centuries of the Christian era, this did not prevent a new civilization from successfully coming to birth in the Far East during those same three hundred years.

Why cannot civilization go on shambling along, from failure

to failure, in the painful, degrading, but not utterly suicidal way in which it has kept going for the first few thousand years of its existence? The answer lies in the recent technological inventions of the modern Western middle class. These gadgets for harnessing the physical forces of non-human nature have left human nature unchanged. The institutions of War and Class are social reflexions of the seamy side of human nature—or what the theologians call original sin—in the kind of society that we call civilization. These social effects of individual human sinfulness have not been abolished by the recent portentous advance in our technological "know-how," but they have not been left unaffected by it either. Not having been abolished, they have been enormously keyed up, like the rest of human life, in respect of their physical potency. Class has now become capable of irrevocably disintegrating Society, and War of annihilating the entire human race. Evils which hitherto have been merely disgraceful and grievous have now become intolerable and lethal, and, therefore, we in this Westernized world in our generation are confronted with a choice of alternatives which the ruling elements in other societies in the past have always been able to shirk—with dire consequences, invariably, for themselves, but not at the extreme price of bringing to an end the history of mankind on this planet. We are thus confronted with a challenge that our predecessors never had to face: We have to abolish War and Class—and abolish them now—under pain, if we flinch or fail, of seeing them win a victory over man which, this time, would be conclusive and definitive.

The new aspect of war is already familiar to Western minds. We are aware that the atom bomb and our many other new lethal weapons are capable, in another war, of wiping out not merely the belligerents but the whole of the human race. But how has the evil of class been heightened by technology? Has not technology already notably raised the minimum standard of living—at any rate in countries that have been specially efficient or specially fortunate in being endowed with the riches of nature and

being spared the ravages of war? Can we not look forward to
seeing this rapidly rising minimum standard raised to so high a
level, and enjoyed by so large a percentage of the human race,
that the even greater riches of a still more highly favoured minority will cease to be a cause of heart-burning? The flaw in this line
of reasoning is that it leaves out of account the vital truth that
man does not live by bread alone. However high the minimum
standard of his material living may be raised, that will not cure
his soul of demanding social justice; and the unequal distribution of this world's goods between a privileged minority and an
underprivileged majority has been transformed from an unavoidable evil into an intolerable injustice by the latest technological
inventions of Western man.[4]

4. *The Unification of the World*

Now we come to the great revolution: a technological revolution by which the West made its fortune, got the better of all the
other living civilizations, and forcibly united them into a single
society of literally world-wide range. The revolutionary Western
invention was the substitution of the Ocean for the Steppe as the
principal medium of world-communication. This use of the
Ocean, first by sailing ships and then by steamships, enabled
the West to unify the whole inhabited and habitable world, including the Americas. . . .

We have reached the Pillars of Hercules and it is time to draw
in sail, for we cannot see clearly very much farther ahead. In
the chapter of history on which we are now entering, the seat of
material power is moving at this moment still farther away from
its pre-da-Gaman locus. From the small island of Britain, lying
a stone's throw from the Atlantic coast of the continent of Asia,
it is moving to the larger island of North America, a bowshot
farther distant. But this transfer of Poseidon's trident from London to New York may prove to have marked the culmination of
the dislocating effects of our current Oceanic age of intercom-
munication; for we are now passing into a new age in which the

material medium of human intercourse is going to be neither the Steppe nor the Ocean, but the Air, and in an air age mankind may succeed in shaking its wings free from their fledgeling bondage to the freakish configuration of the surface—solid or liquid—of the globe.

In an air age the locus of the centre of gravity of human affairs may be determined not by physical but by human geography: not by the lay-out of oceans and seas, steppes and deserts, rivers and mountain-ranges, passes and straits, but by the distribution of human numbers, energy, ability, skill, and character. And, among these human factors, the weight of numbers may eventually come to count for more than its influence in the past. The separate civilizations of the pre-da-Gaman age were created and enjoyed . . . by a tiny sophisticated ruling minority perched on the back of a neolithic peasantry, as Sinbad the Sailor was ridden by the Old Man of the Sea. This neolithic peasantry is the last and mightiest sleeper, before herself, whom the West has waked.

The rousing of this passively industrious mass of humanity has been a slow business. Athens and Florence each flashed her brief candle in the sleeper's drowsy eyes, but each time he just turned onto his side and sank to sleep again. It was left for modern England to urbanize the peasantry with sufficient energy on a large enough scale to set the movement travelling round the circumference of the Earth. The peasant has not taken this awakening kindly. Even in the Americas he has contrived to remain much as he was in Mexico and the Andean Republics, and he has struck new roots on virgin soil in the Province of Quebec. Yet the process of his awakening has been gathering momentum; the French Revolution carried it on to the Continent; the Russian Revolution has propagated it from coast to coast; and, though to-day there are still some fifteen hundred million not yet awakened peasants—about three-quarters of the living generation of mankind—in India, China, Indo-China, Indonesia, Dar-al-Islam, and Eastern Europe, their awakening is now only a matter of time, and, when it has been accomplished, numbers will begin to tell.[5]

Future historians will say, I think, that the great event of the twentieth century was the impact of the Western civilization upon all the other living societies of the world of that day. They will say of this impact that it was so powerful and so pervasive that it turned the lives of all its victims upside down and inside out—affecting the behaviour, outlook, feelings, and beliefs of individual men, women, and children in an intimate way, touching chords in human souls that are not touched by mere external material forces—however ponderous and terrifying. This will be said, I feel sure, by historians looking back on our times even from as short a time hence as A.D. 2047. . . . The historians of A.D. 3047 will, I believe, be chiefly interested in the tremendous counter-effects which, by that time, the victims will have produced in the life of the aggressor. By A.D. 3047, our Western civilization, as we and our Western predecessors have known it, say, for the last twelve or thirteen hundred years, since its emergence out of the Dark Ages, may have been transformed, almost out of all recognition, by a counter-radiation of influences from the foreign worlds which we, in our day, are in the act of engulfing in ours—influences from Orthodox Christendom, from Islam, from Hinduism, from the Far East.

By A.D. 4047 the distinction—which looms large to-day—between the Western civilization, as an aggressor, and the other civilizations, as its victims, will probably seem unimportant. When radiation has been followed by counter-radiation of influences, what will stand out will be a single great experience, common to the whole of mankind: the experience of having one's parochial social heritage battered to bits by collision with the parochial heritages of other civilizations, and then finding a new life—a new common life—springing up out of the wreckage. The historians of A.D. 4047 will say that the impact of the Western civilization on its contemporaries, in the second half of the second millennium of the Christian era, was the epoch-making event of that age because it was the first step towards the unification of mankind into one single society.[6]

5. The Change in Historical Perspective

History, seen in this perspective, makes, I feel, the following call upon historians of our generation and of the generations that will come after ours. If we are to perform the full service that we have the power to perform for our fellow human beings—the important service of helping them to find their bearings in a unified world—we must make the necessary effort of imagination and effort of will to break our way out of the prison walls of the local and short-lived histories of our own countries and our own cultures.[7]

Personally, I do not believe that this antediluvian Western traditional historical outlook is going to last much longer. I have no doubt that a re-orientation is in store for us in our turn, and in our case, I fancy, it will be one in the literal meaning of the word. But why should we wait for History, like some eighteenth-century Prussian drill-sergeant, to take us by the scruff of the neck and twist our heads straight for us? Though our neighbours have recently been re-educated in this unpleasant and humiliating way, we ought surely to do better, for we cannot plead that we have been taken by surprise, as they were. The facts stare us in the face, and, by exercising our historical imagination, we can perhaps anticipate the compulsory education that is already on its way to us. The Greek Stoic philosopher Cleanthes prays Zeus and Fate for grace to follow their lead of his own will without flinching; "for if," he adds, "I quail and rebel, I shall have to follow just the same." . . .[8]

Now what must we Westerners do if we aspire, like Cleanthes, to follow the beck of Zeus and Fate by using our intelligence and exercising our free will, instead of constraining those dread deities to bring us into line by the humiliating method of compulsion?

First, I would suggest, we must readjust our own historical outlook on the lines on which the educated representatives of our sister-societies have been readjusting theirs during these last few generations. Our non-Western contemporaries have grasped the fact that, in consequence of the recent unification of the world, *our* past history has become a vital part of *theirs*. Reciprocally, we mentally still-slumbering Westerners have now to realize, on our part, that, in virtue of the same revolution—a revolution, after all, that has been brought about by ourselves—our neighbours' past is going to become a vital part of our own Western future.

In rousing ourselves to make this effort of imagination we do not have to start quite from the beginning. We have always realized and acknowledged our debt to Israel, Greece, and Rome. But these, of course, are extinct civilizations, and we have managed to pay our homage to them without budging from our traditional self-centred standpoint because we have taken it for granted—in the blindness of our egotism—that our noble selves are those "dead" civilizations' *raison d'être*. We imagined them living and dying for the sake of preparing the way for us—playing John the Baptist to our own role as the Christ (I apologize for the blasphemy of this comparison, but it does bring out sharply how outrageously distorted our outlook has been).

We have latterly also realized the importance, as contributors to our own past, of certain other civilizations which were not only extinct but which had lain buried in oblivion before we disinterred their debris. It is easy for us to be generous in our acknowledgements to Minoans, Hittites, and Sumerians, for their rediscovery has been a feather in our Western scholar's cap, and they have made their reappearance on the stage of history under our patronage.

It will be harder for us to accept the not less plain fact that the past histories of our vociferous, and sometimes vituperative, living contemporaries—the Chinese and the Japanese, the Hindus and the Muslims, and our elder brothers the Orthodox Christians —are going to become a part of our Western past history in a future world which will be neither Western nor non-Western but will inherit all the cultures which we Westerners have now brewed together in a single crucible. Yet this is the manifest truth, when we face it. Our own descendants are not going to be just Western, like ourselves. They are going to be heirs of Confucius and Lao-Tse as well as Socrates, Plato, and Plotinus; heirs of Gautama Buddha as well as Deutero-Isaiah and Jesus Christ; heirs of Zarathustra and Muhammad as well as Elijah and Elisha and Peter and Paul; heirs of Shankara and Ramanuja as well as Clement and Origen; heirs of the Cappadocian Fathers of the Orthodox Church as well as our African Augustine and our Umbrian Benedict; heirs of Ibn Khaldun as well as Bossuet; and heirs (if still wallowing in the Serbonian Bog of politics) of Lenin and Gandhi and Sun Yat-sen as well as Cromwell and George Washington and Mazzini.

A readjustment of historical outlook demands a corresponding revision of methods of historical study. Recapturing, if we can, an old-fashioned mode of thought and feeling, let us confess, with great humility, that, through the providence of God, the historic achievement of Western man has been to do something not simply for himself but for mankind as a whole—something so big that our own parochial history is going to be swallowed up by the results of it. By making history we have transcended our own history. Without knowing what we have been doing we have taken the opportunity offered to us. To be allowed to fulfil oneself by surpassing oneself is a glorious privilege for any of God's creatures.

On this view then—a humble view and yet a proud view too—the main strand of our modern Western history is not the parish-pump politics of our Western society as inscribed on triumphal arches in a half-dozen parochial capitals or recorded in the national and municipal archives of ephemeral "Great Powers." The main strand is not even the expansion of the West over the world —so long as we persist in thinking of that expansion as a private enterprise for the Western society's own. The main strand is the progressive erection, by Western hands, of a scaffolding within which all the once separate societies have built themselves into one. From the beginning, mankind has been partitioned; in our day we have at last become united. The Western handiwork that has made this union possible has not been carried out with open eyes, like David's unselfish labours for the benefit of Solomon; it has been performed in heedless ignorance of its purpose, like the labours of the animalculae that build a coral reef up from the bottom of the sea till at length an atoll rises above the waves. But our Western-built scaffolding is made of less durable materials than that. The most obvious ingredient in it is technology, and man cannot live by technology alone. In the fullness of time, when the oecumenical house of many mansions stands firmly on its own foundations and the temporary Western technological scaffolding falls away—as I have no doubt that it will—I believe it will become manifest that the foundations are firm at last because they have been carried down to the bedrock of religion.[9]

6. *What Shall We Do To Be Saved?*

The problems that have beset and worsted other civilizations have come to a head in our world to-day. We have invented the atomic weapon in a world partitioned between two supremely great powers; and the United States and the Soviet Union stand respectively for two opposing ideologies whose antithesis is so extreme that, as it stands, it seems irreconcilable. Along what path are we to look for salvation in this parlous plight, in which we hold in our hands the choice of life or death not only for ourselves but for the whole human race? Salvation perhaps lies, as so often, in finding a middle way. In politics, this golden mean would be something that was neither the unrestricted sovereignty of parochial states nor the unrelieved despotism of a centralized world government; in economics it would be something that was neither unrestricted private enterprise nor unmitigated socialism.[10] In the life of the spirit, put the secular super-structure back onto religious foundations. Efforts are being made in our Western world to-day to find our way towards each of these goals. If we had arrived at all three of them, we might fairly feel that we had won our present battle for our civilization's survival. But these are, all of them, ambitious undertakings, and it will call for the hardest work and the highest courage to make any progress at all towards carrying any one of them through to achievement.

Of the three tasks, the religious one is, of course, in the long run by far the most important, but the other two are the more urgent, because, if we were to fail in these in the short run, we might lose for ever our opportunity of achieving a spiritual re-birth which cannot just be whistled for at our convenience, but will only come, if it comes at all, at the unhurrying pace at which the deepest tides of spiritual creation flow.

The political task is the most urgent of all. The immediate problem here is a negative one. Faced, as we are, with the pros-pect that—given our present interdependence and present weap-ons—the world is now on the eve of being unified politically by one means or another, we have to stave off the disastrous dénoue-ment of unification by force of arms: the familiar method of the forcible imposition of a *Pax Romana* which is probably the line of least resistance for the resolution of the formidable political forces in whose grip our own world finds itself to-day. Can the United States and the other Western countries manage to co-operate with the Soviet Union through the United Nations? If the United Nations organization could grow into an effective system of world government, that would be much the best solu-tion of our political crux. But we have to reckon with the possi-bility of this enterprise's failing, and to be ready, should it fail, with an alternative to fall back upon. Could the United Nations split, *de facto*, into two groups without a breach of the peace? And, supposing that the whole face of the planet could be parti-tioned peacefully into an American and a Russian sphere, could two worlds on one planet live side by side on a footing of "non-violent non-co-operation" for long enough to give a chance for a gradual mitigation of the present differences in their social and ideological climates? The answer to this question would depend on whether, on these terms, we could buy the time needed to carry out our economic task of finding a middle way between free enterprise and socialism.

These riddles may be hard to read, but they do tell us plainly what we most need to know. They tell us that our future largely depends upon ourselves. We are not just at the mercy of an inexorable fate.[11]

Sources
—

CHAPTER IV: AN HISTORIAN'S VIEW OF THE CRISIS
OF MODERN CIVILIZATON

All selections are from Arnold Toynbee's collection of essays entitled *Civilization on Trial* (Oxford University Press, New York, 1948).

1 "Does History Repeat Itself?", page 29, lines 1-21.

2 *Ibid.*, page 38, lines 17-33; page 39, lines 1-21.

3 "The International Outlook," page 126, lines 17-18; page 127, line 1 and lines 5-33; page 128; page 129, lines 1-25.

4 "The Present Point in History," page 23, lines 10-33; pages 24-25; page 26, lines 1-9.

5 "The Unification of the World and the Change in Historical Perspective," page 70, lines 7-16; page 91, line 33; page 92.

6 "Encounters Between Civilizations," page 214, lines 14-25; page 215, lines 10-33; page 216, lines 1-2.

7 "Civilization on Trial," page 158, lines 29-30; page 159, lines 1-7.

8 "The Unification of the World and the Change in Historical Perspective," page 63, lines 10-27.

9 *Ibid.*, page 88, lines 28-33; pages 89-91.

10 "The Present Point in History," page 27, lines 17-32.

11 "Does History Repeat Itself?", page 39, lines 26-33; pages 40-41.

CHAPTER V

ALBERT EINSTEIN (1879–1955)

Members of the Institute for Advanced Study at Princeton used to look out of their study windows, on sunny days or rainy days or even in occasional blizzards, and see a small plump man with a cap of wind-blown gray hair, carelessly dressed in rumpled slacks and a faded blue sweater over a soft-collared shirt, crossing the lawn to his study in the Institute building. *His* study had a blackboard on its wall, and there the gentle man would write equations, or watch his visitors resort to chalk. This man was Albert Einstein, in his late sixties, already a citizen of the United States, and deeply content with his self-chosen isolation in the small Eastern university town. This man had become in his own lifetime a legend: he was indisputably the greatest scientific genius of the modern world, yet he was known for the radiance of his sympathetic heart as well as for the miraculous creative power of his mind.

The sole creator of that twentieth century revolution in physics known as relativity theory, Einstein also contributed substantially to the development of quantum theory. He had traveled a difficult and lonely path in his epoch-making scientific work. For many years he had had to contend with the shocked rebuffs of the most advanced scientists of the day, who were hard put to it to assimilate the startling changes in fundamental concepts of space, time, mass, energy, gravitation and, ultimately, in the geometry of the world. Paradoxically, by the time the scientific community was prepared to assent enthusiastically to the Einsteinian revolution in physics, and after Einstein's predictions about bending light rays had been dramatically confirmed by two English scientific teams in 1919, Einstein himself was tenaciously pursuing a unifying theory that would embrace in one law large- and small-scale physical phenomena. The fruit of thirty years of his repeated investigations on this vast problem Einstein incorporated in the 1950 edition of *The Meaning of Relativity*. Thus, toward the close of his life Einstein once again experienced the professional skepticism toward his work which he knew of old.

Although Einstein once wrote in an autobiographical essay that "the essential in the being of a man of my type lies precisely in *what* he thinks and *how* he thinks, not in what he does or suffers," and proceeded to a spirited and somewhat technical discussion of the nature of physical theory, he was inveterately a man with an invincible moral conscience and thus a man of serious social belief, ready on occasions of great import to act and to lead. The most momentous action of Einstein's life is easily the fateful letter he addressed to President Roosevelt on August 2, 1939, which simply stated: "Some recent work by E. Fermi and L. Szilard which has been communicated to me in manuscript leads me to expect that the element uranium may be turned into a new and important source of energy in the immediate future. . . . A single bomb of this type . . . exploded in a port . . . might very well destroy the whole port, together with the surrounding territory. . . ." Thus Einstein had made his hard decision, after the many years of service to pacificism and to the ideals of democratic socialism, that it was intolerable to permit the Nazis to get prior hold of such a bomb and that it was imperative for the United States to be the first to develop this devastating weapon.

Einstein's portrait had received a place of honor alongside those of Gandhi and Albert Schweitzer in the headquarters of a European peace society in the 1920's; two decades later he was regarded as the father of the atomic bomb. The principle that explains this apparently violent contrast is a deeply moral one: it is still a "passionate love of social justice" and consequently a whole-souled loathing of militant Fascism which enslaves men, annihilates a race with the methods of the gas chamber. But once the war was won, Einstein's mission was to warn that the peace must be won too. In the last phase of his life, therefore, Einstein protested the strategy of relying on threats of atomic war, which he thought he detected in the policy of the United States more than in that of the Soviet Union. In his ardor for peace and international harmony, he made charitable estimates of Soviet intentions and harsh ones of the free countries where the opinions of great men could be voiced and might be heeded.

Einstein's religious views were a subject of interest and curiosity to the people who had come to regard him as a sainted philosophical scientist. Born in Germany of Swabian Jewish parents who were "entirely irreligious" (in the words of their son), Albert Einstein himself rejected religion as a lad of twelve because he became convinced through his reading of popular scientific books that the stories of the Bible were not true. In his maturity, however, his reverence for nature, his sense of rapt wonder and awe before the irreducible mystery of the world and existence, issued in a form of religion which he quite properly termed "Spinozist." Not a personal God, but a God who is Nature, the "orderly harmony of what exists," such was Einstein's belief. He thought of it as "cosmic religious feeling." This religion as lived, whether in its religious form or divested of it, meant: "Free and self-responsible development of the individual so that he will freely and joyfully put his energies at the service of the community of man."

As a distinguished German intellectual who saw the shape of the coming Hitlerite régime and left that Germany forever, Einstein became increasingly interested in Zionism and attached to the cause of "my people." He welcomed Palestine as the "embodiment of the re-awakening corporate spirit of the whole Jewish nation." The reconciliation of such a position with his normally antinationalistic and internationalist (world government) beliefs was never effectually settled. A life of striving and searching had produced many answers, some of incomparable importance to man's understanding of nature.

THE FAITH OF A SCIENTIST

ALBERT EINSTEIN

1. *The Role of the Scientist Today*

Physicists find themselves in a position not unlike that of Alfred Nobel. Alfred Nobel invented the most powerful explosive ever known up to his time, a means of destruction par excellence. In order to atone for this, in order to relieve his human conscience he instituted his awards for the promotion of peace and for achievements of peace. Today, the physicists who participated in forging the most formidable and dangerous weapon of all times are harassed by an equal feeling of responsibility, not to say guilt. And we cannot desist from warning, and warning again, we cannot and should not slacken in our efforts to make the nations of the world, and especially their governments, aware of the unspeakable disaster they are certain to provoke unless they change their attitude toward each other and toward the task of shaping the future. We helped in creating this new weapon in order to prevent the enemies of mankind from achieving it ahead of us, which, given the mentality of the Nazis, would have meant inconceivable destruction and the enslavement of the rest of the world. We delivered this weapon into the hands of the American and the British people as trustees of the whole of mankind, as fighters for peace and liberty. But so far we fail to see any guarantee of peace, we do not see any guarantee of the freedoms that were promised to the nations in the Atlantic Charter. The war is won, but the peace is not. The great powers, united in fighting, are now divided over the peace settlements. The world was promised freedom from fear, but in fact fear has increased tremendously since the termination of the war. The world was promised freedom from want, but large parts of the world are faced with starvation while others are living in abundance. The nations were promised liberation and justice. But we have witnessed, and are witnessing even now, the sad spectacle of "liberating" armies firing into populations who want their independence and social equality, and supporting in those countries, by force of arms, such parties and personalities as appear to be most suited to serve vested interests. Territorial questions and arguments of power, obsolete though they are, still prevail over the essential demands of common welfare and justice. . . .

The picture of our postwar world is not bright. As far as we, the physicists, are concerned, we are no politicians and it has never been our wish to meddle in politics. But we know a few things that the politicians do not know. And we feel the duty to speak up and to remind those responsible that there is no escape into easy comforts, there is no distance ahead for proceeding little by little and delaying the necessary changes into an indefinite future, there is no time left for petty bargaining. The situation calls for a courageous effort, for a radical change in our whole attitude, in the entire political concept. May the spirit that prompted Alfred Nobel to create his great institution, the spirit of trust and confidence, of generosity and brotherhood among men, prevail in the minds of those upon whose decisions our destiny rests. Otherwise human civilization will be doomed.[1]

2. The Crisis Between the Individual and Society

Innumerable voices have been asserting for some time now that human society is passing through a crisis, that its stability has been gravely shattered. It is characteristic of such a situation that individuals feel indifferent or even hostile toward the group, small or large, to which they belong. In order to illustrate my meaning, let me record here a personal experience. I recently discussed with an intelligent and well-disposed man the threat of another war, which in my opinion would seriously endanger the existence of mankind, and I remarked that only a supra-national organization would offer protection from that danger. Thereupon my visitor, very calmly and coolly, said to me: "Why are you so deeply opposed to the disappearance of the human race?"

I am sure that as little as a century ago no one would have so lightly made a statement of this kind. It is the statement of a man who has striven in vain to attain an equilibrium within himself and has more or less lost hope of succeeding. It is the expression of a painful solitude and isolation from which so many people are suffering in these days. What is the cause? Is there a way out? . . .

Man is, at one and the same time, a solitary being and a social being. As a solitary being, he attempts to protect his own existence and that of those who are closest to him, to satisfy his personal desires, and to develop his innate abilities. As a social being, he seeks to gain the recognition and affection of his fellow human beings, to share in their pleasures, to comfort them in their sorrows, and to improve their conditions of life. Only the existence of these varied, frequently conflicting, strivings accounts for the special character of a man, and their specific combination determines the extent to which an individual can achieve an inner equilibrium and can contribute to the well-being of society. . . .

It is evident . . . that the dependence of the individual upon society is a fact of nature which cannot be abolished—just as in the case of ants and bees. However, while the whole life process of ants and bees is fixed down to the smallest detail by rigid, hereditary instincts, the social pattern and interrelationships of human beings are very variable and susceptible to change. Memory, the capacity to make new combinations, the gift of oral communication have made possible developments among human beings which are not dictated by biological necessities. Such developments manifest themselves in traditions, institutions, and organizations; in literature; in scientific and engineering accomplishments; in works of art. This explains how it happens that, in a certain sense, man can influence his life through his own conduct, and that in this process conscious thinking and wanting can play a part.

Man acquires at birth, through heredity, a biological constitution which we must consider fixed and unalterable, including the natural urges which are characteristic of the human species. In addition, during his lifetime, he acquires a cultural constitution which he adopts from society through communication and through many other types of influences. It is this cultural constitution which, with the passage of time, is subject to change and which determines to a very large extent the relationship between the individual and society. . . .

If we ask ourselves how the structure of society and the cultural attitude of man should be changed in order to make human life as satisfying as possible, we should constantly be conscious of the fact that there are certain conditions which we are unable to modify. As mentioned before, the biological nature of man is, for all practical purposes, not subject to change. Furthermore, technological and demographic developments of the last few centuries have created conditions which are here to stay. In relatively densely settled populations with the goods which are indispensable to their continued existence, an extreme division of labor and a highly-centralized productive apparatus are absolutely necessary. The time—which, looking back, seems so idyllic—is gone forever when individuals or relatively small groups could be completely self-sufficient. It is only a slight exaggeration to say that mankind constitutes even now a planetary community of production and consumption.

I have now reached the point where I may indicate briefly what to me constitutes the essence of the crisis of our time. It concerns the relationship of the individual to society. The individual has become more conscious than ever of his dependence upon society. But he does not experience this dependence as a positive asset, as an organic tie, as a protective force, but rather as a threat to his natural rights, or even to his economic existence. Moreover, his position in society is such that the egotistical drives of his make-up are constantly being accentuated, while his social drives, which are by nature weaker, progressively deteriorate. All human beings, whatever their position in society, are suffering from this process of deterioration. Unknowingly prisoners of their own egotism, they feel insecure, lonely, and deprived of the naive, simple, and unsophisticated enjoyment of life. Man can find meaning in life, short and perilous as it is, only through devoting himself to society.[2]

A man's value to the community depends primarily on how far his feelings, thoughts, and actions are directed towards promoting the good of his fellows. We call him good or bad according to how he stands in this matter. It looks at first sight as if our estimate of a man depended entirely on his social qualities.

And yet such an attitude would be wrong. It is clear that all the valuable things, material, spiritual, and moral, which we receive from society can be traced back through countless generations to certain creative individuals. The use of fire, the cultivation of edible plants, the steam engine—each was discovered by one man.

Only the individual can think, and thereby create new values for society—nay, even set up new moral standards to which the life of the community conforms. Without creative, independently thinking and judging personalities the upward development of society is as unthinkable as the development of the individual personality without the nourishing soil of the community.[3]

What an extraordinary situation is that of us mortals! Each of us is here for a brief sojourn; for what purpose he knows not, though he sometimes thinks he feels it. But from the point of view of daily life, without going deeper, we exist for our fellow-men—in the first place for those on whose smiles and welfare all our happiness depends, and next for all those unknown to us personally with whose destinies we are bound up by the tie of sympathy. A hundred times every day I remind myself that my inner and outer life depend on the labours of other men, living and dead, and that I must exert myself in order to give in the same measure as I have received and am still receiving.[4]

3. Science and Society

There are two ways in which science affects human affairs. The first is familiar to everyone: Directly, and to an even greater extent indirectly, science produces aids that have completely transformed human existence. The second way is educational in character—it works on the mind. Although it may appear less obvious to cursory examination, it is no less incisive than the first.

The most conspicuous practical effect of science is that it makes possible the contriving of things that enrich life, though they complicate it at the same time—inventions such as the steam engine, the railway, electric power and light, the telegraph, radio, automobile, airplane, dynamite, etc. To these must be added the life-preserving achievements of biology and medicine, especially the production of pain relievers and preservative methods of storing food. The greatest practical benefit which all these inventions confer on man I see in the fact that they liberate him from the excessive muscular drudgery that was once indispensable for the preservation of bare existence. Insofar as we may at all claim that slavery has been abolished today, we owe its abolition to the practical consequences of science.

On the other hand, technology—or applied science—has confronted mankind with problems of profound gravity. The very survival of mankind depends on a satisfactory solution of these problems. It is a matter of creating the kind of social institutions and traditions without which the new tools must inevitably bring disaster of the worst kind.

Mechanical means of production in an unorganized economy have had the result that a substantial proportion of mankind is no longer needed for the production of goods and is thus excluded from the process of economic circulation. The immediate consequences are the weakening of purchasing power and the devaluation of labor because of excessive competition, and these give rise, at ever shortening intervals, to a grave paralysis in the production of goods. Ownership of the means of production, on the other hand, carries a power to which the traditional safeguards of our political institutions are unequal. Mankind is caught up in a struggle for adaptation to these new conditions—a struggle that may bring true liberation, if our generation shows itself equal to the task.

Technology has also shortened distances and created new and extraordinarily effective means of destruction which, in the hands of nations claiming unrestricted freedom of action, become threats to the security and very survival of mankind. This situation requires a single judicial and executive power for the entire planet, and the creation of such a central authority is desperately opposed by national traditions. Here too we are in the midst of a struggle whose issue will decide the fate of all of us.

Means of communication, finally—reproduction processes for the printed word, and the radio—when combined with modern weapons, have made it possible to place body and soul under bondage to a central authority—and here is a third source of danger to mankind. Modern tyrannies and their destructive effects show plainly how far we are from exploiting these achievements organizationally for the benefit of mankind. Here too circumstances require an international solution, with the psychological foundation for such a solution not yet laid.

Let us now turn to the intellectual effects that proceed from science. In prescientific times it was not possible by means of thought alone to attain results that all mankind could have accepted as certain and necessary. Still less was there a conviction that all that happens in nature is subject to inexorable laws. The fragmentary character of natural law, as seen by the primitive observer, was such as to foster a belief in ghosts and spirits. Hence even today primitive man lives in constant fear that supernatural and arbitrary forces will intervene in his destiny.

It stands to the everlasting credit of science that by acting on the human mind it has overcome man's insecurity before himself and before nature. In creating elementary mathematics the Greeks for the first time wrought a system of thought whose conclusions no one could escape. The scientists of the Renaissance then devised the combination of systematic experiment with mathematical method. This union made possible such precision in the formulation of natural laws and such certainty in checking them by experience that as a result there was no longer room for basic differences of opinion in natural science. Since that time each generation has built up the heritage of knowledge and understanding, without the slightest danger of a crisis that might jeopardize the whole structure.

The general public may be able to follow the details of scientific research to only a modest degree; but it can register at least one great and important gain: confidence that human thought is dependable and natural law universal.[5]

4. *Science and Religion*

It would not be difficult to come to an agreement as to what we understand by science. Science is the century-old endeavor to bring together by means of systematic thought the perceptible phenomena of this world into as thoroughgoing an association as possible. To put it boldly, it is the attempt at the posterior reconstruction of existence by the process of conceptualization. But when asking myself what religion is I cannot think of the answer so easily. And even after finding an answer which may satisfy me at this particular moment I still remain convinced that I can never under any circumstances bring together, even to a slight extent, all those who have given this question serious consideration.

At first, then, instead of asking what religion is I should prefer to ask what characterizes the aspirations of a person who gives me the impression of being religious: A person who is religiously enlightened appears to me to be one who has, to the best of his ability, liberated himself from the fetters of his selfish desires and is preoccupied with thoughts, feelings, and aspirations to which he clings because of their super-personal value. It seems to me that what is important is the force of this super-personal content and the depth of the conviction concerning its overpowering meaningfulness, regardless of whether any attempt is made to unite this content with a divine Being, for otherwise it would not be possible to count Buddha and Spinoza as religious personalities. Accordingly, a religious person is devout in the sense that he has no doubt of the significance and loftiness of those super-personal objects and goals which neither require nor are capable of rational foundation. They exist with the same necessity and matter-of-factness as he himself. In this sense religion is the age-old endeavor of mankind to become clearly and completely conscious of these values and goals and constantly to strengthen and extend their effect. If one conceives of religion and science according to these definitions then a conflict between them appears impossible. For science can only ascertain what *is*, but not what *should be*, and outside of its domain value judgments of all kinds remain necessary. Religion, on the other hand, deals only with evaluations of human thought and action: it cannot justifiably speak of facts and relationships between facts. . . .

Now, even though the realms of religion and science in themselves are clearly marked off from each other, nevertheless there exist between the two strong reciprocal relationships and dependencies. Though religion may be that which determines the goal, it has, nevertheless, learned from science, in the broadest sense, what means will contribute to the attainment of the goals it has set up. But science can only be created by those who are thoroughly imbued with the aspiration towards truth and understanding. This source of feeling, however, springs from the sphere of religion. To this there also belongs the faith in the possibility that the regulations valid for the world of existence are rational, that is, comprehensible to reason. I cannot conceive of a genuine scientist without that profound faith. The situation may be expressed by an image: Science without religion is lame, religion without science is blind.

Though I have asserted above that in truth a legitimate conflict between religion and science cannot exist I must nevertheless qualify this assertion once again on an essential point, with reference to the actual content of historical religions. This qualification has to do with the concept of God. During the youthful period of mankind's spiritual evolution human fantasy created gods in man's own image, who, by the operations of their will were supposed to determine, or at any rate to influence the phenomenal world. Man sought to alter the disposition of these gods in his own favor by means of magic and prayer. The idea of God in the religions taught at present is a sublimation of that old conception of the gods. Its anthropomorphic character is shown, for instance, by the fact that men appeal to the Divine Being in prayers and plead for the fulfilment of their wishes.

Nobody, certainly, will deny that the idea of the existence of an omnipotent, just and omnibeneficent personal God is able to accord man solace, help, and guidance; also, by virtue of its simplicity it is accessible to the most undeveloped mind. But, on the other hand, there are decisive weaknesses attached to this idea in itself, which have been painfully felt since the beginning of history. That is, if this being is omnipotent then every occurrence, including every human action, every human thought, and every human feeling and aspiration is also His work; how is it possible to think of holding men responsible for their deeds and thoughts before such an almighty Being? In giving out punishment and rewards He would to a certain extent be passing judgment on Himself. How can this be combined with the goodness and righteousness ascribed to Him?

The main source of the present-day conflicts between the spheres of religion and of science lies in this concept of a personal God. It is the aim of science to establish general rules which determine the reciprocal connection of objects and events in time and space. For these rules, or laws of nature, absolutely general validity is required—not proven. It is mainly a program, and faith in the possibility of its accomplishment in principle is only founded on partial successes. But hardly anyone could be found who would deny these partial successes and ascribe them to human self-deception. The fact that on the basis of such laws we are able to predict the temporal behavior of phenomena in certain domains with great precision and certainty is deeply embedded in the consciousness of the modern man, even though he may have grasped very little of the contents of those laws. . .

The more a man is imbued with the ordered regularity of all events the firmer becomes his conviction that there is no room left by the side of this ordered regularity for causes of a different nature. For him neither the rule of human nor the rule of divine will exists as an independent cause of natural events. To be sure the doctrine of a personal God interfering with natural events could never be *refuted*, in the real sense, by science, for this doctrine can always take refuge in those domains in which scientific knowledge has not yet been able to set foot.

But I am persuaded that such behavior on the part of the representatives of religion would not only be unworthy but also fatal. For a doctrine which is able to maintain itself not in clear-light but only in the dark, will of necessity lose its effect on mankind, with incalculable harm to human progress. In their struggle for the ethical good, teachers of religion must have the stature to give up the doctrine of a personal God, that is, give up that source of fear and hope which in the past placed such vast power in the hands of priests. In their labors they will have to avail themselves of those forces which are capable of cultivating the Good, the True, and the Beautiful in humanity itself. This is, to be sure, a more difficult but an incomparably more worthy task. After religious teachers accomplish the refining process indicated they will surely recognize with joy that true religion has been ennobled and made more profound by scientific knowledge.

If it is one of the goals of religion to liberate mankind as far as possible from the bondage of egocentric cravings, desires, and fears, scientific reasoning can aid religion in yet another sense. Although it is true that it is the goal of science to discover rules which permit the association and foretelling of facts, this is not its only aim. It also seeks to reduce the connections discovered to the smallest possible number of mutually independent conceptual elements. It is in this striving after the rational unification of the manifold that it encounters its greatest successes, even though it is precisely this attempt which causes it to run the greatest risk of falling a prey to illusions. But whoever has undergone the intense experience of successful advances made in this domain, is moved by profound reverence for the rationality made manifest in existence. By way of the understanding he achieves a far-reaching emancipation from the shackles of personal hopes and desires, and thereby attains that humble attitude of mind towards the grandeur of reason incarnate in existence, and which in its profoundest depths, is inaccessible to man. This attitude, however, appears to me to be religious, in the highest sense of the word. And so it seems to me that science not only purifies the religious impulse of the dross of its anthropomorphism but also contributes to a religious spiritualization of our understanding of life.[6]

The individual feels the nothingness of human desires and aims and the sublimity and marvellous order which reveal themselves both in nature and in the world of thought. He looks upon individual existence as a sort of prison and wants to experience the universe as a single significant whole. The beginnings of cosmic religious feeling already appear in earlier stages of development—e.g., in many of the Psalms of David and in some of the Prophets. Buddhism, as we have learnt from the wonderful writings of Schopenhauer especially, contains a much stronger element of it.

The religious geniuses of all ages have been distinguished by this kind of religious feeling, which knows no dogma and no God conceived in man's image; so that there can be no Church whose central teachings are based on it. . . .

Only those who realize the immense efforts and, above all, the devotion which pioneer work in theoretical science demands can grasp the strength of the emotion out of which alone such work, remote as it is from the immediate realities of life, can issue. What a deep conviction of the rationality of the universe and what a yearning to understand, were it but a feeble reflection of the mind revealed in this world, Kepler and Newton must have had to enable them to spend years of solitary labour in disentangling the principles of celestial mechanics! Those whose acquaintance with scientific research is derived chiefly from its practical results easily develop a completely false notion of the mentality of the men who, surrounded by a sceptical world, have shown the way to those like-minded with themselves, scattered through the earth and the centuries. Only one who has devoted his life to similar ends can have a vivid realization of what has inspired these men and given them the strength to remain true to their purpose in spite of countless failures. It is cosmic religious feeling that gives a man strength of this sort. A contemporary has said, not unjustly, that in this materialistic age of ours the serious scientific workers are the only profoundly religious people.[7]

Sources

CHAPTER V: THE FAITH OF A SCIENTIST

The selections from Albert Einstein are made from the collections of his letters, essays, articles, and broadcasts which appear in *Out of My Later Years* (Philosophical Library, New York, 1950), denoted as "O"; and *The World As I See It* (Philosophical Library, New York, 1949), denoted as "W."

[1] O, "The War Is Won but Peace Is Not," page 200; page 201, lines 1-13; page 202, lines 27-35; page 203.

[2] O, "Why Socialism?", page 124, lines 24-34; page 125, lines 1-9 and 16-27; page 126, lines 13-35; page 127, lines 1-2 and 12-35; page 128, lines 1-10.

[3] W, "Society and Personality," page 8, lines 27-34; page 9, lines 1-14.

[4] W, "The World As I See It," page 1, lines 8-22.

[5] O, "Science and Society," pages 135-137, lines 1-26.

[6] O, "Science and Religion," page 24, lines 18-32; page 25, lines 1-24; page 26, lines 3-35; page 27, lines 1-28; page 28, lines 18-25, page 29; page 30, lines 1-5.

[7] W, "Religion and Science, page 26, lines 16-32; page 28, lines 4-31.

CHAPTER VI

IGNAZIO SILONE (1900–   )

It can be said of Ignazio Silone that his whole life has been a pilgrimage in the cause of freedom. Yet this essentially truth-seeking artist, who has used his powerful intellect for social justice, creates a sense of loving attachment to his native Abruzzi region in Italy and to its humble peasants. One critic calls him "a sort of Robert Frost of the Abruzzi," but this suggests too little of the cosmic moral scrutiny that gives structure to Silone's method of irony, nor does it suggest enough of that passionate integrity that has made this man an organizer (in the social movement sense) but often also a lonely and courageous rebel.

Silone was born on May 1, 1900, in Pescina dei Marsi, a small village in the Abruzzi Appenines. His family, who were small landholders of the province, saw to it that he received an education in the Catholic schools; but by the time Silone was a youth of seventeen he was secretary of the land workers for the Abruzzi district, representing the peasants whom he knew so well and with whom he had preferred to spend much of his time while he was a schoolboy. His mother and five brothers perished in the 1915 earthquake, and a few years later Silone and a surviving brother left their province to work in the youth and labor cause in Rome.

Silone became one of the founders of the Italian Communist Party, editor of the weekly *Avanguardia* of Rome. In 1921 he visited Russia. Upon his return to Italy, Silone took up his work in Trieste, editing the daily labor paper *Il Lavoratore*, and, as he writes in the following selection, remained in Italy after the passage and enforcement of the special laws against the opponents of Fascism. Thus Silone met the test of highly dangerous, clandestine work, printing illegal newspapers in the knowledge that a warrant for his arrest had been issued. The Fascists seized *Il Lavoratore*, and Silone's brother, who had managed to escape the earthquake that consumed most of his family, was captured and beaten to death by the Fascists in prison. He returned to the Abruzzi, seeking and finding shelter with his friends, the peasants, for some time.

In 1930 Silone broke with the Communist Party, and the next year he was smuggled across the border into Germany, traveling from there to other parts of Europe, encountering imprisonment and exile on several occasions, in different countries. In 1931 he took up residence in Switzerland, where he remained until the end of World War II and the defeat of Fascism. In this period Silone wrote his novels, *Fontamara, Bread and Wine*, and others, as well as a history of the rise of Fascism in Italy, volumes of political essays and dialogues, and important political criticism for Socialist periodicals throughout the world. In 1944 Silone returned to Italy to continue his work as the leading theoretician of the Italian Socialist Party, and manager of the journal *Avanti!*

The bare recital of these "facts" of Silone's life give no hint of the great moral strength of this writer who succeeded in achieving fame during the years of his exile by his strangely moving books. They brought the experience of the totalitarian defamation of the human spirit to a level of human concreteness that aroused the mind and heart of Western European and American intellectuals. In reflecting on his own experience with the ideal of Socialism, which he first thought would be advanced by the Communist Party, but which he learned through years of painful and intimate revelation was the soul of corruption and persecution, Silone comments: "Modern Socialism, after the first world war, fared like the hunter who set out to hunt quail and fell among wolves." From the encounter with wolves, only "whole, real and entire men" were able to save themselves, through questioning, rebellion, personal search, and spiritual suffering. Whether they would be the men to free the spirit of man, which is now forced "to save itself in hiding," partakes of a sacred mystery; but in Silone's judgment "the rediscovery of a Christian heritage in the revolution of our time remains the most important gain that has been made in these last years for the conscience of our generation."

The selection which follows is drawn from a chapter in an unusual book published in 1941, *The God That Failed*, containing autobiographical essays by "the initiates" Arthur Koestler, Ignazio Silone, and Richard Wright, who probe with singular honesty their Communist allegiance in the past and their eventual discovery that Communism is the great betrayal of the hope of human freedom. Here Silone succeeds in evoking, in a brief essay, the feeling which he structures with fine artistry into his fictional writings, that the human person at his highest reach is superior over all the economic and social mechanisms that oppress him and try to rob him of his spiritual independence. It has been pointed out that Silone, even as he champions the oppressed worker, does so in that spirit of individual protest that leaves him unconvinced by slogans like "class consciousness"; for Silone's characters are peasants, not proletarians; and Silone's ultimate brand of faith in Socialism is akin to an aroused sympathy for the hungry, the destitute, the helpless, and those great ones, however obscure, who are ready for martyrdom for the sake of human conviction and belief. What remains of Silone's pilgrimage for social justice and freedom is a stubborn belief in the possibility of an economic order on Socialist lines that is yet based on a true democratic respect for the individual. In one of the stories in Silone's *Mr. Aristotle*, Simplicio, on the verge of death, holds the hand of an old shepherd who has given him shelter, and says: "You know, man could be good!" It is as simple, as complicated, as ancient, and as futuristic as that.

THE GOD THAT FAILED
—
IGNAZIO SILONE

1. *Why I Became a Socialist*

That November evening in Milan, when I wanted to explain to my friends why, at the age of seventeen and still a schoolboy, I had adhered to the Socialism of Zimmerwald, I had to go back, in my memory, step by step, to the beginning of my adolescence; I even had to mention episodes of my childhood, to rediscover the very earliest origins of a view of society which, as it later on assumed a political form, was bound to reveal itself as radical. At the age of seventeen, and in time of war, one does not join a revolutionary movement which is persecuted by the government, unless one's motives are serious.

I grew up in a mountainous district of southern Italy. The phenomenon which most impressed me, when I arrived at the age of reason, was the violent contrast, the incomprehensible, absurd, monstrous contrast between family and private life—in the main decent, honest, and well-conducted—and social relations, which were very often crude and full of hatred and deceit. . . .

I was a child just five years old when, one Sunday, while crossing the little square of my native village with my mother leading me by the hand, I witnessed the cruel, stupid spectacle of one of the local gentry setting his great dog at a poor woman, a seamstress, who was just coming out of church. The wretched woman was flung to the ground, badly mauled, and her dress was torn to ribbons. Indignation in the village was general, but silent. I have never understood how the poor woman ever got the unhappy idea of taking proceedings against the squire; but the only result was to add a mockery of justice to the harm already done. Although, I must repeat, everybody pitied her and many people helped her secretly, the unfortunate woman could not find a single witness prepared to give evidence before the magistrate, nor a lawyer to conduct the prosecution. On the other hand, the squire's supposedly Left-Wing lawyer turned up punctually, and so did a number of bribed witnesses who perjured themselves by giving a grotesque version of what had happened, and accusing the woman of having provoked the dog. The magistrate—a most worthy, honest person in private life—acquitted the squire and condemned the poor woman to pay the costs.

"It went very much against the grain with me," he excused himself a few days later at our house. "On my word of honor, I do assure you, I was very sorry about it. But even if I had been present at the disgusting incident as a private citizen and couldn't have avoided blaming him, still as a judge I had to go by the evidence of the case, and unfortunately it was in favor of the dog. . . ."

I was seven years old when the first election campaign, which I can remember, took place in my district. At that time we still had no political parties, so the announcement of this campaign was received with very little interest. But popular feeling ran high when it was disclosed that one of the candidates was "the Prince." There was no need to add Christian and surname to realize which Prince was meant. He was the owner of the great estate formed by the arbitrary occupation of the vast tracts of land reclaimed in the previous century from the Lake of Fucino. About eight thousand families (that is, the majority of the local population) are still employed today in cultivating the estate's fourteen thousand hectares. The Prince was deigning to solicit "his" families for their vote so that he could become their deputy in parliament. The agents of the estate, who were working for the Prince, talked in impeccably liberal phrases: "Naturally," said they, "naturally, no one will be forced to vote for the Prince, that's understood; in the same way that no one, naturally, can force the Prince to allow people who don't vote for him to work on his land. This is the period of real liberty for everybody; you're free, and so is the Prince." The announcement of these "liberal" principles produced general and understandable consternation among the peasants. For, as may easily be guessed, the Prince was the most hated person in our part of the country. As long as he remained in the invisible Olympus of the great feudal proprietor (none of the eight thousand tenants had seen him, up to then, even from afar) public hatred for him was allowed, and belonged to the same category as curses against hostile deities; such curses, though useless, are satisfying. But now the clouds were being rent, and the Prince was coming down within reach of mortal men. From now on, consequently, they would have to keep their expressions of hatred within the narrow circle of private life and get ready to welcome him with due honors in the village streets.

My father seemed reluctant to accept this kind of logic. He was the youngest of several brothers, all of them peasant proprietors; the youngest, the most restless, and the only one with any inclinations toward insubordination. One evening his older brothers came and urged him, in the common interest, to be prudent and careful. For me (to whom no one paid any attention, for grownups think that children don't understand such things) it was a most instructive evening. "The Prince being a candidate is a real farce," the eldest brother admitted. "Political candidatures should be reserved for lawyers and other such windbags. But as the Prince is a candidate, all we can do is support him." "If the Prince's candidature is a farce," replied my father, "I don't understand why we should support him." "Because we're his dependents, as you know perfectly well." "Not in politics," said my father. "In politics we're free." "We don't cultivate politics, we cultivate the land," they answered him. "As cultivators of the land we depend on the Prince." "There's no mention of politics in our contracts for the land, only of potatoes and beetroots. As voters we're free." "The Prince's bailiff will also be free not to renew our contracts," they answered him. "That's why we're forced to be on his side." "I can't vote for someone merely because I'm forced to," said my father. "I'd feel humiliated." "No one will know how you vote," they answered him. "In the secrecy of the polling booth you can vote as you like, freely. But during the electioneering campaign we must be on the Prince's side, all of us together." "I'd be pleased to do it if I wasn't ashamed to," said my father, "but, do believe me, I'd be too much ashamed." To settle it, my uncles and my father reached this compromise: he would not come out either on the Prince's side or against him.

The Prince's election tour was prepared by the civil authorities, the police, the carabineers, and the agents of the estate. One Sunday, the Prince deigned to pass through the principal villages in the constituency, without stopping and without making any speeches. This tour of his was remembered for a long time in our district, mainly because he made it in a motorcar, and it was the first time we had seen one. The word "motorcar" itself had not yet found a place in our everyday language, and the peasants called it a "horseless carriage. . . ." That Sunday the entire population of the village had gone to meet the Prince on the road by which he was due to arrive. There were numerous visible signs of the collective admiration and affection for the Prince. The crowds were dressed up in their best, and were in a perfectly understandable state of excitement. The "horseless carriage" arrived late, and roared through the crowd and the village, without stopping and without even slowing down, leaving a thick white dust cloud behind it. . . .

Two days later a strange little old man arrived from Rome; he wore glasses, and had a black stick and a small suitcase. Nobody knew him. He said he was an oculist and had put himself up as candidate against the Prince. A few people gathered round him out of curiosity, mainly children and women, who had not the right to vote. I was among the children, in my short trousers and with my schoolbooks under my arm. We begged the old man to make a speech. He said to us: "Remind your parents that the vote is secret. Nothing else." Then he said, "I am poor; I live by being an oculist; but if any of you have anything wrong with your eyes I'm willing to treat them for nothing." So we brought him an old woman who sold vegetables. She had bad eyes, and he cleaned them up and gave her a little phial with drops in it and explained how to use it. Then he said to us (we were only a group of children): "Remind your parents that the vote is secret," and he went away. . . . Great was everybody's surprise when it became known that in the secrecy of the polling booths an enormous majority had voted against the Prince and for the unknown oculist. It was a great scandal. . . .

In 1915 an earthquake of exceptional violence destroyed a large part of our province and killed, in thirty seconds, about fifty thousand people. I was surprised to see how much my fellow-villagers took this appalling catastrophe as a matter of course. The geologists' complicated explanations, reported in the newspapers, aroused their contempt. In a district like ours, where so many injustices go unpunished, people regarded the recurrent earthquakes as a phenomenon requiring no further explanation. In fact, it was astonishing that earthquakes were not more frequent. An earthquake buries rich and poor, learned and illiterate, authorities and subjects alike beneath its ruined houses. Here lies, moreover, the real explanation of the Italians' well-known powers of endurance when faced with the cataclysms of nature. An earthquake achieves what the law promises but does not in practice maintain—the equality of all men. . . .

What seemed to the poor people of our part of the world a much more serious calamity than any natural cataclysm was what happened *after* the earthquake. The State reconstruction program was carried out to the accompaniment of innumerable intrigues, frauds, thefts, swindles, embezzlements, and dishonesty of every kind. An acquaintance of mine, who had been sacked by one of the government departments concerned, gave me some information of this sort about certain criminal acts which were being committed by the head engineers of the department. Impressed rather than surprised, I hastened to pass on the facts to some persons in authority, whom I knew to be upright and honest, so that they could denounce the criminals. Far from denying the truth of what I told them, my honorable friends were in a position to confirm it. But, even then, they advised me not to get mixed up in it or to get worked up, in my simplicity, about things of that kind. "You're young," they said to me affectionately, "you must finish your studies, you've got your career to think of, you shouldn't compromise yourself with things that don't concern you." "Of course," I said, "it would be better for the denunciation to come from grown-up people like yourselves, people with authority, rather than from a boy of seventeen."

They were horrified. "We are not madmen," they answered. "We shall mind our own business and nobody else's."

I then talked the matter over with some reverend priests, and then with some of my more courageous relations. All of them, while admitting that they were already aware of the shameful things that were happening, begged me not to get mixed up in that hornets' nest, but to think of my studies, of my career, and of my future. "With pleasure," I replied, "but isn't one of you ready to denounce the thieves?" "We are not madmen," they replied, scandalized, "these things have nothing to do with us."

I then began to wonder seriously whether it mightn't be a good thing to organize, together with some other boys, a new "revolution" that would end up with a good bonfire of the corrupt engineers' offices; but I was dissuaded by the acquaintance who had given me the proof of their crooked dealings: a bonfire, he pointed out, would destroy the proofs of the crimes. He was older and more experienced than myself; he suggested I should get the denunciation printed in some newspaper. But which newspaper? "There's only one," he explained, "which could have any interest in publishing your denunciation, and that's the Socialist paper." So I set to work and wrote three articles, the first of my life, giving a detailed exposure of the corrupt behavior of State engineers in my part of the country, and sent them off to *Avanti*. The first two were printed at once and aroused much comment among the readers of the paper, but none at all among the authorities. The third article did not appear, because, as I learned later, a leading Socialist intervened with the editorial staff. This showed me that the system of deception and fraud oppressing us was much vaster than at first appeared, and that its invisible ramifications extended even into Socialism. However, the partial denunciation which had appeared unexpectedly in the press contained enough material for a number of law-suits, or at least for a board of enquiry; but nothing happened. . . .[1]

2. *The Lure of Communism*

I realize that the progress which I have been tracing in these pages is too summary to seem anything but strained. And if I touch on this objection now, it is not to refute it or to swear to the absolute truth of my explanations; I can guarantee their sincerity, not their objectivity. I am myself sometimes astonished to find, when I go back over that remote, almost prehistoric, period of our lives with my contemporaries, how they cannot remember at all, or only very vaguely, incidents which had a decisive influence on me; whereas on the contrary, they can clearly recall other circumstances which to me were pointless and insignificant. Are they, these contemporaries of mine, all "unconscious accomplices"? And by what destiny or virtue does one, at a certain age, make the important choice, and become "accomplice" or "rebel"? From what source do some people derive their spontaneous intolerance of injustice, even though the injustice affects only others? And that sudden feeling of guilt at sitting down to a well-laden table, when others are having to go hungry? And that pride which makes poverty and prison preferable to contempt?

I don't know. Perhaps no one knows. At a certain point, even the fullest and deepest confession becomes a mere statement of fact and not an answer. Anyone who has reflected seriously about himself or others knows how profoundly secret are certain decisions, how mysterious and unaccountable certain vocations.

There was a point in my rebellion where hatred and love coincided; both the facts which justified my indignation and the moral motives which demanded it stemmed directly from the district where I was born. This explains, too, why everything I have happened to write up to now, and probably everything I shall ever write, although I have traveled and lived abroad, is concerned solely with this same district, or more precisely with the part of it which can be seen from the house where I was born—not more than thirty or forty kilometers on one side or the other. It is a district, like the rest of the Abruzzi, poor in secular history, and almost entirely Christian and medieval in its formation. The only buildings worthy of note are churches and monasteries. Its only illustrious sons for many centuries have been saints and, stone-carvers. The conditions of human existence have always been particularly difficult there; pain has always been accepted there as first among the laws of nature, and the Cross welcomed and honored because of it. Franciscanism and anarchy have always been the two most accessible forms of rebellion for lively spirits in our part of the world. The ashes of skepticism have never suffocated, in the hearts of those who suffered most, the ancient hope of the Kingdom of God on earth, the old expectation of charity taking the place of law, the old dream of Gioacchino da Fiore, of the "Spirituali," of the Celestimisto.* And this is a fact of enormous, fundamental importance; in a disappointed, arid, exhausted, weary country such as ours, it constitutes real riches, it is a miraculous reserve. The politicians are unaware of its existence, the clergy are afraid of it; only the saints, perhaps, know where to find it. What for us has always been much more difficult, if not impossible, has been to discern the ways and means to a political revolution, *hic et nunc*, to the creation of a free and ordered society.

I thought I had reached this discovery, when I moved to the town and made my first contact with the workers' movement. It was a kind of flight, a safety exit from unbearable solitude, the sighting of *terra firma*, the discovery of a new continent. . . .[2]

. . . By then the imperious necessity of understanding, of realizing, of comparing the development of the action in which I was engaged with the motives which had originally led me into it, had taken entire possession of me and left me no more peace. And if my poor literary work has any meaning, in the ultimate analysis, it consists of this: a time came when writing meant, for me, an absolute necessity to testify, an urgent need to free myself from

---

* Followers of Pope Celestine V, an Abruzzi hermit who, elected Pope in August, 1294, abdicated three and a half months later. He was canonized in 1313.

an obsession, to state the meaning and define the limits of a painful but decisive break, and of a vaster allegiance that still continues. For me writing has not been, and never could be, except in a few favored moments of grace, a serene aesthetic enjoyment, but rather the painful and lonely continuation of a struggle. As for the difficulties and imperfections of self-expression with which I sometimes have to wrestle, they arise, not from lack of observation of the rules of good writing, but rather from a conscience which, while struggling to heal certain hidden and perhaps incurable wounds, continues obstinately to demand that its integrity be respected. For to be sincere is obviously not enough, if one wants to be truthful. . . .[8]

For me to join the Party of Proletarian Revolution was not just a simple matter of signing up with a political organization; it meant a conversion, a complete dedication. Those were still the days when to declare oneself a Socialist or a Communist was equivalent to throwing oneself to the winds, and meant breaking with one's parents and not finding a job. If the material consequences were harsh and hard, the difficulties of spiritual adaptation were no less painful. My own internal world, the "Middle Ages," which I had inherited and which were rooted in my soul, and from which, in the last analysis, I had derived my initial aspiration to revolt, were shaken to their foundations, as though by an earthquake. Everything was thrown into the melting-pot, everything became a problem. Life, death, love, good, evil, truth, all changed their meaning or lost it altogether. It is easy enough to court danger when one is no longer alone; but who can describe the dismay of once and for all renouncing one's faith in the individual immortality of the soul? It was too serious for me to be able to discuss it with anyone; my Party comrades would have found it a subject for mockery, and I no longer had any other friends. So, unknown to anyone, the whole world took on a different aspect. How men are to be pitied!

The conditions of life imposed on the Communists by the Fascist conquest of the State were very hard. But they also served

to confirm some of the Communists' political theses, and provided an opportunity to create a type of organization which was
in no way incompatible with the Communist mentality. So I too
had to adapt myself, for a number of years, to living like a for-
eigner in my own country. One had to change one's name, abandon every former link with family and friends, and live a false
life to remove any suspicion of conspiratorial activity. The Party
became family, school, church, barracks; the world that lay beyond it was to be destroyed and built anew. The psychological
mechanism whereby each single militant becomes progressively
identified with the collective organization is the same as that used
in certain religious orders and military colleges, with almost identical results. Every sacrifice was welcomed as a personal contribution to the "price of collective redemption"; and it should be
emphasized that the links which bound us to the Party grew
steadily firmer, not in spite of the dangers and sacrifices involved,
but because of them. This explains the attraction exercised by
Communism on certain categories of young men and of women,
on intellectuals, and on the highly sensitive and generous people
who suffer most from the wastefulness of bourgeois society. . . .[4]

3. *Communist Tyranny*

It is not surprising that the first internal crises which shook the
Communist International left me more or less indifferent. These
crises originated from the fact that the main parties which had
adhered to the new International, even after the formal acceptance of the twenty-one conditions laid down by Lenin to govern
admission, were far from homogeneous. . . .

These internal crises took place in a sphere far removed from
my own and so I was not involved. I do not say this boastfully; on
the contrary, I am merely trying to explain the situation. The increasing degeneration of the Communist International into a
tyranny and a bureaucracy filled me with repulsion and disgust,
but there were some compelling reasons which made me hesitate
to break with it: solidarity with comrades who were dead or in

prison, the nonexistence at that time of any other organized anti-Fascist force in Italy, the rapid political, and in some cases also moral, degeneration of many who had already left Communism, and finally the illusion that the International might be made healthy again by the proletariat of the West, in the event of some crisis occurring within the Soviet regime.

Between 1921 and 1927, I had repeated occasion to go to Moscow and take part, as a member of Italian Communist delegations, in a number of congresses and meetings of the Executive. What struck me most about the Russian Communists, even in such really exceptional personalities as Lenin and Trotsky, was their utter incapacity to be fair in discussing opinions that conflicted with their own. The adversary, simply for daring to contradict, at once became a traitor, an opportunist, a hireling. *An adversary in good faith* is inconceivable to the Russian Communists. What an aberration of conscience this is, for so-called materialists and rationalists absolutely in their polemics to uphold the primacy of morals over intelligence! To find a comparable infatuation one has to go back to the Inquisition.

Just as I was leaving Moscow, in 1922, Alexandra Kollontaj said to me: "If you happen to read in the papers that Lenin has had me arrested for stealing the silver spoons in the Kremlin, that simply means that I'm not entirely in agreement with him about some little problem of agricultural or industrial policy." Kollontaj had acquired her sense of irony in the West and so only used it with people from the West. But even then, in those feverish years of building the new regime, when the new orthodoxy had not yet taken complete possession of cultural life, how difficult it was to reach an understanding with a Russian Communist on the simplest, and for us most obvious, questions; how difficult, I don't say to agree, but at least to understand each other, when talking of what liberty means for a man of the West, even for a worker. I spent hours one day trying to explain to one of the directors of the State publishing house, why she ought at least to be ashamed of the atmosphere of discouragement and intimidation in which Soviet writers lived. She could not understand what I was trying to tell her.

"Liberty"—I had to give examples—"is the possibility of doubting, the possibility of making a mistake, the possibility of searching and experimenting, the possibility of saying 'no' to any authority—literary, artistic, philosophic, religious, social, and even political." "But that," murmured this eminent functionary of Soviet culture in horror, "that is counter-revolution. . . ." [5]

4. *The Stalinist Counterrevolution*

Besides internal differences resulting from its own heterogeneous composition, the Communist International felt the repercussions of every difficulty of the Soviet State. After Lenin's death, it was clear that the Soviet State could not avoid what seems to be the destiny of every dictatorship: the gradual and inexorable narrowing of its political pyramid. The Russian Communist Party, which had suppressed all rival parties and abolished any possibility of general political discussion in the Soviet assemblies, itself suffered a similar fate, and its members' political views were rapidly ousted by the policy of the Party machine. From that moment, every difference of opinion in the controlling body was destined to end in the physical extinction of the minority. The Revolution, which had extinguished its enemies, began to devour its favorite sons. The thirsty gods gave no more truce.

In May, 1927, as a representative of the Italian Communist Party, I took part with Togliatti in an extraordinary session of the enlarged Executive of the Communist International. Togliatti had come from Paris, where he was running the political secretariat of the Party, and I from Italy, where I was in charge of the underground organization. We met in Berlin and went on to Moscow together. . . . At the first sitting which we attended, I had the impression that we had arrived too late. We were in a small office in the Communist International Headquarters. The German Thälmann was presiding, and immediately began reading out a proposed resolution against Trotsky, to be presented at the full session. This resolution condemned, in the most violent terms, a document which Trotsky had addressed to the Political Office of the Russian Communist Party. The Russian delegation at that day's session of the Senior-convent was an exceptional one: Stalin, Rikov, Bukharin and Manuilsky. At the end of the reading Thälmann asked if we were in agreement with the proposed resolution. The Finn Ottomar Kuusinen found that it was not strong enough. . . . As no one else asked to speak, after consulting Togliatti, I made my apologies for having arrived late and so not having been able to see the document which was to be condemned. "To tell the truth," Thälmann declared candidly, "we haven't seen the document either."

Preferring not to believe my ears, I repeated my objection in other words: "It may very well be true," I said, "that Trotsky's document may be condemned, but obviously I cannot condemn it before I've read it."

"Neither have we," repeated Thälmann, "neither have the majority of the delegates present here, except for the Russians, read the document. . . ."

At this point Stalin intervened. He was standing over at one side of the room, and seemed the only person present who was calm and unruffled.

"The Political Office of the Party," said Stalin, "has considered that it would not be expedient to translate and distribute Trotsky's document to the delegates of the International Executive, because there are various allusions in it to the policy of the Soviet State. . . ."

Ernst Thälmann asked me if I were satisfied with Stalin's explanation. "I do not contest the right of the Political Office of the Russian Communist Party to keep any document secret," I said. "But I do not understand how others can be asked to condemn an unknown document." At this, indignation against myself and Togliatti, who appeared to agree with what I had said, knew no bounds. . . .

The only person who remained calm and imperturbable was

Stalin. He said, "If a single delegate is against the proposed resolution, it should not be presented." Then he added, "Perhaps our
Italian comrades are not fully aware of our internal situation. I
propose that the sitting be suspended until tomorrow and that
one of those present should be assigned the task of spending the
evening with our Italian comrades and explaining our internal
situation to them." The Bulgarian Vasil Kolarov was given this
ungrateful task.

He carried it out with tact and good humor. He invited us to
have a glass of tea that evening in his room at the Hotel Lux. And
he faced up to the thorny subject without much preamble. "Let's
be frank," he said to us with a smile. "Do you think I've read
that document? No, I haven't. . . . My dear Italian friends, this
isn't a question of documents. . . . It's a question of a struggle for
power between two hostile, irreconcilable groups. One's got to
choose. I, for my part, have already chosen, I'm for the majority
group. Whatever the minority says or does, whatever document
it draws up against the majority, I repeat to you that I'm for the
majority. Documents don't interest me. We aren't in an academy
here." He refilled our glasses with tea and scrutinized us with the
air of a schoolmaster obliged to deal with two unruly youngsters.
"Do I make myself clear?" he asked, addressing me specifically.

"Certainly," I replied, "very clear indeed." "Have I persuaded
you?" he asked again. "No," I said. "And why not?" he wanted
to know. "I should have to explain to you," I said, "why I'm
against Fascism. . . ."

Next morning, in the Senior-convent, the scene of the day before was repeated. An unusual atmosphere of nervousness per-
vaded the little room into which a dozen of us were packed.
"Have you explained the situation to our Italian comrades?"
Stalin asked Kolarov. "Fully," the Bulgarian assured him. "If a
single delegate," Stalin repeated, "is against the proposed resolution, it cannot be presented in the full session. A resolution
against Trotsky can only be taken unanimously. Are our Italian

comrades," he added turning to us, "favorable to the proposed resolution?"

After consulting Togliatti, I declared: "Before taking the resolution into consideration, we must see the document concerned. . . ."

"The proposed resolution is withdrawn," said Stalin. After which, we had the same hysterical scene as the day before, with the indignant, angry protests of Kuusinen, Rakosi, Pepper and the others. Thälmann argued from our "scandalous" attitude that the whole trend of our anti-Fascist activity in Italy was most probably wrong, and that if Fascism was still so firmly entrenched in Italy it must be our fault. He asked because of this that the policy of the Italian Communist Party should be subjected to a thorough sifting. . . .

In Berlin, on my way back, I read in the paper that the Executive of the Communist International had severely rebuked Trotsky for a document he had prepared about recent events in China. I went to the offices of the German Communist Party and asked Thälmann for an explanation. "This is untrue," I said to him sharply.

But he explained that the statutes of the International authorized the Presidium, in case of urgency, to adopt any resolution in the name of the Executive. . . .[6]

5. My Continuing Faith in Socialism

I felt at that time like someone who has had a tremendous blow on the head and keeps on his feet, walking, talking and gesticulating, but without fully realizing what has happened.

Realization came, however, slowly and with difficulty during the course of the succeeding years. And to this day I go on thinking it over, trying to understand better. If I have written books, it has been to try and understand and to make others understand. I am not at all certain that I have reached the end of my efforts. The truth is this: the day I left the Communist Party was a very sad one for me, it was like a day of deep mourning, the mourning for my lost youth. And I come from a district where mourning is worn longer than elsewhere. It is not easy to free oneself from an experience as intense as that of the underground organization of the Communist Party. Something of it remains and leaves a mark on the character which lasts all one's life. One can, in fact, notice how recognizable the ex-Communists are. They constitute a category apart, like ex-priests and ex-regular officers. The number of ex-Communists is legion today. "The final struggle," I said jokingly to Togliatti recently, "will be between the Communists and the ex-Communists. . . ."

Consideration of the experience I have been through has led me to a deepening of the motives for my separation which go very much further than the circumstantial ones by which it was produced. But my faith in Socialism (to which I think I can say my entire life bears testimony) has remained more alive than ever in me. In its essence, it has gone back to what it was when I first revolted against the old social order; a refusal to admit the existence of destiny, an extension of the ethical impulse from the restricted individual and family sphere to the whole domain of human activity, a need for effective brotherhood, an affirmation of the superiority of the human person over all the economic and social mechanisms which oppress him. As the years have gone by, there has been added to this an intuition of man's dignity and a feeling of reverence for that which in man is always trying to outdistance itself, and lies at the root of his eternal disquiet. But I do not think that this kind of Socialism is in any way peculiar to me. The "mad truths" recorded above are older than Marxism; toward the second half of the last century they took refuge in the workers' movement born of industrial capitalism, and continue to remain one of its most enduring founts of inspiration. I have repeatedly expressed my opinion on the relations between the Socialist Movement and the theories of Socialism; these relations are by no means rigid or immutable. With the development of new studies, the theories may go out of fashion or be discarded, but the movement goes on. It would be inaccurate, however, with regard to the old quarrel between the doctrinaires and the empiricists of the workers' movement, to include me among the latter. I do not conceive Socialist policy as tied to any particular theory, but to a faith. The more Socialist theories claim to be "scientific," the more transitory they are; but Socialist values are permanent. The distinction between theories and values is not sufficiently recognized, but it is fundamental. On a group of theories one can found a school; but on a group of values one can found a culture, a civilization, a new way of living together among men.[7]

Sources

—

CHAPTER VI: THE GOD THAT FAILED

All selections are from Ignazio Silone's contribution to the volume of essays entitled *The God That Failed*, edited by Richard Crossman (Harper & Brothers, New York, 1949).

[1] Page 82, lines 13-28; page 83, lines 2-29; page 86, lines 7-36; page 87; page 88, lines 1-8; 13-21; 27-36; page 89, lines 1-6; 14-17; page 92, lines 14-29; page 93, lines 7-36; page 94, lines 1-26.

[2] Page 96, lines 13-27; page 97; page 98, lines 1-9.

[3] Page 81, lines 22-36; page 82, lines 1-6.

[4] Page 98, lines 14-26; page 99, lines 1-24.

[5] Page 99, lines 29-34; page 100, lines 26-36; page 101; page 102, lines 1-6.

[6] Page 105, lines 27-36; page 106, lines 1-8; lines 26-30; page 107, lines 2-4; lines 10-21; lines 28-36; page 108, lines 15-21; lines 28-36; page 109, lines 1-4; line 8; lines 15-27; line 37; page 110, lines 1-11; lines 16-24; page 111, lines 26-34; page 112, lines 31-34.

[7] Page 113, lines 1-17; lines 29-36; page 114.

CHAPTER VII

E. M. FORSTER (1879–   )

E. M. Forster properly identifies himself as a humanist, tracing his philosophical descent from Erasmus and Montaigne. One should add to that lineage, which has something of a cool skepticism in its veins, a seasoning dash of qualified romanticism and a quite personal and unobtrusive disposition toward charity. Mr. Forster has been called "one of the sanest writers alive," and if sanity can be purified of the least trace of dullness, the phrase is apt. His novel *A Passage to India,* published in 1924, is probably the one best-known and most appreciated in America; however, some critics maintain that his first novel, *Where Angels Fear to Tread,* which introduced his major themes, and his masterpiece, *Howards End,* are both more integral works of art.

Actually, E. M. Forster is more than one of the great English-speaking writers of our times. He is a literary figure who has been called "master" of the Cambridge-Bloomsbury school, and one could number among his disciples his great friend the late Virginia Woolf and the talented novelist Elizabeth Bowen. Like other complex contemporary writers, Forster is deeply involved in literary criticism, although here his achievement is not comparable to that of T. S. Eliot.

Forster is the critic and conscience of the upper-middle-class English who are products of the public school and human examples of "the undeveloped heart." To stir up the complacent, to test them by forcing them to confront the socially "untouchable" member of the un-English society, or the English lower class, to drive toward that wholeness of feeling and spontaneity that must crack apart a social-layered human existence is part of Forster's work. Yet there is no message in him of a "social" kind, only the quest for a richer individualized humanity. His devotion to England has such depth and assur-

126

ance that he can put the most disquieting questions before it (as he did in A Passage to India) without forgetting that he is essentially engaged in "a family quarrel." Perhaps what Forster very early saw as the tragic flaw of the totalitarian conscience, the "stupid barbarism, which smashes at problems instead of disentangling them," is what sustains his faith in the alternative habit of liberalism, without the usual illusion that the mixture of human good-and-evil can be purified into separate essences. Therefore, only two (not three) cheers for democracy!

Edward Morgan Forster was born in London, on the opening day of the year 1879. Through his mother's family, Forster could claim an inheritance of intellectual middle-class distinction; from his father, who was an architect, of mixed English and Welsh ancestry, he might claim something less solid but more liberating, a taste for imaginative creation. Forster has written of his early education when he was a "day boy" at Tonbridge School, where his painful sensations at "being out of it" were accompanied by a vivid perception of the more ruinous fate that "being in it" would have meant. Balm for his wounded spirit was found at King's College, Cambridge, with which center of learning he has maintained a lifelong affectionate connection. There, as a student, he won the friendship of G. Lowes Dickinson, with whom, some years later, he journeyed to India. Shortly after college, Forster visited Italy, where some of his early novels were written. When he returned to England in 1907, he lectured at the Working Men's College, then finished his novel A Room with a View and, in 1910, Howards End. Prior to World War I, Forster was engaged in literary journalism, tried his hand at playwriting, and on the trip to India with Dickinson began to take notes for a novel about the Indians, the British colonial administration, and the problem of empire. During World War I, Forster engaged in war work in Alexandria and did not return to London until peace was declared. A second trip to India in 1921 permitted him to complete his notes for the novel and in 1924 he published A Passage to India, which was awarded several literary prizes, including the James Tait Black Memorial Prize. In 1927 Forster was invited to deliver the annual Clark Lectures at King's College, Cambridge, and chose for his theme Aspects of the Novel, which appeared later as a book under the same title.

Although Forster is constitutionally at a far remove from political actionism, his concern for culture, and its inevitable dependence upon freedom, has made him acutely aware of the political developments of the century. Surveying the period from the First to the Second World War, he has called it "the sinister corridor of our age." In an anti-Nazi broadcast in World War II, Forster said: "By profession, I am a writer. I know nothing about economics or politics, but I am deeply interested in what is conveniently called culture, and I want it to prosper all over the world." In this commitment, Forster entered the fight against totalitarianism, against its principle of censorship, and against the enemy within, whose intolerance, racial prejudice, or fanaticism poisons the atmosphere in which individual liberty breathes. In a book on Forster, Lionel Trilling appraises the man: "He is one of the thinking people who were never led by thought to suppose they could be more than human and who, in bad times, will not become less."

The selections below are taken from *Two Cheers for Democracy*, a book of collected essays, published in 1951.

THE DEFENSE OF INDIVIDUALISM
—

E. M. FORSTER

1. *The Belief in Persons*

I do not believe in Belief. But this is an age of faith, and there are so many militant creeds that, in self-defence, one has to formulate a creed of one's own. Tolerance, good temper and sympathy are no longer enough in a world which is rent by religious and racial persecution, in a world where ignorance rules, and science, who ought to have ruled, plays the subservient pimp. Tolerance, good temper and sympathy—they are what matter really, and if the human race is not to collapse they must come to the front before long. But for the moment they are not enough, their action is no stronger than a flower, battered beneath a military jack-boot. They want stiffening, even if the process coarsens them. Faith, to my mind, is a stiffening process, a sort of mental starch, which ought to be applied as sparingly as possible. I dislike the stuff. I do not believe in it, for its own sake, at all. Herein I probably differ from most people, who believe in Belief, and are only sorry they cannot swallow even more than they do. My law-givers are Erasmus and Montaigne, not Moses and St. Paul. My temple stands not upon Mount Moriah but in that Elysian Field where even the immoral are admitted. My motto is: "Lord, I disbelieve—help thou my unbelief."

I have, however, to live in an Age of Faith—the sort of epoch I used to hear praised when I was a boy. It is extremely unpleasant really. It is bloody in every sense of the word. And I have to keep my end up in it. Where do I start?

With personal relationships. Here is something comparatively solid in a world full of violence and cruelty. Not absolutely solid, for Psychology has split and shattered the idea of a "Person," and has shown that there is something incalculable in each of us, which may at any moment rise to the surface and destroy our normal balance. We don't know what we are like. We can't know what other people are like. How, then, can we put any trust in personal relationships, or cling to them in the gathering political storm? In theory we cannot. But in practice we can and do. Though A is not unchangeably A or B unchangeably B, there can still be love and loyalty between the two. For the purpose of living one has to assume that the personality is solid, and the "self" is an entity, and to ignore all contrary evidence. And since to ignore evidence is one of the characteristics of faith, I certainly can proclaim that I believe in personal relationships.

Starting from them, I get a little order into the contemporary chaos. One must be fond of people and trust them if one is not to make a mess of life, and it is therefore essential that they should not let one down. They often do. The moral of which is that I must, myself, be as reliable as possible, and this I try to be.

But reliability is not a matter of contract—that is the main difference between the world of personal relationships and the world of business relationships. It is a matter for the heart, which signs no documents. In other words, reliability is impossible unless there is a natural warmth. Most men possess this warmth, though they often have bad luck and get chilled. Most of them, even when they are politicians, *want* to keep faith. And one can, at all events, show one's own little light here, one's own poor little trembling flame, with the knowledge that it is not the only light that is shining in the darkness, and not the only one which the darkness does not comprehend. Personal relations are despised today. They are regarded as bourgeois luxuries, as products of a time of fair weather which is now past, and we are urged to get rid of them, and to dedicate ourselves to some movement or cause instead. I hate the idea of causes, and if I had to choose between betraying my country and betraying my friend, I hope I should have the guts to betray my country. Such a choice may scandalise the modern reader, and he may stretch out his patriotic hand to the telephone at once and ring up the police. It would not have shocked Dante, though. Dante places Brutus and Cassius in the lowest circle of Hell because they had chosen to betray their friend Julius Caesar rather than their country Rome. Probably one will not be asked to make such an agonising choice. Still, there lies at the back of every creed something terrible and hard for which the worshipper may one day be required to suffer, and there is even a terror and a hardness in this creed of personal relationships, urbane and mild though it sounds. Love and loyalty to an individual can run counter to the claims of the State. When they do—down with the State, say I, which means that the State would down me.[1]

2. *The Challenge of Our Time*

Temperamentally, I am an individualist. Professionally, I am a writer, and my books emphasize the importance of personal relationships and the private life, for I believe in them. What can a man with such an equipment, and with no technical knowledge, say about the Challenge of our Time? [2]

If we are to answer the Challenge of our Time successfully, we must manage to combine the new economy and the old morality. The doctrine of *laisser-faire* will not work in the material world. It has led to the black market and the capitalist jungle. We must have planning, or millions of people will have nowhere to live, and nothing to eat. On the other hand, the doctrine of *laisser-faire* is the only one that seems to work in the world of the spirit; if you plan and control men's minds you stunt them, you get the censorship, the secret police, the road to serfdom, the community of slaves. Our economic planners sometimes laugh at us when we are afraid of totalitarian tyranny resulting from their efforts—or rather they sneer at us, for there is some deep connection between planning and sneering which psychologists should explore. But the danger they brush aside is a real one. They assure us that the new economy will evolve an appropriate morality, and that when all people are properly fed and housed, they will have an outlook which will be right, because they are the people. I cannot swallow that. I have no mystic faith in the people. I have in the individual. He seems to me a divine achievement and I mistrust any view which belittles him. If anyone calls you a wretched little individual—and I've been called that—don't you take it lying down. You are important because everyone else is an individual too—including the person who criticises you. In asserting your personality you are playing for your side.

That then is the slogan with which I would answer, or partially answer, the Challenge of our Time. We want the New Economy with the Old Morality. We want planning for the body and not for the spirit. But the difficulty is this: where does the body stop and the spirit start? In the Middle Ages a hard and fast line was drawn between them, and according to the mediaeval theory of the Holy Roman Empire men rendered their bodies to Caesar and their souls to God. But the theory did not work. The Emperor, who represented Caesar, collided in practice with the Pope, who represented Christ. And we find ourselves in a similar dilemma today. Suppose you are planning the world-distribution of food. You can't do that without planning world population. You can't do that without regulating the number of births and interfering with family life. You must supervise parenthood. You are meddling with the realms of the spirit, of personal relationship, although you may not have intended to do so. And you are brought back again to that inescapable arbiter, your own temperament. When there is a collision of principles would you favour the individual at the expense of the community as I would? Or would you prefer economic justice for all at the expense of personal freedom?

In a time of upheaval like the present, this collision of principles, this split in one's loyalties, is always occurring.[3]

3. *Order and Art for Art's Sake*

I am really supposed to be speaking from the standpoint of the creative artist. You will gather what a writer, who also cares for men and women and for the countryside, must be feeling in the world today. Uncomfortable, of course. Sometimes miserable and indignant. But convinced that a planned change must take place if the world is not to disintegrate, and hopeful that in the new economy there may be a sphere both for human relationships, and for the despised activity known as art. What ought the writer, the artist, to do when faced by the Challenge of our Time? Briefly, he ought to express what he wants and not what he is told to express by the planning authorities. He ought to impose a discipline on himself rather than accept one from outside. And that discipline may be esthetic, rather than social or moral; he may wish to practise art for art's sake. That phrase has been foolishly used and often raises a giggle. But it is a profound phrase. It indicates that art is a self-contained harmony. Art is valuable not because it is educational (though it may be), not because it is recreative (though it may be), not because everyone enjoys it (for everybody does not), not even because it has to do with beauty. It is valuable because it has to do with order, and creates little worlds of its own, possessing internal harmony, in the bosom of this disordered planet.[4]

It is to the conception of order that I would now turn. This is important to my argument, and I want to make a digression, and glance at order in daily life, before I come to order in art.

In the world of daily life, the world which we perforce inhabit, there is much talk about order, particularly from statesmen and politicians. They tend, however, to confuse order with orders, just as they confuse creation with regulations. Order, I suggest, is something evolved from within, not something imposed from without; it is an internal stability, a vital harmony, and in the social and political category it has never existed except for the convenience of historians. Viewed realistically, the past is really a series of *dis*orders, succeeding one another by discoverable laws, no doubt, and certainly marked by an increasing growth of human interference, but disorders all the same. So that, speaking as a writer, what I hope for today is a disorder which will be more favourable to artists than is the present one, and which will provide them with fuller inspirations and better material conditions. It will not last—nothing lasts—but there have been some advantageous disorders in the past—for instance, in ancient Athens, in Renaissance Italy, eighteenth-century France, periods in China and Persia—and we may do something to accelerate the next one. But let us not again fix our hearts where true joys are not to be found. We were promised a new order after the first world war through the League of Nations. It did not come, nor have I faith in present promises, by whomsoever endorsed. The implacable offensive of Science forbids. We cannot reach social and political stability for the reason that we continue to make scientific discoveries and to apply them, and thus to destroy the arrangements which were based on more elementary discoveries. If Science would discover rather than apply—if, in other words, men were more interested in knowledge than in power—mankind would be in a far safer position, the stability statesmen talk about would be a possibility, there could be a new order based on vital harmony, and the earthly millennium might approach. But Science shows no signs of doing this: she gave us the internal combustion engine, and before we had digested and assimilated it with terrible pains into our social system, she harnessed the atom, and destroyed any new order that seemed to be evolving. How can man get into harmony with his surroundings when he is constantly altering them? . . .

I do want to emphasise that order in daily life and in history, order in the social and political category, is unattainable under our present psychology.

Where is it attainable? Not in the astronomical category, where it was for many years enthroned. The heavens and the earth have become terribly alike since Einstein. No longer can we find a reassuring contrast to chaos in the night sky and look up with George Meredith to the stars, the army of unalterable law, or listen for the music of the spheres. Order is not there. In the entire universe there seem to be only two possibilities for it. The first of them—which again lies outside my terms of reference —is the divine order, the mystic harmony, which according to all religions is available for those who can contemplate it. We must admit its possibility, on the evidence of the adepts, and we must believe them when they say that it is attained, if attainable, by prayer. "O thou who changest not, abide with me," said one of its poets. "*Ordina questo amor, o tu che m'ami*," said another: "Set love in order, thou who lovest me." The existence of a divine order, though it cannot be tested, has never been disproved.

The second possibility for order lies in the esthetic category, which is my subject here: the order which an artist can create in his own work, and to that we must now return. A work of art, we are all agreed, is a unique product. But why? It is unique not because it is clever or noble or beautiful or enlightened or original or sincere or idealistic or useful or educational—it may embody any of those qualities—but because it is the only material object in the universe which may possess internal harmony. All the others have been pressed into shape from outside, and when their mould is removed they collapse. The work of art stands up by itself, and nothing else does. It achieves something which has often been promised by society, but always delusively. Ancient Athens made a mess—but the Antigone stands up. Renaissance Rome made a mess—but the ceiling of the Sistine got painted. James I made a mess—but there was *Macbeth*. Louis XIV—but there was *Phèdre*. Art for art's sake? I should just think so, and more so than ever at the present time. It is the one orderly product which our muddling race has produced. It is the cry of a thousand sentinels, the echo from a thousand labyrinths; it is the lighthouse which cannot be hidden: *c'est le meilleur témoignage que nous puissions donner de notre dignité.*[5]

4. *Tolerance*

Everybody is talking about reconstruction. Our enemies have their schemes for a new order in Europe, maintained by their secret police, and we on our side talk of rebuilding London or England, or western civilisation, and we make plans how this is to be done. Which is all very well, but when I hear such talk, and see the architects sharpening their pencils and the contractors getting out their estimates, and the statesmen marking out their spheres of influence, and everyone getting down to the job, a very famous text occurs to me: "Except the Lord build the house, they labour in vain who build it." Beneath the poetic imagery of these words lies a hard scientific truth, namely, unless you have a sound attitude of mind, a right psychology, you cannot construct or reconstruct anything that will endure. The text is true, not only for religious people, but for workers whatever their outlook, and it is significant that one of our historians, Dr. Arnold Toynbee, should have chosen it to preface his great study of the growth and decay of civilisations. Surely the only sound foundation for a civilisation is a sound state of mind. . . .

What state of mind is sound? Here we may differ. Most people, when asked what spiritual quality is needed to rebuild civilisation, will reply "Love." Men must love one another, they say; nations must do likewise, and then the series of cataclysms which is threatening to destroy us will be checked.

Respectfully but firmly, I disagree. Love is a great force in private life; it is indeed the greatest of all things: but love in public affairs does not work. It has been tried again and again: by the Christian civilisations of the Middle Ages, and also by the French Revolution, a secular movement which reasserted the Brotherhood of Man. And it has always failed. The idea that nations should love one another, or that business concerns or marketing boards should love one another, or that a man in Portugal should love a man in Peru of whom he has never heard —it is absurd, unreal, dangerous. It leads us into perilous and vague sentimentalism. "Love is what is needed," we chant, and then sit back and the world goes on as before. The fact is we can only love what we know personally. And we cannot know much. In public affairs, in the rebuilding of civilisation, something much less dramatic and emotional is needed, namely, tolerance. Tolerance is a very dull virtue. It is boring. Unlike love, it has always had a bad press. It is negative. It merely means putting up with people, being able to stand things. No one has ever written an ode to tolerance, or raised a statue to her. Yet this is the quality which will be most needed after the war. This is the sound state of mind which we are looking for. This is the only force which will enable different races and classes and interests to settle down together to the work of reconstruction.[6]

5. *Two Cheers for Democracy*

This brings me along to Democracy, "even Love, the Beloved Republic, which feeds upon Freedom and lives." Democracy is not a Beloved Republic really, and never will be. But it is less hateful than other contemporary forms of government, and to that extent it deserves our support. It does start from the assumption that the individual is important, and that all types are needed to make a civilisation. It does not divide its citizens into the bossers and the bossed—as an efficiency-regime tends to do. The people I admire most are those who are sensitive and want to create something or discover something, and do not see life in terms of power, and such people get more of a chance under a democracy than elsewhere. They found religions, great or small, or they produce literature and art, or they do disinterested scientific research, or they may be what is called "ordinary people," who are creative in their private lives, bring up their children decently, for instance, or help their neighbours. All these people need to express themselves; they cannot do so unless society allows them liberty to do so, and the society which allows them most liberty is a democracy.

Democracy has another merit. It allows criticism, and if there is not public criticism there are bound to be hushed-up scandals. That is why I believe in the Press, despite all its lies and vulgarity, and why I believe in Parliament. Parliament is often sneered at because it is a Talking Shop. I believe in it *because* it is a talking shop. . . .

So Two Cheers for Democracy: one because it admits variety and two because it permits criticism. Two cheers are quite enough: there is no occasion to give three. Only Love the Beloved Republic deserves that.[7]

6. *Force Versus Creation*

What about Force, though? While we are trying to be sensitive and advanced and affectionate and tolerant, an unpleasant question pops up: does not all society rest upon force? If a government cannot count upon the police and the army, how can it hope to rule? And if an individual gets knocked on the head or sent to a labour camp, of what significance are his opinions?

This dilemma does not worry me as much as it does some. I realise that all society rests upon force. But all the great creative actions, all the decent human relations, occur during the intervals when force has not managed to come to the front. These intervals are what matter. I want them to be as frequent and as lengthy as possible, and I call them "civilisation." Some people idealise force and pull it into the foreground and worship it, instead of keeping it in the background as long as possible. I think they make a mistake, and I think that their opposites, the mystics, err even more when they declare that force does not exist. I believe that it exists, and that one of our jobs is to prevent it from getting out of its box. It gets out sooner or later, and then it destroys us and all the lovely things which we have made. But it is not out all the time, for the fortunate reason that the strong are so stupid. . . .

So that is what I feel about force and violence. It is, alas! the ultimate reality on this earth, but it does not always get to the front. Some people call its absences "decadence"; I call them "civilisation" and find in such interludes the chief justification for the human experiment. I look the other way until fate strikes me. Whether this is due to courage or to cowardice in my own case I cannot be sure. But I know that if men had not looked the other way in the past, nothing of any value would survive. The people I respect most behave as if they were immortal and as if society was eternal. Both assumptions are false: both of them must be accepted as true if we are to go on eating and working and loving, and are to keep open a few breathing holes for the human spirit. No millennium seems likely to descend upon humanity; no better and stronger League of Nations will be instituted; no form of Christianity and no alternative to Christianity will bring peace to the world or integrity to the individual; no "change of heart" will occur. And yet we need not despair, indeed, we cannot despair; the evidence of history shows us that men have always insisted on behaving creatively under the shadow of the sword; that they have done their artistic and scientific and domestic stuff for the sake of doing it, and that we had better follow their example under the shadow of the aeroplanes. Others, with more vision or courage than myself, see the salvation of humanity ahead, and will dismiss my conception of civilisation as paltry, a sort of tip-and-run game. Certainly it is presumptuous to say that we *cannot* improve, and that Man, who has only been in power for a few thousand years, will never learn to make use of his power. All I mean is that, if people continue to kill one another as they do, the world cannot get better than it is, and that since there are more people than formerly, and their means for destroying one another superior, the world may well get worse. What is good in people—and consequently in the world—is their insistence on creation, their belief in friendship and loyalty for their own sakes; and though Violence remains and is, indeed, the major partner in this muddled establishment, I believe that creativeness remains too, and will always assume direction when violence sleeps. So, though I am not an optimist, I cannot agree with Sophocles that it were better never to have been born. And although, like Horace, I see no evidence that each batch of births is superior to the last, I leave the field open for the more complacent view. This is such a difficult moment to live in, one cannot help getting gloomy and also a bit rattled, and perhaps short-sighted.[8]

7. *Belief in Aristocracy of the Sensitive*

In search of a refuge, we may perhaps turn to hero-worship. But here we shall get no help, in my opinion. Hero-worship is a dangerous vice, and one of the minor merits of a democracy is that it does not encourage it, or produce that unmanageable type of citizen known as the Great Man. It produces instead different kinds of small men—a much finer achievement. But people who cannot get interested in the variety of life, and cannot make up their own minds, get discontented over this, and they long for a hero to bow down before and to follow blindly. It is significant that a hero is an integral part of the authoritarian stock-in-trade today. An efficiency-regime cannot be run without a few heroes stuck about it to carry off the dullness—much as plums have to be put into a bad pudding to make it palatable. One hero at the top and a smaller one each side of him is a

favourite arrangement, and the timid and the bored are com-
forted by the trinity, and, bowing down, feel exalted and strengthened.

No, I distrust Great Men. They produce a desert of uniformity around them and often a pool of blood too, and I always feel
a little man's pleasure when they come a cropper. . . . I believe
in aristocracy, though—if that is the right word, and if a demo-
crat may use it. Not an aristocracy of power, based upon rank
and influence, but an aristocracy of the sensitive, the considerate and the plucky. Its members are to be found in all nations
and classes, and all through the ages, and there is a secret understanding between them when they meet. They represent the true
human tradition, the one permanent victory of our queer race
over cruelty and chaos. Thousands of them perish in obscurity, a
few are great names. They are sensitive for others as well as for
themselves, they are considerate without being fussy, their pluck
is not swankiness but the power to endure, and they can take a
joke. . . . Again and again Authority, seeing their value, has tried
to net them and to utilise them as the Egyptian Priesthood or
the Christian Church or the Chinese Civil Service or the Group
Movement, or some other worthy stunt. But they slip through the
net and are gone; when the door is shut, they are no longer in the
room; their temple, as one of them remarked, is the Holiness of
the Heart's Affection, and their kingdom, though they never
possess it, is the wide-open world.

With this type of person knocking about, and constantly
crossing one's path if one has eyes to see or hands to feel, the
experiment of earthly life cannot be dismissed as a failure. But
it may well be hailed as a tragedy, the tragedy being that no
device has been found by which these private decencies can be
transmitted to public affairs. As soon as people have power they
go crooked and sometimes dotty as well, because the possession
of power lifts them into a region where normal honesty never
pays. . . . The Saviour of the future—if ever he comes—will not

preach a new Gospel. He will merely utilise my aristocracy, he will make effective the good will and the good temper which are already existing. . . .

The above are the reflections of an individualist and a liberal who has found liberalism crumbling beneath him and at first felt ashamed. Then, looking around, he decided there was no special reason for shame, since other people, whatever they felt, were equally insecure. And as for individualism—there seems no way of getting off this, even if one wanted to. The dictator-hero can grind down his citizens till they are all alike, but he cannot melt them into a single man. That is beyond his power. He can order them to merge, he can incite them to mass-antics, but they are obliged to be born separately, and to die separately, and, owing to these unavoidable termini, will always be running off the totalitarian rails. The memory of birth and the expectation of death always lurk within the human being, making him separate from his fellows and consequently capable of intercourse with them. Naked I came into the world, naked I shall go out of it! And a very good thing too, for it reminds me that I am naked under my shirt, whatever its colour.[9]

Sources

—

CHAPTER VII: THE DEFENSE OF INDIVIDUALISM

All selections are from E. M. Forster's collection of essays, articles, and broadcasts entitled *Two Cheers for Democracy* (Harcourt, Brace and Company, New York, 1951).

[1] "What I Believe," pages 67-68; page 69, lines 1-12.
[2] "The Challenge of Our Time," page 55, lines 17-21.
[3] *Ibid.*, page 57, lines 4-37; page 58, lines 1-16.
[4] *Ibid.*, page 59, lines 16-37 and line 1 of page 60.
[5] "Art for Art's Sake," page 90, lines 3-37; page 91, lines 1-5 and 17-37; page 92, lines 1-21.

6 "Tolerance," page 44, lines 1-18; page 45, lines 1-39.

7 "What I Believe," page 69, lines 13-37; page 70, lines 13-16.

8 *Ibid.*, page 70, lines 17-37; page 71, lines 21-37; page 72, lines 1-26.

9 *Ibid.*, page 72, lines 27-37; page 73, lines 1-9 and 21-32; page 74, lines 10-26; page 75, lines 9-12; page 76, lines 13-29.

CHAPTER VIII

JOHN MAURICE CLARK (1884–   )

John Maurice Clark, one of the foremost American economists, has played a leading role in redirecting the work of economists to the urgent social issues of our time. He pioneered in assimilating the fact of business cycles into theory and in elaborating the major features of our mixed economy. In performing this task, Clark broke through the simplified, static, and marginalistic assumptions of the "orthodox" economics taught by his distinguished father, John Bates Clark. The constructive side of his work has resulted in what is essentially an integrated series of explorations to account for the more realistic and dynamic aspects of our economy and to examine the great problems of human freedom and economic agency in their contemporary setting.

Clark was born in Northampton, Massachusetts, in 1884. He was educated in the first decade of this century at Amherst College, Columbia and Chicago universities when the prevailing "assumptions of contentment" dominated the thought and policy of economics. On these assumptions of *laissez-faire*, the operation of the competitive market results in equating the real demands of consumers with the real costs of the producers under conditions of fully utilizing resources. Clark's early work, in papers prepared to persuade his professional colleagues, exposed the inadequacies of the older theories and fashioned new tools of analysis to attack the problems of unutilized resources, imperfect market mechanisms, and distorted resource allocations in the light of human ends and social costs. By the early twenties these inquiries issued in two constructive books which have become classics in their field: *Studies in the Economics of Overhead Costs* and *The Social Control of Business*.

After 1929, Clark deepened his inquiries and shifted his attention

143

to the discovery and advocacy of instrumentalities to deal with the problems of the depression, war, demobilization, and inflation. His study of business cycles had advanced far enough to result in the volumes *Strategic Factors in Business Cycles* (1934) and *Economics of Planning Public Works* (1935). Both of these pre-Keynesian studies did much to focus the economists' attention on macro-economic factors operating in the economy considered as a whole, and to convince a wider public of the directive role of government fiscal and monetary policies in expanding national income, production, and employment. During this period, Clark served as an economic adviser to the government, to the National Planning Board (1934) and the National Recovery Administration (1934–1935). With our entry into the war, he became an adviser to the Office of Price Administration (1940–1941). Before the war was over, he turned to an analysis of the *Demobilization of Wartime Economic Controls* (1944) to examine how to achieve ample employment under a voluntary system, in which government and private activities play complementary roles. After the war, as the pressures of inflation continued to mount, Clark concentrated on the problem of the private and public measures that should be undertaken to achieve continued economic growth without inflation. "Man needs to belong to a community smaller and more personal than the overpowering state; but the units that meet this need—including trade unions—are not parts of an integrated community, but monopolistic groups, at war with others. To resolve these conflicts without destroying liberty seems to require, first, that the powers of these groups be fairly well balanced, and second, that they be responsibly exercised. The means of accomplishing this will tax our qualities of citizenship and our powers of social invention."

John Maurice Clark's qualities of citizenship and powers of inventing new means to meet the pressing issues of our time have not been confined to American society. He has persuasively written of the need to accept our role in a wider world community, of the Communist threat to that community, and of the challenge of the underdeveloped areas. He joined a distinguished international group of economists in advising the United Nations on measures for economic development. In all his work, he has shown deep concern with the need "to defend, develop and improve a way of life consistent with the welfare, freedom and dignity of the individual, against the implacable drive of totalitarian Communism for anti-democratic world domination." The selection from his *Alternative to Serfdom* reflects Clark's preoccupation with economic means for human ends.

John Maurice Clark has been Professor Emeritus of Columbia University since 1953 and appropriately holds the John Bates Clark Professorship.

ALTERNATIVE TO SERFDOM
—
JOHN MAURICE CLARK

1. *Is This Decay or Transition?*

Professor Shotwell has spoken of the "anarchy in which we are living today: the most dangerous since the fall of Rome." No one can doubt the dangers; and no one can be sure, except as an act of faith or despair, whether this is the inevitable confusion of a great transition or the death of a civilization—a civilization whose roots have rotted until they will no longer sustain the great weight of its trunk and the vast spread of its branches. We know this civilization still contains much sound timber; but civilizations that still contained much sound timber have fallen before this. The balance that tells the story of survival or decay may be a very delicate one, like the margin between defeat and victory in any close battle.

Decay may not necessarily mean that individuals are inherently worse than they were. The fact seems to be rather that it takes better individuals to hold society together when it grows more complicated, and when old disciplines have been weakened by the growth of intellectual and moral freedom and individualism. Strong individuals have conquered this freedom; and now all have it, whether or not they have grown up to the demands it makes. They reject old leaderships and disciplines, and most of them accept new ones; but the new ones may be made in the image of their prejudices, group interests, and resentments rather than the requirements of a sound social structure. And groups have gained such power that, under leadership that plays on these disruptive forces, they can shatter society rather than hold it together. The old sanctions that supported morality have kept their hold on some and lost it for others. And the content of codes is changing, with different codes for different classes. Community aid is more readily accepted. But chiefly the old code of irresponsible self-interest persists, after outgrowing the checks that once minimized its dangers. The rebuilding of a generally accepted code is the kind of process that might normally take centuries, and in the meantime disaster could come.

One wonders if a people ever before faced the task of building a code of social conduct, and the spiritual basis on which it must rest, with so little willingness to accept leadership or authority except in matters of group interest that conflict with the interests of other groups. The skepticism of the age has been useful in puncturing the myths with which false leaders misled the people in their own interests; but if it goes to the lengths of discrediting all ideas other than those of fairly obvious self-interest—as it is capable of doing—it can destroy our capacity, as a people, for working together in a reasonable degree of freedom.

It is well to realize the seriousness of this crisis. But the most useful faith on which to proceed is the faith that this is transition, not decay. Indeed, we were living in a transition throughout the nineteenth century: a transition that baffled Henry Adams, who saw more deeply into it than most. The forms of freedom we then enjoyed were transitional forms, though many thought of them as final. But we can still hope that freedom itself is more than a passing episode, possibly only in a brief interval before the logic of the industrial revolution has fully worked itself out. And this hope seems to be more than mere unreasoning optimism. Back of the shifting moral codes, normal man still seems incurably bent on living by some code that his fellows approve. There is discipline and leadership within groups; and between groups there is more recognition of the need of accommodation than often appears in public statements which take the form of political special pleading, with all the shortcomings to which that form of discourse is regularly subject.

The thing we call "capitalism" is on the defensive, and the defensive does not win many wars. The initiative rests with other forces. There seems to be no going back to old-fashioned atomistic competition; and if there were, this would not solve the problem of security. We must go forward, on a basis in which security is included. But outright collectivism is, for us, on the defensive also, especially the centralized variety. And a decentralized collectivism, which might preserve more flexibility and freedom, is not the sort of thing one invents out of whole cloth. It would have to evolve, and would depend on the development of much the same voluntary restraints and disciplines that are needed to make our present mixed system work. So the present question is: in what constructive direction can we move forward? What positive structure can we build out of the forces that have the initiative at present? [1]

2. The Individual, the Community, and the State

We need to define the natural rights of man in a new setting, and with a new content. The idea of natural rights has been discredited, largely because it was associated with a set of specific rules embodying an obsolescent form and degree of individualism, attaching to it an unwarranted claim to permanence, and applying formal contractual equality to a society whose differentiated functions no longer fitted this framework. But underlying this is the conception of the nature of man—his needs, reactions, and capacities—and of the arrangements he needs in order to fulfill his individual nature and to do his job in society. These are his natural rights, which society cannot deny without suffering a penalty rooted in the nature of society and of man. But the procedures that embody them do not remain fixed. And, with some basic exceptions, these procedures are not the same for business executive and sharecropper, for physician, professor, and coal-miner. With changing conditions, and changing knowledge of man himself, each generation must discover them afresh.

Underlying all this, and subject to development and modification by it, are our basic ideas of the relation of the individual, the community, and the state. As to this, we have been living in a world of conflict between false absolutes—the absolute community or the absolute state, and the absolute individual. Our liberal civilization has been built on the myth of the absolute individual, whom the state and the community exist to serve; the community being an arithmetic sum of such individuals, and the state their agent, serving them best by giving them maximum liberty to serve themselves. Over against this theory, and taking advantage of its excesses and shortcomings, has arisen the doctrine of the totalitarian state, under which the individual exists to serve the community, of which the state is the embodiment; and the state's power embraces everything in life. In practice this means power that is not only unlimited, but irresponsible.

Our abhorrence of this doctrine should not lead us to support its extreme opposite, which leads to the apotheosis of irresponsible private self-interest. For neither of these one-sided theories is the truth about man and society, and neither is a sound basis for building a social constitution. A good society is one that makes demands on its members—demands that call out the full exercise of their powers—and in which these demands are prevailingly accepted voluntarily. Even our excessively individualistic society recognizes the supremacy of the state when it is attacked, though it takes special pains to maintain as much personal freedom as possible, even in wartime.

It is socially safe for individuals to concede the supremacy of the community only if the community is the kind that finds its life and welfare in those of its members and in their sound relations to one another. And it is safe for the community to regard its welfare as consisting in that of its members, and accordingly to give their individual purposes large scope, only if they are social animals and not self-seeking monsters or machines—if they take one another's purposes and needs into account and regard themselves as basically responsible for behaving as members of a community. With this kind of individuals, in this kind of community, the two antithetical conceptions cease to be irreconcilable and can unite in a working synthesis, with conflict reduced to a matter of adjusting the details of marginal issues.

In this kind of community the state is the most tangibly powerful agency of the community, but not the only one. And while it needs to have ultimate supreme power of coercion—setting to one side the thorny question of an ultimate right of revolution— it can get on with a limited exercise of coercive powers and still maintain orderly community life. In proportion as the social responsibility of the members is imperfect, the result will be turbulent; but if a strong, basic sense of responsibility persists, the turbulence will stop short of chaos. The state will have no need to set itself up, as Nazi Germany did, as the complete embodiment of the community, coercing the individual's entire existence. Instead, we shall have many groups representing parts of the community. In so far as they do not conflict with others, they are minor societies in themselves; and in so far as they do conflict, they must adjust or be subordinated.[2]

3. Needed: An Economic Community

For some hundred and seventy years we have deluded ourselves with the idea that irresponsible self-interest could organize a community in which men not only could progress, but could live in dignity and harmony while doing it. We have trusted to a mechanical market, which promotes goods and neglects men, and to a politics, too little moral, which represents particular interest better than community need. Meanwhile two great correctives— the neighborhood community and religion—have been waning in their power to bring us together. In too many everyday matters a man is a member of some economic group first and an American afterward. We may deplore this, but the real thing to take to heart is the fact that society has given cause for this attitude, through generations of neglect of important needs, and of blindness to what man is, and what a community is.

We are waking up to some of the more obvious and tangible needs and beginning to make material provision for them. On the human and spiritual side, we are beginning to grope toward common standards, or at least toward a basis on which we can live together with the standards we possess. But we have long arrears to make up. We must learn the working meaning of the truth that a community is not merely something to which one looks for benefits, though it has that side, but is also something to which one owes obligations; and that gains must be justified by contributions, not only to customers, or even to an industry, but to the common enterprise as a whole. This truth needs to be rediscovered after generations of life in a world in which each was expected to look out for himself alone.

The neglected needs can only in part be looked after by the state. In large part they are promoted by groups, contending to advance their interests at the expense of the customary status of other groups. This is a natural and healthy way of making necessary changes, if the groups recognize the social stake in what they are doing, and if, between groups, power is evenly enough balanced to avoid exposing any group to the proverbial corrupting effect of power that is unchecked. President Bryn J. Hovde, of the New School of Social Research, has recently made a pregnant statement of the necessary conditions. "Freedom is voluntary association with other individuals who are also free. Therefore individual liberty can not coincide with the power to exploit other individuals or to suppress their liberties. . . . The individual . . . must understand the conditions of his own life in order to decide wisely that he will put up with so and so much law or regimentation in order to enjoy such and such freedom. Only that individual is free, as free as possible that is, who in the privacy of his own mind limits his own liberty in the interest of the greatest possible freedom for all. A society composed of such free individuals will be able to digest all the changes of technology and of social relationships, and will be able to transform into orderly evolution the dynamic forces that would otherwise create revolution."

This sets a high and exacting standard. In so far as it contemplates control by law, every individual is not free to choose how far such control shall go. So this requires him to accept voluntarily a collective decision that will seldom draw the line precisely where he would have chosen to draw it. He will force the line to be drawn too far on the side of regimentation unless, in many matters, he limits his liberty without waiting for law to do it for him. And the principles guiding such limitation, while easy to accept in the abstract, are very difficult to apply to concrete cases, especially one's own case. Those who have new rights to conquer cannot easily visualize the duties that go with them, or even the fact that new rights carry new duties and are forfeit otherwise. Still harder to realize are the dangers of power without adequate social purpose. When all these requirements have been measurably met, we can claim to be an economic community.[3]

4. Religious Needs and Community

The needs and capacities of man for building a community include religious needs and capacities. The search should be for elements contributing constructively to this task. And it should be emphasized that an evolutionary view of the origins of religious ideas is no proof of the soundness or unsoundness of their present forms, but may contribute both toward tolerance and toward acceptance of such evolution as is still going on. The ultimate end is to bring together in the task of community-building people whose religious views will remain diverse.

Man starts interpreting the things he does not understand about his cosmos in terms of the kinds of things he does understand, as the personal doings of benevolent and malevolent spirits. Ultimately comes the conception of a single benevolent, just, and all-powerful being, to whom, in our Occidental theologies, the destiny of every individual is of moment. This structure has been refined as man became more humane, and its cosmology has been partially and tardily adjusted to growing scientific knowledge. It is compounded of attitudes of awe and reverence toward cosmic forces, and of intellectual propositions; of great cosmic and human insights, imperfectly apprehended and formulated, and of logical deductions from these formulations. And logic, thus applied, can be a terrible force. The Inquisition was utterly and ruthlessly logical, granted its premises. The structure includes the spirit of human brotherhood, and formal moral precepts, rewards and punishments, hope of victory for the good and promise of defeat for evil. It acts through effects on personal motives, and through pressure on objective social practices.

The medieval church united theology and moral discipline, controlling economic and social conduct. Its standards were customary, affording both some protection for the common man and a bulwark for the established order. It had temporal power to an extent no longer possible. It was universal, and its discipline was backed by the penalties of a very real and physical hell. The extension of modern business enterprise alone would probably have emasculated this discipline, but the Protestant Reformation robbed the church of the universality necessary to the control of universal economic practices, and extended individualism into the religious basis of ethics, while science was weakening the hold of dogma.

Protestantism temporarily lost interest in objective control of social practices, and was peculiarly exposed to attack by radicals as the "opiate of the masses." Now that it is trying to make up for lost time in this field, its power is limited by the historically irreversible changes I have noted. Adherence is voluntary, hell has become a vague hypothesis, and the population, in terms of the attitudes religion tries to lay hold of, is bafflingly heterogeneous, including many who are frankly irreligious. The state of Tennessee includes both Dayton, where Scopes was tried for teaching evolution, and Oak Ridge, where the atomic age was born. The church faces no easy task in trying to reintroduce adequate precepts of social morality into an economic structure that is firmly established and has grown up for something like a hundred and seventy years on the theory that it could get on very well without them.

One is tempted to conceive a scientist, unwilling to rely on supernatural forces inconsistent with scientific cause and effect, but in whom science had not atrophied the sense of the common man's apprehension of the things religion deals with, and to ask what he would make of them in a world from which inherited theological and cosmological dogmas had been erased. Would he see that man's social heritage includes external supports, the real nature of which is lost for the common man if they are reduced to the formulas of psychology and social science? Would he see that man's racial heritage includes something in his unconscious being stronger than his conscious faculties, fairly describable as a cosmic force, so that each man includes in himself perhaps a bit of eternity, and surely a bit of the enduring life of the race?

Would he perhaps see that this scientific reality is a part of the universal forces of nature around which men have built their conceptions of gods; and that these conceptions, by laying hold of this reality, come nearer the truth than a blank scientific mechanism that ignores this reality? That it represents a power in which man lives and which lives in man, and does for him many of the things that received religion expresses, in its own way, in countless scriptural texts? I suspect that this is possible, and that such material needs to be a part of religious concepts that can be real to a people to whom scientific ways of thinking have thoroughly permeated. With emphasis on such a conception, differences between particular sects might not loom so large.

One thing such a scientist would surely see is that, to make man's life express the socially constructive side of this racial heritage, it is not enough to preach to individuals whose daily doings are organized on a strictly individualistic basis. But he would also see that the individualistic basis is changing. Impersonal market laws no longer overrule all individual latitude of action and all responsibility. The responsible agencies are only partly social, but they have unused potentialities of a social sort. These need to be made effective in the structure of daily doings, or the revived attempt to make Christian ethics effective in temporal affairs will fail. And we have reached a state in which, unless it succeeds measurably, our civilization will not endure.[4]

5. *The Perilous Adventure of Intelligence*

If this unconventional excursion into the realms of human nature and human needs has driven home one truth, it is that intelligence is a perilous adventure. It finds ways of gratifying wants that primitive nature did not allow to be gratified. It makes demands on us at which our unconscious nature may rebel. It builds "rational" bases for social conduct and then proceeds to debunk and destroy the bases it has built. It professes principles that sanction and stimulate ambitions which society cannot fully gratify or appease, and which may therefore destroy it.

Man's reactions do not adapt themselves perfectly to the needs of different situations; they are blundering or imperfectly discriminating; and this applies to all, from the crudest instincts to the "highest" achievements, in the shape of ethical absolutes, or moral codes of the specific sort, or the theological creeds that Tennyson spoke of as "broken lights." The creeds leave insufficient room for diverse degrees and kinds of cosmic insight; the codes fail to do justice to the infinite variety of human personality and situation. Our traditional code of "economic virtues" has been transformed and needs a new balance between self-interest and community responsibility. It has ignored man's needs as a social animal and must make a place for them. We have never yet built a "great society" on the combined basis of freedom and progressive social morality. That unprecedented task is what we now face.

Our economic life and thinking have emphasized quantity of gratifications, of marketable sorts, without reference to what is gratified and what is denied. They have stressed power of attaining ends without reference to the human purposes for which it is used; and power without social purpose has become a Moloch, which has brought our civilization to the brink of chaos and destruction. It is becoming a commonplace that Hitler was able to fill this void largely because he gave his people a purpose. We need no such purpose, nor any overruling collective purpose, except where society itself is threatened. But we do need a collective apprehension of the purposes of a society that understandingly furthers the needs and purposes of its members. . . .[5]

Why does a state need an organized community back of it, to the constitution of which its own constitution corresponds? Because otherwise the alternative is coercion or chaos. If the community is itself well knit, it can call on the state to do various things that the state can best do; but coercion will be needed only to keep recalcitrant minorities within bounds. But if within the society there is a "state of nature" that approximates a state of war, then the state either will fail to maintain tolerable order, or will do it at the cost of general and indiscriminate coercion, and either way personal liberty is lost.

And at present the economic groups into which we are organized are too near this condition, bringing the alternative of coercion or chaos too close for either comfort or safety. These groups are too large, too sophisticated, too consciously and rationally purposeful, to organize themselves into a community of the "natural" sort of which anthropologists tell us, as found, for example, in the South Sea Islands before white civilization submerged them. The organizing of these warring groups must be done by the more deliberate kind of action associated with the theory of the "social contract." In fact, we seem to be in a stage of human development to which some form of "social contract" theory may, for the first time, be applicable on the scale of a "great society." But not for the whole job of organizing a community. There must be an underlying feeling of a common bond, if only the danger of mutual annihilation, to furnish a basis for a willingness to recognize mutual rights and responsibilities. And so we come back to our central theme.

This calls for an adventure in reconstruction, for which no happy outcome can be guaranteed. The world is in the grip of a mighty struggle. On one side are forces driving toward chaos and anarchy, political, social, economic, and moral. On the other side are forces of centralized control. Between them stand the forces and men who are trying desperately to salvage a workable basis for a humane and ordered community, in which some effective degree of freedom and democracy may be kept alive, without wrecking society by their undisciplined exercise and disruptive excesses. There is no point in asking, in the Year of Atomic Energy II, for a world safe for freedom and democracy. Society is condemned to live dangerously—of that much we can be sure. Our fighting chance depends on developing the capacity for generous and constructive thinking and acting, beneath the sword of Damocles.[6]

Sources

CHAPTER VIII: ALTERNATIVE TO SERFDOM

All selections are from J. M. Clark's lectures entitled *Alternative to Serfdom* (Alfred A. Knopf, New York, 1948).

[1] Pages 119-120; page 121, lines 1-15.
[2] Page 19, lines 12-32; page 20; page 21, lines 1-24.
[3] Page 150, lines 27-32; pages 151-152.
[4] Page 54, lines 21-31; pages 55-57.
[5] Page 59, lines 5-31; page 60.
[6] Page 6; page 7, lines 1-12.

CHAPTER IX

ERICH FROMM (1900–)

The importance of Erich Fromm's revision of Freudian psychoanalysis was brought forcefully to the attention of the American reading public by the appearance of his brilliant book *Escape from Freedom*, in 1941. Fromm contributed an original and penetrating study of the psychological and social causes that had permitted the development of totalitarian dictatorship in the modern world. In abandoning the Freudian view of man as a fundamentally antisocial creature, with fixed biological drives, whom society must domesticate and check, Fromm developed a dynamic view of man with physiological needs, to be sure, but with equally imperative needs to achieve significant relatedness to the world and to himself.

Fromm's thesis is that new-found freedom resulting from the growth of many powers of individual conscience and outward control, since the Renaissance, is accompanied by a growing sense of precariousness, loneliness, and isolation. The dilemma of the character type which emerges in modern Western culture is that freedom for this relatively unique responsible self has become a *burden*; the negative "freedom from" older forms of control has not issued in a positive "freedom to" lead a productive and self-realizing life. His discussion of the typical mechanisms by which the least successful moderns contrive to "escape from freedom" threw new light not only on totalitarianism and its zealots, but on the grave problems that must be understood and eased if man's freedom is to survive.

Apart from the intrinsic importance of Dr. Fromm's analysis of man in the social scene, he is one of the few genuine scholars who has the talent to translate psychiatric concepts into language that a lay audience not only can understand but also often enjoy. The breadth of his interests and the scope of his past training permit him to bring to

his analysis the richness of philosophical knowledge, historical awareness, and literary and artistic perception. *Man for Himself,* which
appeared in 1947, forms a positive and constructive sequel to *Escape
from Freedom.* Other stimulating but perhaps less durable studies
have been *Psychoanalysis and Religion* (1950, the Terry Lectures at
Yale), *The Forgotten Language* (1951, an interesting study of dreams,
fairy tales, and myths), and his most recent book, *The Sane Society.*

Erich Fromm was born in Frankfurt, Germany, in 1900. He studied
sociology and psychology at the universities of Heidelberg, Frankfurt,
and Munich, receiving his doctoral degree from Heidelberg in 1922.
His formal training in psychoanalysis was received at the Psychoanalytic Institute in Berlin, and it was here that his explorations of psychoanalysis as applied to culture and society began. Dr. Fromm came to
America as a visiting lecturer at the Chicago Psychoanalytic Institute
in 1933, spent the next three years doing research at the International
Institute of Social Research, Columbia University, and in 1940 became a naturalized American citizen. Since that time he has been
closely associated with the Washington Institute of Psychiatry
(founded by Harry Stack Sullivan), and he is a fellow of the New
York Academy of Science. He has lectured at Columbia University
and at Bennington College, and from 1952 on has been a professor at
the National University of Mexico.

As Fromm has brought the latest social-scientific techniques to the
exploration of man's character and his primary set of moral values, he
has perfected a kind of marriage between Aristotelian self-realization
and pragmatic humanism. Personally, he has stressed the nature of
productive solutions to the problems of man's isolation—creative
work, humanistic, anti-authoritarian conscience, courage, love, pride,
and hope in man's ability to take himself, his life, and happiness
seriously. In a recent small study called "The Art of Loving," Erich
Fromm declared: "Love is the only sane and satisfactory answer to
the problem of human existence." Both the worth-whileness of this
personal solution and the complexity of attaining it may be inferred
from the fact that Dr. Fromm is now married to his third wife.

MAN FOR HIMSELF

—

ERICH FROMM

1. *The Problem*

A spirit of pride and optimism has distinguished Western culture in the last few centuries: pride in reason as man's instrument for his understanding and mastery of nature; optimism in the fulfillment of the fondest hopes of mankind, the achievement of the greatest happiness for the greatest number.

Man's pride has been justified. By virtue of his reason he has built a material world the reality of which surpasses even the dreams and visions of fairy tales and utopias. He harnesses physical energies which will enable the human race to secure the material conditions necessary for a dignified and productive existence, and although many of his goals have not yet been attained there is hardly any doubt that they are within reach and that the *problem of production*—which was the problem of the past—is, in principle, solved. Now, for the first time in his history, man can perceive that the idea of unity of the human race and the conquest of nature for the sake of man is no longer a dream but a realistic possibility. Is he not justified in being proud and in having confidence in himself and in the future of mankind?

Yet modern man feels uneasy and more and more bewildered. He works and strives, but he is dimly aware of a sense of futility with regard to his activities. While his power over matter grows, he feels powerless in his individual life and in society. While creating new and better *means* for mastering nature, he has become enmeshed in a network of those means and has lost the vision of the end which alone gives them significance—*man himself*. While becoming the master of nature, he has become the slave of the machine which his own hands built. With all his knowledge about matter, he is ignorant with regard to the most important and fundamental questions of human existence: what man is, how he ought to live, and how the tremendous energies *within* man can be released and used productively.

The contemporary human crisis has led to a retreat from the hopes and ideas of the Enlightenment under the auspices of which our political and economic progress had begun. The very idea of progress is called a childish illusion, and "realism," a new word for the utter lack of faith in man, is preached instead. The idea of the dignity and power of man, which gave man the strength and courage for the tremendous accomplishments of the last few centuries, is challenged by the suggestion that we have to revert to the acceptance of man's ultimate powerlessness and insignificance. This idea threatens to destroy the very roots from which our culture grew.

The ideas of the Enlightenment taught man that he could trust his own reason as a guide to establishing valid ethical norms and that he could rely on himself, needing neither revelation nor the authority of the church in order to know good and evil. The motto of the Enlightenment, "dare to know," implying "trust your knowledge," became the incentive for the efforts and achievements of modern man. The growing doubt of human autonomy and reason has created a state of moral confusion where man is left without the guidance of either revelation or reason. The result is the acceptance of a relativistic position which proposes that value judgments and ethical norms are exclusively matters of taste or arbitrary preference and that no objectively valid statement can be made in this realm. But since man can not live without values and norms, this relativism makes him an easy prey for irrational value systems. He reverts to a position which the Greek Enlightenment, Christianity, the Renaissance, and the eighteenth-century Enlightenment had already overcome. The demands of the State, the enthusiasm for magic qualities of powerful leaders, powerful machines, and material success become the sources for his norms and value judgments.

Are we to leave it at that? Are we to consent to the alternative between religion and relativism? Are we to accept the abdication of reason in matters of ethics? Are we to believe that the choices between freedom and slavery, between love and hate, between truth and falsehood, between integrity and opportunism, between life and death, are only the results of so many subjective preferences?

Indeed, there is another alternative. Valid ethical norms can be formed by man's reason and by it alone. Man is capable of discerning and making value judgments as valid as all other judgments derived from reason. The great tradition of humanistic ethical thought has laid the foundations for value systems based on man's autonomy and reason. These systems were built on the premise that in order to know what is good or bad for man one has to know the nature of man. They were, therefore, also fundamentally psychological inquiries.[1]

2. *The Contributions and Limitations of Freud*

The most important contribution, perhaps, is the fact that psychoanalytic theory is the first modern psychological system the subject matter of which is not isolated aspects of man but his total personality. Instead of the method of conventional psychology, which had to restrict itself to the study of such phenomena as could be isolated sufficiently to be observed in an experiment, *Freud* discovered a new method which enabled him to study the total personality and to understand what makes man act as he does. This method, the analysis of free associations, dreams, errors, transference, is an approach by which hitherto "private" data, open only to self-knowledge and introspection, are made "public" and demonstrable in the communication between subject and analyst. The psychoanalytic method has thus gained access to phenomena which do not otherwise lend themselves to observation. At the same time it uncovered many emotional experiences which could not be recognized even by introspection because they were repressed, divorced from consciousness.

At the beginning of his studies Freud was mainly interested in neurotic symptoms. But the more psychoanalysis advanced, the more apparent it became that a neurotic symptom can be understood only by understanding the character structure in which it is embedded. The neurotic *character*, rather than the symptom, became the main subject matter of psychoanalytic theory and therapy. In his pursuit of the study of the neurotic character Freud laid new foundations for a science of character (characterology), which in recent centuries had been neglected by psychology and left to the novelists and playwrights.

Psychoanalytic characterology, though still in its infancy, is indispensable to the development of ethical theory. All the virtues and vices with which traditional ethics deals must remain ambiguous because they often signify by the same word different and partly contradictory human attitudes; they lose their ambiguity only if they are understood in connection with the character structure of the person of whom a virtue or vice is predicated. A virtue isolated from the context of character may turn out to be nothing valuable (as, for instance, humility caused by fear or compensating for suppressed arrogance); or a vice will be viewed in a different light if understood in the context of the whole character (as, for instance, arrogance as an expression of insecurity and self-depreciation). This consideration is exceedingly relevant to ethics; it is insufficient and misleading to deal with isolated virtues and vices as separate traits. The subject matter of ethics is *character*, and only in reference to the character structure as a whole can value statements be made about single traits or actions. *The virtuous or the vicious character, rather than single virtues or vices, is the true subject matter of ethical inquiry.*

No less significant for ethics is the psychoanalytic concept of *unconscious* motivation. While this concept, in a general form, dates back to Leibniz and Spinoza, Freud was the first to study unconscious strivings empirically and in great detail, and thus to lay the foundations of a theory of human motivations. The evolution of ethical thought is characterized by the fact that value judgments concerning human conduct were made in reference to the motivations underlying the act rather than to the act itself. Hence the understanding of unconscious motivation opens up a new dimension for ethical inquiry. Not only "what is lowest," as Freud remarked, "but also what is highest in the Ego can be unconscious" and be the strongest motive for action which ethical inquiry can not afford to ignore.

In spite of the great possibilities which psychoanalysis provides for the scientific study of values, Freud and his school have not made the most productive use of their method for the inquiry into ethical problems; in fact, they did a great deal to confuse ethical issues. The confusion springs from Freud's relativistic position, which assumes that psychology can help us to understand the *motivation* of value judgments but can not help in establishing the *validity* of the value judgments themselves.

Freud's relativism is indicated most distinctly in his theory of the Super-Ego (conscience). According to this theory, anything can become the content of conscience if only it happens to be part of the system of commands and prohibitions embodied in the father's Super-Ego and the cultural tradition. *Conscience in this view is nothing but internalized authority.* Freud's analysis of the Super-Ego is the analysis of the "authoritarian conscience" only. . . .

However, Freud's position is by no means consistently relativistic. He displays a passionate faith in truth as the aim toward which man must strive, and he believes in man's capacity thus to strive since he is by nature endowed with reason. This anti-relativistic attitude is clearly expressed in his discussions of "a philosophy of life." He opposes the theory that truth is "only the product of our own needs and desires, as they are formulated under varying external conditions"; in his opinion such an "anarchistic" theory "breaks down the moment it comes in contact with practical life." His belief in the power of reason and its capacity to unify mankind and to free man from the shackles of superstition has the pathos characteristic of the Enlightenment philosophy. This faith in truth underlies his concept of psychoanalytic cure. Psychoanalysis is the attempt to uncover the truth about oneself. In this respect Freud continues the tradition of thought which, since Buddha and Socrates, believes in truth as the power that makes man virtuous and free, or—in Freud's terminology—"healthy." The aim of analytic cure is to replace the irrational (the id) by reason (the ego). The analytic situation may be defined from this standpoint as one where two people—the analyst and the patient—devote themselves to the search for truth. The aim of the cure is the restoring of health, and the remedies are truth and reason. To have postulated a situation based upon radical honesty within a culture in which such frankness is rare is perhaps the greatest expression of Freud's genius.[2]

3. Humanistic Ethics

Humanistic ethics, for which "good" is synonymous with good for man and "bad" with bad for man, proposes that in order to know *what* is good for man we have to know his nature. *Humanistic ethics is the applied science of the "art of living" based upon the theoretical "science of man."* Here as in other arts, the excellence of one's achievement ("virtus") is proportional to the knowledge one has of the science of man and to one's skill and practice. But one can deduce norms from theories only on the premise that a certain activity is chosen and a certain aim is desired. The premise for medical science is that it is desirable to cure disease and to prolong life; if this were not the case, all the rules of medical science would be irrelevant. Every applied science is based on an axiom which results from an act of choice: namely, that the end of the activity is desirable. There is, however, a difference between the axiom underlying ethics and that of other arts. We can imagine a hypothetical culture where people do not want paintings or bridges, but not one in which people do not want to live. The drive to live is inherent in every organism, and man can not help wanting to live regardless of what he would like to think about it.* The choice between life and death is more apparent than real; man's real choice is that between a good life and a bad life.

It is interesting at this point to ask why our time has lost the concept of *life as an art*. Modern man seems to believe that reading and writing are arts to be learned, that to become an architect, an engineer, or a skilled worker warrants considerable study, but that *living* is something so simple that no particular effort is required to learn how to do it. Just because everyone "lives" in some fashion, life is considered a matter in which everyone qualifies as an expert. But it is not because of the fact that man has mastered the art of living to such a degree that he has lost the sense of its difficulty. The prevailing lack of genuine joy and happiness in the process of living obviously excludes such an explanation. Modern society, in spite of all the emphasis it puts upon happiness, individuality, and self-interest, has taught man to feel that not his happiness (or if we were to use a theological term, his salvation) is the aim of life, but the fulfillment of his duty to work, or his success. Money, prestige, and power have become his incentives and ends. He acts under the illusion that his actions benefit his self-interest, though he actually serves everything else but the interests of his real self. Everything is important to him except his life and the art of living. He is for everything except for himself.

If ethics constitutes the body of norms for achieving excellence in performing the art of living, its most general principles must follow from the nature of life in general and of human existence in particular. In most general terms, the nature of all life is to preserve and affirm its own existence. All organisms have an inherent tendency to preserve their existence: it is from this fact

* Suicide as a pathological phenomenon does not contradict this general principle.

that psychologists have postulated an "instinct" of self-preservation. The first "duty" of an organism is to be alive.

"To be alive" is a dynamic, not a static, concept. *Existence and the unfolding of the specific powers of an organism are one and the same.* All organisms have an inherent tendency to actualize their specific potentialities. *The aim of man's life,* therefore, is to be understood as *the unfolding of his powers according to the laws of his nature.*

Man, however, does not exist "in general." While sharing the core of human qualities with all members of his species, he is always an individual, a unique entity, different from everybody else. He differs by his particular blending of character, temperament, talents, dispositions, just as he differs at his fingertips. He can affirm his human potentialities only by realizing his individuality. The duty to be alive is the same as the duty to become oneself, to develop into the individual one potentially is.

To sum up, *good in humanistic ethics is the affirmation of life, the unfolding of man's powers. Virtue is responsibility toward his own existence.* Evil constitutes the crippling of man's powers; *vice is irresponsibility toward himself.* These are the first principles of an objectivistic humanistic ethics.[3]

4. *The Productive Orientation*

The assumption that man has an inherent drive for growth and integration does not imply an abstract drive for perfection as a particular gift with which man is endowed. It follows from the very nature of man, from the principle that *the power to act creates a need to use this power and that the failure to use it results in dysfunction and unhappiness.* The validity of this principle can be easily recognized with regard to the physiological functions of man. Man has the power to walk and to move; if he were prevented from using this power severe physical discomfort or illness would result. Women have the power to bear children and to nurse them; if this power remains unused, if a woman does not become a mother, if she can not spend her power to bear and love a child, she experiences a frustration which can be remedied only by increased realization of her powers in other realms of her life. Freud has called attention to another lack of expenditure as a cause of suffering, that of sexual energy, by recognizing that the blocking of sexual energy can be the cause of neurotic disturbances. While Freud overvalued the significance of sexual satisfaction, his theory is a profound *symbolic* expression of the fact that man's failure to use and to spend what he has is the cause of sickness and unhappiness. The validity of this principle is apparent with regard to psychic as well as physical powers. Man is endowed with the capacities of speaking and thinking. If these powers were blocked, the person would be severely damaged. Man has the power to love, and if he can not make use of his power, if he is incapable of loving, he suffers from this misfortune even though he may try to ignore his suffering by all kinds of rationalizations or by using the culturally patterned avenues of escape from the pain caused by his failure.

The reason for the phenomenon that not using one's powers results in unhappiness is to be found in the very condition of human existence. Man's existence is characterized by existential dichotomies. . . . He has no other way to be one with the world and at the same time to feel one with himself, to be related to others and to retain his integrity as a unique entity, but by making productive use of his powers. If he fails to do so, he can not achieve inner harmony and integration; he is torn and split, driven to escape from himself, from the feeling of powerlessness, boredom and impotence which are the necessary results of his failure. Man, being alive, can not help wishing to live and the only way he can succeed in the act of living is to use his powers, to spend that which he has.[4]

A preliminary approach to the understanding of *productive thinking* may be made by examining the difference between reason and intelligence.

Intelligence is man's tool for attaining practical goals with the aim of discovering those aspects of things the knowledge of which is necessary for manipulating them. The goal itself or, what is the same, the premises on which "intelligent" thinking rests are not questioned, but are taken for granted and may or may not be rational in themselves. This particular quality of intelligence can be seen clearly in an extreme case, in that of the paranoid person. His premise, for instance, that all people are in conspiracy against him, is irrational and false, but his thought processes built upon this premise can in themselves show a remarkable amount of intelligence. In his attempt to prove his paranoid thesis he connects observations and makes logical constructions which are often so cogent that it is difficult to prove the irrationality of his premise. The application of mere intelligence to problems is, of course, not restricted to such pathological phenomena. Most of our thinking is necessarily concerned with the achievement of practical results, with the quantitative and "superficial" aspects of phenomena without inquiring into the validity of implied ends and premises and without attempting to understand the nature and quality of phenomena.

Reason involves a third dimension, that of depth, which reaches to the essence of things and processes. While reason is not divorced from the practical aims of life (and I shall show presently in what sense this is true), it is not a mere tool for immediate action. Its function is to know, to understand, to grasp, to relate oneself to things by comprehending them. It penetrates through the surface of things in order to discover their essence, their hidden relationships and deeper meanings, their "reason." It is, as it were, not two-dimensional but "perspectivistic," to use Nietzsche's term; i.e., it grasps all conceivable perspectives and dimensions, not only the practically relevant ones. Being concerned with the essence of things does not mean being concerned with something "behind" things, but with the essential, with the generic and the universal, with the most general and pervasive traits of phenomena, freed from their superficial and accidental (logically irrelevant) aspects.[5]

Reason, man's blessing, is also his curse; it forces him to cope everlastingly with the task of solving an insoluble dichotomy. Human existence is different in this respect from that of all other organisms; it is in a state of constant and unavoidable disequilibrium. Man's life cannot "be lived" by repeating the pattern of his species; *he* must live. Man is the only animal that can be *bored*, that can be *discontented*, that can feel evicted from paradise. Man is the only animal for whom his own existence is a problem which he has to solve and from which he cannot escape. He cannot go back to the prehuman state of harmony with nature; he must proceed to develop his reason until he becomes the master of nature, and of himself.

The emergence of reason has created a dichotomy within man which forces him to strive everlastingly for new solutions. The dynamism of his history is intrinsic to the existence of reason which causes him to develop and, through it, to create a world of his own in which he can feel at home with himself and his fellow men. Every stage he reaches leaves him discontented and perplexed, and this very perplexity urges him to move toward new solutions. There is no innate "drive for progress" in man; it is the contradiction in his existence that makes him proceed on the way he set out. Having lost paradise, the unity with nature, he has become the eternal wanderer (Odysseus, Oedipus, Abraham, Faust); he is impelled to go forward and with everlasting effort to make the unknown known by filling in with answers the blank spaces of his knowledge. He must give account to himself of himself, and of the meaning of his existence. He is driven to overcome this inner split, tormented by a craving for "absoluteness," for another kind of harmony which can lift the curse by which he was separated from nature, from his fellow men, and from himself.[6]

5. *Faith as a Character Trait*

Faith is not one of the concepts that fits into the intellectual climate of the present-day world. One usually associates faith with God and with religious doctrines, in contradistinction to rational and scientific thinking. The latter is assumed to refer to the realm of facts, distinguished from a realm transcending facts where scientific thinking has no place, and only faith rules. To many, this division is untenable. If faith can not be reconciled with rational thinking, it has to be eliminated as an anachronistic remnant of earlier stages of culture and replaced by science dealing with facts and theories which are intelligible and can be validated.

The modern attitude toward faith was reached after a long drawn-out struggle against the authority of the church and its claim to control any kind of thinking. Thus skepticism with regard to faith is bound up with the very advance of reason. This constructive side of modern skepticism, however, has a reverse side which has been neglected.

Insight into the character structure of modern man and the contemporary social scene leads to the realization that the current widespread lack of faith no longer has the progressive aspect it had generations ago. Then the fight against faith was a fight for emancipation from spiritual shackles; it was a fight against irrational belief, the expression of faith in man's reason and his ability to establish a social order governed by the principles of freedom, equality, and brotherliness. Today the lack of faith is the expression of profound confusion and despair. Once skepticism and rationalism were progressive forces for the development of thought; now they have become rationalizations for relativism and uncertainty. The belief that the gathering of more and more facts will inevitably result in knowing the truth has become a superstition. Truth itself is looked upon, in certain quarters, as a metaphysical concept, and science as restricted to the task of gathering information. Behind a front of alleged rational certainty, there is a profound uncertainty which makes people ready to accept or to compromise with any philosophy impressed upon them.

Can man live without faith? Must not the nursling have "faith in his mother's breast"? Must we all not have faith in our fellow men, in those whom we love and in ourselves? Can we live without faith in the validity of norms for our life? Indeed, without faith man becomes sterile, hopeless, and afraid to the very core of his being. . . .

The history of science is replete with instances of faith in reason and vision of truth. Copernicus, Kepler, Galileo, and Newton were all imbued with an unshakable faith in reason. For this Bruno was burned at the stake and Spinoza suffered excommunication. At every step from the conception of a rational vision to the formulation of a theory, *faith* is necessary: faith in the vision as a rationally valid aim to pursue, faith in the hypothesis as a likely and plausible proposition, and faith in the final theory, at least until a general consensus about its validity has been reached. This faith is rooted in one's own experience, in the confidence in one's power of thought, observation, and judgment. While irrational faith is the acceptance of something as true only *because* an authority or the majority say so, rational faith is rooted in an independent conviction based upon one's own productive observing and thinking.

Thought and judgment are not the only realm of experience in which rational faith is manifested. In the sphere of human relations, faith is an indispensable quality of any significant friendship or love. "Having faith" in another person means to be certain of the reliability and unchangeability of his fundamental attitudes, of the core of his personality. By this I do not mean that a person may not change his opinions but that his basic motivations remain the same; that, for instance, his capacity or respect for human dignity is part of his self, not subject to change.

In the same sense we have faith in ourselves. We are aware of the existence of a self, of a core in our personality which is unchangeable and which persists throughout our life in spite of varying circumstances and regardless of certain changes in opinions and feelings. It is this core which is the reality behind the word "I" and on which our conviction of our own identity is based. Unless we have faith in the persistence of our self, our feeling of identity is threatened and we become dependent on other people whose approval then becomes the basis for our feeling of identity with ourselves. Only the person who has faith in himself is able to be faithful to others because only he can be sure that he will be the same at a future time as he is today and, therefore, to feel and to act as he now expects to. Faith in oneself is a condition of our ability to promise something, and since, as Nietzsche pointed out, man can be defined by his capacity to promise, that is one of the conditions of human existence.

Another meaning of having faith in a person refers to the faith we have in the potentialities of others, of ourselves, and of mankind. The most rudimentary form in which this faith exists is the faith which the mother has toward her newborn baby: that it will live, grow, walk, and talk. However, the development of the child in this respect occurs with such regularity that the expectation of it does not seem to require faith. It is different with those potentialities which can fail to develop: the child's potentialities to love, to be happy, to use his reason, and more specific potentialities like artistic gifts. They are the seeds which grow and become manifest if the proper conditions for their development are given, and they can be stifled if they are absent. One of the most important of these conditions is that the significant persons in a child's life have faith in these potentialities. The presence of this faith makes the difference between education and manipulation. Education is identical with helping the child realize his potentialities. The opposite of education is manipulation, which is based on the absence of faith in the growth of potentialities and on the conviction that a child will be right only if the adults put into him what is desirable and cut off what seems to be undesirable. There is no need of faith in the robot since there is no life in it either.

The faith in others has its culmination in faith in *mankind*. In the Western world this faith was expressed in religious terms in the Judaeo-Christian religion, and in secular language it has found its strongest expression in the progressive political and social ideas of the last 150 years. Like the faith in the child, it is based on the idea that the potentialities of man are such that given the proper conditions they will be capable of building a social order governed by the principles of equality, justice, and love. Man has not yet achieved the building of such an order, and therefore the conviction that he can requires faith. But like all rational faith this, too, is not wishful thinking but based upon the evidence of the past achievements of the human race and on the inner experience of each individual, on his own experience of reason and love. . . .

Man cannot live without faith. The crucial question for our own generation and the next ones is whether this faith will be an irrational faith in leaders, machines, success, or the rational faith in man based on the experience of our own productive activity.[7]

Sources
—

CHAPTER IX: MAN FOR HIMSELF

All selections in this chapter are taken from Erich Fromm's *Man for Himself* (Rinehart and Company, Inc., New York, 1947).

[1] Pages 3-5; page 6, lines 1-17.

[2] Page 31, lines 15-23; pages 32-33; page 34, lines 1-14; page 35, lines 14-30; page 36, lines 1-11.

[3] Page 18, lines 5-30; page 19; page 20, lines 1-19.

[4] Page 217, lines 4-30; page 220, lines 1-20.

[5] Page 102; page 103, lines 1-10.

[6] Page 40, lines 16-29; page 41, lines 1-19.

[7] Page 197, lines 14-29; page 198, lines 1-28; page 205, lines 14-31; pages 206-207; page 208, lines 1-3; page 210, lines 14-18.

SELECTIONS FROM RELIGIOUS PHILOSOPHERS

PART THREE

SELECTIONS FROM RELIGIOUS PHILOSOPHERS

CHAPTER X

MARTIN BUBER (1878–   )

Martin Buber, who has been described as a tiny man with a huge head and a flowing white beard, resembling a prophet of old, is considered the greatest living Jewish philosopher. His original religious-philosophical thought has exerted an immense influence on thinkers of different faiths, including Father D'Arcy of England and Paul Tillich and Reinhold Niebuhr in the United States.

The book which presents his basic ideas, *I and Thou,* has been hailed in the pages of the Catholic periodical *Commonweal* as "one of the epoch-making books of our generation." The title of this book suggests that the central relationship Buber wishes to enstate is a dialogue between "I," man, and "Thou," God. In Buber's terms, the disease of the modern world is the substitution for this saving dialogue of the corrupt "I-It" relationship, which ignores the living God and the spiritual potentialities of man. In carrying this thought further, Buber contends that the "I-It" extends in turn to man, making a thing of him, and precluding the life of ideals and aspirations which is the proper response of a man of whole being to the natural and spiritual environment which continually addresses him.

Buber was born in Vienna in 1878, and spent his early youth in Lemberg at the home of his grandfather, a Hebrew scholar and leader of the Galician Haskalah, or Enlightenment. Visiting a nearby town, Sadagora, Buber saw the Hasidic rabbis, descendants of the *Zaddikim,* or "perfect men," advising people who were more superstitious than religious. Despite the debased state of the mystical Jewish tradition then, Buber was inflamed by the thought of the authority of the holy man who could lead a community united by love for God. In his memoir *My Road to Hasidism,* he wrote: "This luminous idea I found in the dirty little town of Sadagora." But when he was no longer a child, Buber received a thorough education in philosophy, art, and literature at the universities of Vienna, Berlin, Leipzig, and Zurich. Some of these years he spent alienated from the Hasidic tradition and from Judaism itself. His spiritual malaise appears to have been cured in 1899, at the University of Leipzig where he was converted to Zionism, which he accepted not only as a political movement but as a religious idea.

In 1901 Buber worked as editor of the Vienna *Die Welt*, a Zionist journal; and the next year he assisted in founding *Jüdischer Verlag*, a prominent Jewish publishing house. After the First World War, Buber founded and edited *Der Jude*, which became the leading organ of German-speaking Jewry. For the decade 1923–1933, Buber held the chair of Comparative Religion at Frankfurt University; and in 1933, when Jewish students were excluded from educational institutions by the Nazis, he became Director of the Central Office for Jewish Adult Education in Germany. But in 1938 Buber fled Germany and took up his life in the country whose ideals he could approve. He became Professor of Social Philosophy at the Hebrew University in Jerusalem, occupying this position until his retirement in 1951. He is now Professor Emeritus. In the year of his retirement, however, he visited the United States on a lecture tour; on one occasion he addressed an audience of 2,500 people in Carnegie Hall. He has won several awards, including one of "World Brotherhood" from Union Theological Seminary, and an honorary doctorate from the University of Aberdeen, Scotland.

Of Buber's numerous writings, about nineteen have been translated into English, and tend to fall into the following groups: philosophy and sociology, Zionism and Hasidism, biblical studies, translations. In collaboration with Franz Rosenzweig, he produced a translation of the Bible into German which has been universally praised as a faithful and beautiful text. Buber's social and political philosophy in such books as *Between Man and Man, Paths in Utopia*, and partly in *Israel and the World*, condemn Soviet Socialism and also large-scale centralist collectivism which he finds characteristic of European social democratic thought. He emphasizes a decentralized form of religious Socialism, founded upon village communities whose individual members wish to live in human and divine emotional interaction, and who are blessed with the desire to learn the art of "creative companionship." A sympathetic critic has remarked of Buber's philosophy and theology that "the only valid name we can give to Dr. Buber's writing is teaching."

HEBREW HUMANISM
—
MARTIN BUBER

1. *In the Midst of Crisis*

For the last three decades we have felt that we were living in the initial phases of the greatest crisis humanity has ever known. It grows increasingly clear to us that the tremendous happenings of the past years, too, can be understood only as symptoms of this crisis. It is not merely the crisis of one economic and social system being superseded by another, more or less ready to take its place; rather all systems, old and new, are equally involved in the crisis. What is in question, therefore, is nothing less than man's whole existence in the world.

Ages ago, far beyond our calculation, this creature "Man" set out on his journey; from the point of view of Nature a well-nigh incomprehensible anomaly; from the point of view of the spirit an incarnation hardly less incomprehensible, perhaps unique; from the point of view of both a being whose very essence it was to be threatened with disaster every instant, both from within and without, exposed to deeper and deeper crises. During the ages of his earthly journey man has multiplied what he likes to call his "power over Nature" in increasingly rapid tempo, and he has borne what he likes to call the "creations of his spirit" from triumph to triumph. But at the same time he has felt more and more profoundly, as one crisis succeeded another, how fragile all his glories are; and in moments of clairvoyance he has come to realize that in spite of everything he likes to call "progress" he is not travelling along the high-road at all, but is picking his precarious way along a narrow ledge between two abysses. The graver the crisis becomes the more earnest and consciously responsible is the knowledge demanded of us; for although what is demanded is a deed, only that deed which is born of knowledge will help to overcome the crisis. In a time of great crisis it is not enough to look back to the immediate past in order to bring the enigma of the present nearer to solution: we have to bring the stage of the journey we have now reached face to face with its beginnings, so far as we can picture them.

The essential thing among all those things which once helped man to emerge from Nature and, notwithstanding his feebleness as a natural being, to assert himself—more essential even than the making of a "technical" world out of things expressly formed for the purpose—was this: that he banded together with his own kind for protection and hunting, food gathering and work; and did so in such a way that from the very beginning and thereafter to an increasing degree he faced the others as more or less independent entities and communicated with them as such, addressing and being addressed by them in that manner. This creation of a "social" world out of persons at once mutually dependent and independent differed in kind from all similar undertakings on the part of animals, just as the technical work of man differed in kind from all the animals' works. Apes, too, make use of some stick they happen to have found, as a lever, a digging-tool or a weapon; but that is an affair of chance only: they cannot conceive and produce a tool as an object constituted so and not otherwise and having an existence of its own. And again, many of the insects live in societies built up on a strict division of labour; but it is just this division of labour that governs absolutely their relations with one another; they are all as it were tools; only, their own society is the thing that makes use of them for its "instinctive" purposes; there is no improvisation, no degree, however modest, of mutual independence, no possibility of "free" regard for one another, and thus no person-to-person relationship. Just as the specific technical creations of man mean the conferring of independence on things, so his specific social creation means the conferring of independence on beings of his own kind. It is in the light of this specifically human idiosyncrasy that we have to interpret man's journey with all its ups and downs, and so also the point we have reached on this journey, our great and particular crisis. . . .

In the monstrous confusion of modern life, only thinly disguised by the reliable functioning of the economic and State-apparatus, the individual clings desperately to the collectivity. The little society in which he was embedded cannot help him; only the great collectivities, so he thinks, can do that, and he is all too willing to let himself be deprived of personal responsibility: he only wants to obey. And the most valuable of all goods —the life between man and man—gets lost in the process; the autonomous relationships become meaningless, personal relationships wither; and the very spirit of man hires itself out as a functionary. The personal human being ceases to be the living member of a social body and becomes a cog in the "collective" machine. Just as his degenerate technology is causing man to lose the feel of good work and proportion, so the degrading social life he leads is causing him to lose the feel of community—just when he is so full of the illusion of living in perfect devotion to his community. . . .

The real essence of community is to be found in the fact— manifest or otherwise—that it has a centre. The real beginning of a community is when its members have a common relation to the centre overriding all other relations: the circle is described by the radii, not by the points along its circumference. And the originality of the centre cannot be discerned unless it is discerned as being transpicuous to the light of something divine. All this is true; but the more earthly, the more creaturely, the more attached the centre is, the truer and more transpicuous it will be. This is where the "social" element comes in. Not as something separate, but as the all-pervading realm where man stands the test; and it is here that the truth of the centre is proved.[1]

2. Between Man and Man

True community among men cannot come into being until each individual accepts full responsibility for the other; particularly, that a crisis in the community, such as that of today, can only be overcome if the individual charges himself with a share in the situation, and discharges it as a personal responsibility. Contemporary man, and unfortunately young men as well as old, evades this demand for steadfastness, escaping into membership in a "collective," for which he needs decide only once and which, from that moment on, relieves him of all further worry about responsibility. Now, so he thinks, he can unconcernedly co-operate toward a common end without having to ask himself whether this or that means to the desired end is really worthy and adequate, or whether an end which was desecrated because it was attained by such means has anything still in common with the end which it was the original hope to achieve. By this I do not mean to say that our younger generation should not work in collectives and in and for groups. On the contrary! Membership in a group need not constitute escape from more and more new and different responsibilities; it can be the place for the truest and most serious responsibility, and its constant test. When the membership is of such a nature, the responsible human being can prove himself more wholly and profoundly there than anywhere else. The individual—and this holds for young and old alike—must be able to belong to his group with passionately active and passionately combative love. At the same time, however, he must refuse to let the power of any slogan coined within the group prevent him from standing up for what is right, for worthy and adequate rather than unworthy and inadequate means. He must have the courage to stand up for true realization and against mere empty accomplishment, and to pledge his entire existence not only to fight the world without in behalf of the just demand of his group, but to fight within the group against false interpretations and applications of that demand, with the whole of his responsible personality.

The collective is not the only factor which threatens the individual with the loss of personality. His most intimate province, the real content of his personal relationships has become subject to question. I am referring to the prejudice against spontaneity which is cropping up everywhere in the life patterns of the younger generation. This too originated in a well-founded protest against the modern forms of the overestimation of the personal sphere of feeling and the sentimentalizing of life. But with these something of inestimable value has been given up: the unreserved spontaneity between men. A certain impersonality occupies the space between man and man, often begetting a strange distrust even in kindred spirits, an attitude of assumed superiority in a critical appraisal and dismissal of one's fellow which creates a sense of distance in nearness. It has become very rare for one person to open up spontaneously to another. He holds back, observes, calculates, and criticizes. The other no longer is a personal world like myself, a world which I can understand and affirm from the vantage of my own; he is a sum of qualities which are more or less useful to me; he is an aggregate of forces which I regard as excellent or poor prospects for my exploitation. Nothing is substantially changed if the cause in regard to which I weighed his usability is not a personal but a common cause. Even if it is a common cause, let me point out that this impersonal analysis of a comrade makes barren the soil on which the community is based, and destroys the secret of its organic life, which can prosper only when a spontaneous relationship between each and every member can unfold unimpeded. When the innermost possession, personal love itself, is treated as a means to further the mechanism of life, and made subject to it, then what is innermost must die too.[2]

3. *The Power of Faith*

All the prejudices which I have brought to your attention are, in one way or another, connected with the ultimate or rather with the penultimate prejudice, that against faith. For this, too, there is reason and even some justification in the fact that the religious institutions and procedures which are supposed to be objective expressions of the reality of faith are so often and in so many different ways contrary to true faith and to the truth of faith. They have become stumbling blocks in the path of the true believer; they have placed themselves in opposition to his humble life, and on the side of whatever happens to be powerful and accepted as valid in this world. This error, which is in the foreground of our time, has affected the souls of the generations which grew up in a time of crisis; it has invalidated their faith. Here again, the right has been abandoned along with the wrong. Real faith does not mean professing what we hold true in a ready-made formula. On the contrary: it means holding ourselves open to the unconditional mystery which we encounter in every sphere of our life and which cannot be comprised in any formula. It means that, from the very roots of our being, we should always be prepared to live with this mystery as one being lives with another. Real faith means the ability to endure life in the face of this mystery. The forms in which the mystery approaches us are nothing but our personal experiences. At times it is very difficult to live with the mystery, and to be constant to it in the midst of these ever new, unforeseen, surprising, precipitating and overpowering experiences. But there is something which can help us and there are helpers. There is the living transmission of those who have really lived with the mystery, and above all those who are of our kind and who had our tidings. They help us through the pure strength with which they experienced the mystery, faced it, and engaged their lives to it. For to believe means to engage oneself.[3]

It is the signature of our time that the spirit imposes no obligations. We proclaim the rights of the spirit, we formulate its laws, but they enter only into books and discussions, not into our lives. They float in mid-air above our heads, rather than walk the earth in our midst. Everything except everyday life belongs to the realm of the spirit. Instead of union, a false relationship obtains between the spirit and everyday life. This relationship may shape up as spurious idealism, toward which we may lift our gaze without incurring any obligation to recover from the exigencies of earth; or it may present itself as spurious realism, which regards the spirit as only a function of life and transforms its unconditionality into a number of conditional characters: psychological, sociological, and others. It is true that some contemporaries realize all the corroding consequences of this separation of two interdependent entities, a corrosion which is bound to penetrate into deeper and deeper strata, until the spirit is debased into a willing and complacent servant of whatever powers happen to rule the world. The men of whom I am speaking have pondered over how this corrosion can be halted, and have appealed to religion as the only power which is still capable of bringing about a new union between spirit and world. But what goes by the name of religion nowadays will never bring about such a union. For nowadays "religion" itself is part of the detached spirit. It is one of the subdivisions—one which is in high favor, to be sure—of the structure erected over and above life, one of the rooms on the top floor, with a very special atmosphere of its own. But this sort of religion is not an entity which includes all of life and, in this its present status, can never become one. It has lost its unity and so it cannot lead man to inner unity. It has adapted to this twofold character of human existence. To exert an influence on contemporary man, religion itself would have to return to reality. And religion was always real only when it was free of fear, when it shouldered the load of concreteness instead of rejecting it as something belong to another realm, when it made the spirit incarnate, and sanctified everyday life.[4]

In our use of the word, "spirit" does not indicate something which gradually developed in the history of mankind. Spirit is not a late bloom on the tree Man, but what constitutes man. The fact that man is a unit of substance which cannot be grasped if we regard it merely as a phenomenon of nature, the fact that there is a category of existence called Man, is based on the particular human consciousness. Spirit, then, is not just one human faculty among others. It is man's totality that has become consciousness, the totality which comprises and integrates all his capacities, powers, qualities, and urges. When a man thinks, he thinks with his entire body; spiritual man thinks even with his fingertips. Spiritual life is nothing but the existence of man, insofar as he possesses that true human conscious totality, which is not the result of development; it goes back to the origin of mankind, though it may unfold differently in different individuals.[5]

The world is given to the human beings who perceive it, and the life of man is itself a giving and receiving. The events that occur to human beings are the great and small, untranslatable but unmistakable signs of their being addressed; what they do and fail to do can be an answer or a failure to answer. Thus the whole history of the world, the hidden, real world history, is a dialogue between God and his creature; a dialogue in which man is a true, legitimate partner, who is entitled and empowered to speak his own independent word out of his own being.

I am far from wishing to contend that the conception and experience of the dialogical situation are confined to Judaism. But I am certain that no other community of human beings has entered with such strength and fervor into this experience as have the Jews.

What is presupposed when one is serious about the lived dialogue, regarding the moment as word and answer, is, of course, that one is serious about the appointment of Man to the earth.

In the strongest contrast to the Iranian conception with all its later ramifications, the Jewish conception is that the happenings of this world take place not in the sphere between two principles, light and darkness, or good and evil, but in the sphere between

God and men, these mortal, brittle human beings who yet are able to face God and withstand his word.

The so-called evil is fully and as a primary element included in the power of God, who "forms the light, and creates darkness" (Isa. 45:7). The divine sway is not answered by anything which is evil in itself, but by the individual human beings, through whom alone the so-called evil, the directionless power, can become real evil. Human choice is not a psychological phenomenon but utter reality, which is taken up into the mystery of the One who is. Man is truly free to choose God or to reject him, and to do so not in a relationship of faith which is empty of the content of this world, but in one which contains the full content of the everyday. The "Fall" did not happen once and for all and become an inevitable fate, but it continually happens here and now in all its reality. In spite of all past history, in spite of all his inheritance, every man stands in the naked situation of Adam: to each, the decision is given. It is true that this does not imply that further events are deducible from that decision; it only implies that the human being's choice is that side of reality which concerns him as one called upon to act. . . .

The great question which is more and more deeply agitating our age is this: How can we act? Is our action valid in the sight of God, or is its very foundation broken and unwarranted? The question is answered as far as Judaism is concerned by our being serious about the conception that man has been appointed to this world as an originator of events, as a real partner in the real dialogue with God.

This answer implies a refusal to have anything to do with all separate ethics, any concept of ethics as a separate sphere of life, a form of ethics which is all too familiar in the spiritual history of the West. Ethical life has entered into religious life, and cannot be extracted from it. There is no responsibility unless there is One to whom one is responsible, for there is no reply where there is no appeal. In the last resort, "religious life" means concreteness itself, the whole concreteness of life *without reduction*, grasped dialogically, included in the dialogue.[6]

4. *The Faith of Judaism*

The fealty of the Jew is the substance of his soul. The living God to whom he has pledged himself appears in infinite manifestations in the infinite variety of things and events; and this acts both as an incentive and as a steadying influence upon those who owe him allegiance. In the abundance of his manifestations they can ever and again recognize the One to whom they have entrusted themselves and pledged their faith. The crucial word which God himself spoke of this rediscovery of his presence was spoken to Moses from the midst of the burning bush: "I shall be there as I there shall be" (Exod. 3:14). He is ever present to his creature, but always in the form peculiar to that moment, so that the spirit of man cannot foretell in the garment of what existence and what situation God will manifest himself. It is for man to recognize him in each of his garments. I cannot straightaway call any man a pagan; I know only of the pagan in man. But insofar as there is any paganism, it does not consist in not discerning God, but in not recognizing him as ever the same; the Jewish in man, on the contrary, seems to me to be the ever renewed rediscernment of God. . . .

I see the soul of Judaism as elliptically turning round two centers.

One center of the Jewish soul is the primeval experience that God is wholly raised above man, that he is beyond the grasp of man, and yet that he is present in an immediate relationship with these human beings who are absolutely incommensurable with him, and that he faces them. To know both these things at the same time, so that they cannot be separated, constitutes the living core of every believing Jewish soul; to know both, "God in heaven," that is, in complete hiddenness, and man "on earth," that is, in the fragmentation of the world of his senses and his understanding; God in the perfection and incomprehensibility of his being, and man in the abysmal contradiction of this strange existence from birth to death—and between both, immediacy!

The pious Jews of pre-Christian times called their God "Father"; and when the naively pious Jew in Eastern Europe uses that name today, he does not repeat something which he has learned, but he expresses a realization which he has come upon himself of the fatherhood of God and the sonship of man. It is not as though these men did not know that God is also utterly distant; it is rather that they know at the same time that however far away God is, he is never unrelated to them, and that even the man who is farthest away from God cannot cut himself off from the mutual relationship. In spite of the complete distance between God and man, they know that when God created man he set the mark of his image upon man's brow, and embedded it in man's nature, and that however faint God's mark may become, it can never be entirely wiped out.

According to Hasidic legend, when the Baal Shem conjured up the demon Sammael, he showed him this mark on the forehead of his disciples, and when the master bade the conquered demon begone, the latter prayed, "Sons of the living God, permit me to remain a little while to look at the mark of the image of God on your faces." God's real commandment to men is to realize this image.

"Fear of God," accordingly, never means to the Jews that they ought to be afraid of God, but that, trembling, they ought to be aware of his incomprehensibility. The fear of God is the creaturely knowledge of the darkness to which none of our spiritual powers can reach, and out of which God reveals himself. Therefore, "the fear of God" is rightly called "the beginning of knowledge" (Ps. III:10). It is the dark gate through which man must pass if he is to enter into the love of God. He who wishes to avoid passing through this gate, he who begins to provide himself with a comprehensible God, constructed thus and not otherwise, runs the risk of having to despair of God in view of the actualities of history and life, or of falling into inner falsehood. Only through the fear of God does man enter so deep into the love of God that he cannot again be cast out of it.

But fear of God is just a gate; it is not a house in which one can comfortably settle down—he who should want to live in it in adoration would neglect the performance of the essential commandment. God is incomprehensible, but he can be known through a bond of mutual relationship. God cannot be fathomed by knowledge, but he can be imitated. The life of man who is unlike God can yet be an *imitatio Dei*. "The likeness" is not closed to the "unlike." This is exactly what is meant when the Scripture instructs man to walk in God's way and in his footsteps. Man cannot by his own strength complete any way or any piece of the way, but he can enter on the path, he can take that first step, and again and again that first step. Man cannot "be like unto God," but with all the inadequacy of each of his days, he can follow God at all times, using the capacity he has on that particular day—and if he has used the capacity of that day to the full, he has done enough. This is not a mere act of faith; it is an entering into the life that has to be lived on that day with all the active fulness of a created person. This activity is within man's capacity: uncurtailed and not to be curtailed, the capacity is present through all the generations. God concedes the right to abridge this central property of decision to no primordial "Fall," however far-reaching in its effects, for the intention of God the Creator is mightier than the sin of man. The Jew knows from his knowledge of creation and of creatureliness that there may be burdens inherited from prehistoric and historic times, but that there is no overpowering original sin which could prevent the late-comer from deciding as freely as did Adam; as freely as Adam let God's hand go the late-comer can clasp it. We are dependent on grace; but we do not do God's will when we take it upon ourselves to begin with grace instead of beginning with ourselves. Only our beginning, our having begun, poor as it is, leads us to grace. God made no tools for himself, he needs none; he created for himself a partner in the dialogue of time and one who is capable of holding converse.

In this dialogue God speaks to every man through the life which he gives him again and again. Therefore man can only answer God with the whole of life—with the way in which he lives this given life. The Jewish teaching of the wholeness of life is the other side of the Jewish teaching of the unity of God. Because God bestows not only spirit on man, but the whole of his existence, from its "lowest" to its "highest" levels as well, man can fulfil the obligations of his partnership with God by no spiritual attitude, by no worship, on no sacred upper story; the whole of life is required, every one of its areas and every one of its circumstances. There is no true human share of holiness without the hallowing of the everyday. Whilst Judaism unfolds itself through the history of its faith, and so long as it does unfold itself through that history, it holds out against that "religion" which is an attempt to assign a circumscribed part to God, in order to satisfy him who bespeaks and lays claim to the whole. But this unfolding of Judaism is really an unfolding, and not a metamorphosis. . . .

The second focus of the Jewish soul is the basic consciousness that God's redeeming power is at work everywhere and at all times, but that a state of redemption exists nowhere and never. The Jew experiences as a person what every openhearted human being experiences as a person: the experience, in the hour when he is most utterly forsaken, of a breath from above, the nearness, the touch, the mysterious intimacy of light out of darkness; and the Jew, as part of the world, experiences, perhaps more intensely than any other part, the world's lack of redemption. He feels this lack of redemption against his skin, he tastes it on his tongue, the burden of the unredeemed world lies on him. Because of this almost physical knowledge of his, he *cannot* concede that the redemption has taken place; he knows that it has not. It is true that he can discover prefigurations of redemption in past history, but he always discovers only that mysterious intimacy of light out of darkness which is at work everywhere and at all times; no redemption which is different in kind, none which by its nature would be unique, which would be conclusive for future ages, and which had but to be consummated. Most of all, only through a denial of his own meaning and his own mission would it be possible for him to acknowledge that in a world which still remains unredeemed an anticipation of the redemption had been effected by which the human soul—or rather merely the souls of men who in a specific sense are believers—had been redeemed. . . .

Though robbed of their real names, these two foci of the Jewish soul continue to exist for the "secularized" Jew too, insofar as he has not lost his soul. They are, first, the immediate relationship to the Existent One, and second, the power of atonement at work in an unatoned world. In other words, first, the *non-incarnation* of God who reveals himself to the "flesh" and is present to it in a mutual relationship, and second, the unbroken continuity of human history, which turns toward fulfilment and decision. These two centres constitute the ultimate division between Judaism and Christianity.

We "unify" God, when living and dying we profess his unity; we do not unite ourselves with him. The God in whom we believe, to whom we are pledged, does not unite with human substance on earth. But the very fact that we do not imagine that we can unite with him enables us the more ardently to demand "that the world shall be perfected under the kingship of the Mighty One."

We feel salvation happening; and we feel the unsaved world. No savior with whom a new redeemed history began has appeared to us at any definite point in history. Because we have not been stilled by anything which has happened, we are wholly directed toward the coming of that which is to come. . . .

Now to the Christian the Jew is the incomprehensibly obdurate man, who declines to see what has happened; and to the Jew the Christian is the incomprehensibly daring man, who affirms in an unredeemed world that its redemption has been accomplished. This is a gulf which no human power can bridge. But it does not prevent the common watch for a unity to come to us from God, which, soaring above all of your imagination and all of ours, affirms and denies, denies and affirms what you hold and what we hold, and which replaces all the creedal truths of earth by the ontological truth of heaven which is one.

It behooves both you and us to hold inviolably fast to our own true faith, that is to our own deepest relationship to truth. It behooves both of us to show a religious respect for the true faith of the other. This is not what is called "tolerance," our task is not to tolerate each other's waywardness but to acknowledge the real relationship in which both stand to the truth. Whenever we both, Christian and Jew, care more for God himself than for our images of God, we are united in the feeling that our Father's house is differently constructed than our human models take it to be.[7]

5. *The Eclipse of God*

What is it that we mean when we speak of an eclipse of God which is even now taking place? Through this metaphor we make the tremendous assumption that we can glance up to God with our "mind's eye," or rather being's eye, as with our bodily eye to the sun, and that something can step between our existence and His as between the earth and the sun. That this glance of the being exists, wholly unillusory, yielding no images yet first making possible all images, no other court in the world attests than that of faith. It is not to be proved; it is only to be experienced; man has experienced it. And that other, that which steps in between, one also experiences, today. I have spoken of it since I have recognized it, and as exactly as my perception allowed me.

The double nature of man, as the being that is both brought forth from "below" and sent from "above," results in the duality of his basic characteristics. These cannot be understood through the categories of the individual man existing-for-himself, but only through the categories of his existing as man-with-man. As a being who is sent, man exists over against the existing being before which he is placed. As a being who is brought forth, he finds himself beside all existing beings in the world, beside which he is set. The first of these categories has its living reality in the relation I-Thou, the second has its reality in the relation I-It. The second always brings us only to the aspects of an existing being, not to that being itself. Even the most intimate contact with another remains covered over by an aspect if the other has not become Thou for me. Only the first relation, that which establishes essential immediacy between me and an existing being, brings me just thereby not to an aspect of it but to that being itself. To be sure, it brings me only to the existential meeting with it; it does not somehow put me in a position to view it objectively in its being. As soon as an objective viewing is established, we are given only an aspect and ever again only an aspect. But it is also only the relation I-Thou in which we can meet God at all, because of Him, in absolute contrast to all other existing beings, no objective aspect can be attained. Even a vision yields no objective viewing, and he who strains to hold fast an afterimage after the cessation of the full I-Thou relation has already lost the vision.

It is not the case, however, that the I in both relations, I-Thou and I-It, is the same. Rather where and when the beings around one are seen and treated as objects of observation, reflection, use, perhaps also of solicitude or help, there and then another I is spoken, another I manifested, another I exists than where and when one stands with the whole of one's being over against another being and steps into an essential relation with him. Everyone who knows both in himself—and that is the life of man, that one comes to know both in himself and ever again both—knows whereof I speak. Both together build up human existence; it is only a question of which of the two is at any particular time the architect and which is his assistant. Rather, it is a question of whether the I-Thou relation remains the architect, for it is self-evident that it cannot be employed as assistant. If it does not command, then it is already disappearing.

In our age the I-It relation, gigantically swollen, has usurped, practically uncontested, the mastery and the rule. The I of this relation, an I that possesses all, makes all, succeeds with all, this I that is unable to say Thou, unable to meet a being essentially, is the lord of the hour. This selfhood that has become omnipotent, with all the It around it, can naturally acknowledge neither God nor any genuine absolute which manifests itself to men as of non-human origin. It steps in between and shuts off from us the light of heaven.

Such is the nature of this hour. But what of the next? It is a modern superstition that the character of an age acts as fate for the next. One lets it prescribe what is possible to do and hence what is permitted. One surely cannot swim against the stream, one says. But perhaps one can swim with a new stream whose source is still hidden? In another image, the I-Thou relation has gone into the catacombs—who can say with how much greater power it will step forth! Who can say when the I-It relation will be directed anew to its assisting place and activity!

The most important events in the history of that embodied possibility called man are the occasionally occurring beginnings of new epochs, determined by forces previously invisible or unregarded. Each age, is of course, a continuation of the preceding one, but a continuation can be confirmation and it can be refutation.

Something is taking place in the depths that as yet needs no name. To-morrow even it may happen that it will be beckoned to from the heights, across the heads of the earthly archons. The eclipse of the light of God is no extinction; even to-morrow that which has stepped in between may give way.[8]

Sources

––

CHAPTER X: HEBREW HUMANISM

Most of the selections are from Martin Buber's collection of essays and articles entitled *Israel and the World* (Schocken Books, Inc., New York, 1948), denoted as "I." The other selections are from *Paths in Utopia* (The Macmillan Company, New York, 1950), denoted as "P," and *The Eclipse of God* (Harper and Brothers, New York, 1952), denoted as "E."

[1] P, page 129; page 130, lines 1-36; page 132, lines 9-26; page 135, lines 9-21.

[2] "The Prejudices of Youth," I, page 47, lines 2-34; page 48.

[3] *Ibid.*, page 49.

[4] "The Man of Today and the Jewish Bible," I, page 90, lines 10-34; page 91, lines 1-11.

[5] "The Power of the Spirit," I, page 175, lines 5-20.

[6] "The Faith of Judaism," I, page 16, lines 7-34; page 17, lines 1-16; page 18, lines 27-34; page 19, lines 1-8.

[7] "The Two Foci of the Jewish Soul," I, page 29, line 32; page 30, lines 1-18 and 24-34; pages 31-32; page 33, lines 1-21; page 34, lines 31-34; page 35, lines 1-20; page 38, lines 27-34; page 39, lines 1-14; page 40, lines 1-21.

[8] E, page 164, lines 12-26; pages 165-167.

CHAPTER XI

JACQUES MARITAIN (1882–   )

The French philosopher Jacques Maritain has for many years been a central figure in the Neo-Scholastic movement of the twentieth century. He has brought a depth of scholarship and flexible imagination to his interpretations of the philosophy of St. Thomas Aquinas, a subject on which he has lectured in universities all over the Western world—Louvain, Geneva, Fribourg, Milan, Oxford, Santander, the universities of Chicago, Princeton, Columbia, the Angelicum in Rome and the Institute of Medieval Studies in Toronto, Canada. However, in the words of a friendly critic, "What is compelling about him is *not* his Thomism, but his capacity for constant intellectual growth." Maritain's preoccupation has been with all the intellectual and spiritual currents of the contemporary world, as evidenced by his writings on formal logic, theory of knowledge, the history of philosophy, art, and aesthetics, the theory of the state, and particularly on the relationship between Christianity and democracy, education, and on vital questions of our times such as Nazism, anti-Semitism, war and peace. There is much in his thought that is close to Personalism and Humanism; and he has written trenchantly of "Freedom in the Modern World" without yielding his belief that "the penetration by Christianity and the Gospel truths into the heart of the social and cultural life . . . is indispensable to the human fulfilment and perfection of all civilization."

Because of Maritain's commanding position as a representative of modern Catholicism, few people realize that he is a Catholic convert. Jacques Maritain was born on November 18, 1882, to a family whose home maintained an atmosphere of liberal Protestantism. His mother, who had been born a Catholic, became a Protestant when her father remarried after the death of her mother, and accepted his new wife's Protestant religion. Jacques Maritain was educated at the Sorbonne, and appears to have been deeply dissatisfied with the somewhat skeptical academic philosophy and materialistic science which were taught there. He became a disciple of the late Henri Bergson, accepting the philosophy of intuition, which years later he characterized as "an irrational philosophy of pure movement." While studying at the Sorbonne, he met a fellow student, Raïssa Oumancoff, a Russian Jewish *émigrée* whom he married in 1904. The young couple, both professional students of philosophy, continued their search for "the Absolute" which they ultimately found, not in philosophy itself but in religion, under the influence of the ardent faith of Léon Bloy and Charles Péguy. In June of 1908 Jacques and Raïssa Maritain were baptized in the Catholic Church, a conversion that shocked both their families, although in time a reconciliation was effected.

Maritain spent some time in an intensive study of St. Thomas' *Summa Theologiae* under the Dominican Father Clerissac at Versailles; and several of his early books, like *Antimoderne* (1922) and *Three Reformers* (1928), argue explicitly for a Thomistic revival in the modern world. Maritain won greater critical acclaim, however, for his subsequent books, such as *Art and Scholasticism, Christianity and Democracy, True Humanism, The Rights of Man and Natural Law, Man and the State,* and *The Range of Reason.* Raïssa Maritain, who is herself a writer and poet, collaborated with her husband on *Prayer and Intelligence.* In the late 1940's, Maritain was at the Vatican as French Ambassador to the Holy See. He also spent some time writing in America at the Princeton Institute for Advanced Study.

Maritain has been credited with inspiring a wave of conversions to Catholicism on the part of Western intellectuals, especially in the field of the arts. Even where he has not created converts, his influence has been felt, as is evident in T. S. Eliot's remark that Maritain is in his judgment "the most powerful force in contemporary philosophy."

THEOCENTRIC HUMANISM

—

JACQUES MARITAIN

1. *The Present Need To Reconcile Science and Wisdom*

. . . The coming of the atomic age has suddenly exposed to the world the terrible countenance of this problem. Man no longer believes that science and technical skills can by themselves ensure the progress and happiness of the race. Rather he is filled with terror at the sight of the destruction and calamities science and technical skills can bring about. Men of science are examining themselves; and it is with profound respect and in a sincere attempt to discern the bearing of the drama involved, that we must consider the anguish of a scientist of genius like Albert Einstein.

It is not enough to draw the attention of the peoples to the world-destroying catastrophes which the discoveries of modern physics may well lead to, if another armed conflict should occur. Fear is not enough to make men wise. And it is not enough to tell them that these same discoveries, if used for purposes of peace, can open unprecedented vistas of prosperity and freedom to the human race. A possibility is not enough to create happiness. What is required of human intelligence is an awareness of the fact that we have entered a crucial age in our history, a period when, under pain of death, the gigantic implements of power obtained by the scientific mastery of matter must be made subject to reason, in overcoming the irrational temptations to which human beings are liable, especially in their collective existence. It is also necessary to understand that there is an inner hierarchy and a vital inter-connection among the virtues of the human soul, so that, whereas the province of science deals with the *means*, the realm of *ends* pertains to something which is not science, and is not commensurable with it, and is called wisdom. We can be assured of neither peace, nor liberty, nor dignity in the world of tomorrow so long as, in the structures of civilization and in the consciousness of men (and of the scientists themselves) science and wisdom are not reconciled, and the practical applications of science are not rigorously submitted to right ethical will and to the true ends of human life. There was a time when we expected science to solve or do away with problems of ethics, metaphysics and religion; then we counted on the scientists to constitute one day the spiritual authority which would lead mankind toward the green pastures of necessary progress. Today we have to defend science against those who, after asking of it more than it could give, now accuse it, just as unreasonably, of being bankrupt. And, on the other hand, we see men of science engaged in a serious internal examination, in which is questioned the relationship between their conscience as men and the possible use of their work as scientists. We even see them in danger of being treated by the states as mere industrial ore made particularly valuable by its output in terms of discoveries. Thus it is the very dignity of science and of the scientist which is at stake; and it is to maintain and preserve this dignity, as well as to direct the applications of science toward the welfare of the world and not toward its destruction, that mankind stands in need of a powerful renewal of the disciplines of wisdom, and of a re-integration of ethical, metaphysical and religious truths into its culture, and of that reconciliation of science and wisdom which I have mentioned above.[1]

2. The Failure of Secularized Civilization

. . . The great undertaking of secularized Christian man has achieved splendid results for everyone but man *himself*; in what concerns man himself things have turned out badly—and this is not surprising.

The process of secularization of the Christian man concerns above all the idea of man and the philosophy of life which developed in the modern age. In the concrete reality of human history, a process of growth occurred at the same time great human conquests were achieved, owing to the natural movement of civilization and to the primitive impulse, the evangelical one, toward the democratic ideal. At least the civilization of the nineteenth century remained Christian in its real though forgotten or disregarded principles, in the secularized remnants involved in its very idea of man and civilization; in the religious freedom—thwarted as this may have been at certain moments and in certain countries—that it willingly or unwillingly preserved; even in the very emphasis on reason and human grandeur which its freethinkers used as a weapon against Christianity; and finally in the secularized feeling which inspired, despite a wrong ideology, its social and political improvements, and its great hopes.

But the split had progressively increased between the real behavior of this secularized Christian world and the moral and spiritual principles which had given it its meaning and its internal consistency, and which it came to ignore. Thus this world seemed emptied of its own principles; it tended to become a universe of words, a nominalistic universe, a dough without leaven. It lived and endured by habit and by force acquired from the past, not by its own power; it was pushed forward by a *vis a tergo*, not by an internal dynamism. It was utilitarian, its supreme rule was utility. Yet utility which is not a means toward a goal is of no use at all. It was capitalistic (in the nineteenth-century sense of this word, which is the genuine and unmitigated sense), and capitalist civilization enabled the initiatives of the individual to achieve tremendous conquests over material nature. Yet, as Werner Sombart observed, the man of this age was neither "ontologic" nor "erotic"; that is to say, he had lost the sense of Being because he lived in signs and by signs, and he had lost the sense of Love because he did not enjoy the life of a person dealing with other persons, but he underwent the hard labor of enrichment for the sake of enrichment.

Despite the wrong ideology I have just described, and the disfigured image of man which is linked to it, our civilization bears in its very substance the sacred heritage of human and divine values which depends on the struggle of our forefathers for freedom, on Judaeo-Christian tradition, and on classical antiquity, and which has been sadly weakened in its efficiency but not at all destroyed in its potential reserves.

The most alarming symptom in the present crisis is that, while engaged in a death struggle for the defense of these values, we have too often lost faith and confidence in the principles on which what we are defending is founded, because we have more often than not forgotten the true and authentic principles and because, at the same time, we feel more or less consciously the weakness of the insubstantial ideology which has preyed upon them like a parasite.[2]

3. The Idea of a New Christian Civilization

A new age of Christendom, if it is to come, will be an age of reconciliation of that which was disjoined, the age of a "secular" Christian civilization, in which temporal things, philosophical and scientific reason, and civil society, will enjoy their autonomy and at the same time recognize the quickening and inspiring role that spiritual things, religious faith, and the Church play from their higher plane. Then a Christian philosophy of life would guide a community vitally, not decoratively Christian, a community of human rights and of the dignity of the human person, in which men belonging to diverse racial stocks and to diverse spiritual lineages would work at a temporal common task which was truly human and progressive.

In the last analysis, I would say that from the end of the Middle Ages—a moment at which the human creature, while awakening to itself, felt itself oppressed and crushed in its loneliness—modern times have longed for a rehabilitation of the human creature. They sought this rehabilitation in a separation from God. It was to be sought in God. The human creature claims the right to be loved; it can be really and efficaciously

loved only in God. It must be respected in its very connection
with God and because it receives everything—and its very dignity
—from Him. After the great disillusionment of "anthropocentric
humanism" and the atrocious experience of the anti-humanism
of our day, what the world needs is a new humanism, a "theocentric" or integral humanism which would consider man in all
his natural grandeur and weakness, in the entirety of his
wounded being inhabited by God, in the full reality of nature,
sin, and sainthood. Such a humanism would recognize all that is
irrational in man, in order to tame it to reason, and all that is
supra-rational, in order to have reason vivified by it and to open
man to the descent of the divine into him. Its main work would
be to cause the Gospel leaven and inspiration to penetrate the
secular structures of life—a work of sanctification of the temporal order.

This "humanism of the Incarnation" would care for the
masses, for their right to a temporal condition worthy of man
and to spiritual life, and for the movement which carries labor
toward the social responsibility of its coming of age. It would
tend to substitute for materialistic-individualistic civilization,
and for an economic system based on the fecundity of money,
not a collectivistic economy but a "Christian-personalistic" democracy. This task is joined to today's crucial effort to preserve
freedom from totalitarian aggression, and to a simultaneous work
of reconstruction which requires no less vigor. It is also joined to
a thorough awakening of the religious conscience. One of the
worst diseases of the modern world . . . is its dualism, the disso-
ciation between the things of God and the things of the world.
The latter, the things of the social, economic, and political life,
have been abandoned to their own carnal law, removed from the
exigencies of the Gospel. The result is that it has become more
and more impossible to live with them. At the same time, Christian ethics, not really permeating the social life of people, became in this connection—I do not mean in itself or in the
Church, I mean in the world, in the general cultural behavior—

a universe of formulas and words; and this universe of formulas and words was in effect made subservient in practical cultural behavior to the real energies of this same temporal world existentially detached from Christ.

In addition, modern civilization, which pays dearly today for the past, seems as if it were pushed by the self-contradiction and blind compulsions suffered by it, toward contrasting forms of misery and intensified materialism. To rise above these blind compulsions we need an awakening of liberty and of its creative forces, of which man does not become capable by the grace of the state or any party pedagogy, but by that love which fixes the center of his life infinitely above the world and temporal history. In particular, the general paganization of our civilization has resulted in man's placing his hope in force alone and in the efficacy of hate, whereas in the eyes of an integral humanism a political ideal of justice and civic friendship, requiring political strength and technical equipment, but inspired by love, is alone able to direct the work of social regeneration.[3]

4. Catholicism and the Democratic Faith`

As concerns . . . the revitalized democracy we are hoping for, the only solution is of the *pluralistic* type. Men belonging to very different philosophical or religious creeds and lineages could and should co-operate in the common task and for the common welfare of the earthly community, provided they similarly assent to the charter and basic tenets of a society of free men.

For a society of free men implies an essential charter and basic tenets which are at the core of its very existence, and which it has the duty of defending and promoting. One of the errors of individualist optimism was to believe that in a free society "truth," as to the foundations of civil life, as well as the decisions and modes of behavior befitting human dignity and freedom, would automatically emerge from the conflicts of individual forces and opinions supposedly immune from any irrational trends and disintegrating pressures; the error lay in conceiving of free society as a perfectly *neutral* boxing-ring in which all possible ideas about society and the bases of social life meet and battle it out, without the Body Politic's being concerned with the maintenance of any common conditions and inspiration. Thus democratic society, in its concrete behavior, had no *concept* of itself, and freedom, disarmed and paralyzed, lay exposed to the undertakings of those who hated it, and who tried by all means to foster in men a vicious desire to become free from freedom.

If it is to conquer totalitarian trends and to be true to its own mission, a renewed democracy will have its own concept of man and society, and its own philosophy, its own faith, enabling it to educate people for freedom and to defend itself against those who would use democratic liberties to destroy freedom and human rights. No society can live without a basic common inspiration and a basic common faith.

But the all-important point to be noted here is that this faith and inspiration, this philosophy and the concept of itself which democracy needs, all these do not belong in themselves to the order of religious creed and eternal life but to the temporal or secular order of earthly life, of culture and civilization. Even more, they are matters of *practical* rather than theoretical or dogmatic agreement: I mean that they deal with practical convictions which the human mind can try to justify—rightly or wrongly— from quite different, even conflicting philosophical outlooks; probably because they depend basically on simple, "natural" apperceptions, of which the human heart becomes capable with the progress of moral conscience. Thus it is that men possessing quite different, even opposite, metaphysical or religious outlooks, can converge, not by virtue of any identity of doctrine, but by virtue of an analogical similitude in practical principles, toward the same practical conclusions, and can share in the same practical democratic faith, provided that they similarly revere, perhaps for quite diverse reasons, truth and intelligence, human dignity, freedom, brotherly love, and the absolute value of moral good. . . .

Here, if we want to be thorough in our thought and do not fear words, we should point out that where faith is—divine or human—there are also heretics who threaten the unity of the community, either religious or civil. In the "sacral" society the heretic was the breaker of religious unity. In a lay society of free men the heretic is the breaker of "the common democratic beliefs and practices," the totalitarian, the one who denies freedom —his neighbor's freedom—and the dignity of the human person, and the moral power of law. We do not wish him to be burned, or expelled from the city, or outlawed, or put in a concentration camp. But the democratic community should defend itself against him, by keeping him out of its leadership, through the power of a strong and informed public opinion, and even by handing him over to justice when his activity endangers the security of the state—and over and above all by strengthening everywhere a philosophy of life, intellectual convictions, and constructive work which would make his influence powerless. . . . [4]

5. To Serve the Tasks of Peace

. . . If the work of peace is to be prepared in the thought of men and in the consciousness of nations, it is on the condition that minds come to be deeply convinced of principles like the following: Good politics is first and foremost a politics that is just;—every people should strive to understand the psychology, the development and traditions, the material and moral needs, the proper dignity and historic calling of the other peoples, because every people should look out not only for its own advantages but for the common good of the assembly of nations;—this awakening of mutual understanding and of the sense of the civilized community, though it supposes (given the age-old habits of human history) a sort of spiritual revolution, nevertheless answers requirements of public emergency in a world which, from now on, is one world for life or for death, while it remains disastrously divided as to political passions and interests;—to place national interest above everything is a sure means of losing everything;—a community of free men is only conceivable if it recognizes that truth is the expression of what *is*, and right the expression of what is *just*, and not of what is most expedient at a given time for the interest of the human group;—it is not permissible to take the life of an innocent man because he has become a useless and costly burden to the nation, or because he impedes the successful undertakings of any group whatsoever;—the human person is endowed with a dignity which the very good of the community presupposes and must, for its own sake, respect, and is also endowed, whether as a civic, or as a social or working person, with certain fundamental rights and fundamental obligations;—the common good comes before private interests;—the world of labor has a right to the social transformations required by its coming of age in human history, and the masses have a right to participate in the common treasure of culture and of the spirit;—the domain of consciences is inviolable;—men of various beliefs and spiritual lineages must recognize each other's rights as fellow-citizens in the civilized community;—it is the duty of the state, for the very sake of the common good, to respect religious freedom as well as freedom of research;—the basic equality of men makes prejudices of race, class or caste, and racial discrimination, offences against human nature and the dignity of the person as well as a deep-seated threat to peace.

If a state of peace worthy of the name, firm and enduring, is to be established one day among the peoples of the world, this will depend not only upon the economic, political and financial arrangements reached by diplomats and statesmen, nor will it depend solely upon the juridical building up of a truly supra-national co-ordinating organism endowed with efficient means of action; it will depend also upon the deep adherence of men's consciousness to practical principles like those I have recalled. And, to state things as they are, it will depend also upon that *bigger soul* which, according to Bergson, our world, become technically greater, needs, and upon a victorious outpouring of that supreme and free energy which comes to us from on high, and whose name we know—whatever may be our religious denomination or school of thought—to be brotherly love, a name which has been pronounced in such a manner by the Gospels that it has stirred the conscience of man for all time.[5]

6. A Faith To Live By

A faith to live by? That is the topic of an inquiry I was requested to answer some years ago. I wonder whether these words satisfactorily present the question. What is necessary? What do we desperately need? A faith to live by? Or a faith to live for, a faith to live and die for? Just because our very life is at stake we are compelled to rediscover a faith to live and die for.

In the conception of many of our contemporaries faith, a faith to live by, far from being defined by any intrinsic and incontrovertible truth superior to man and human life, is merely something measured by human feeling or human needs, and destined to comfort human life's intellectual and social order, man's security in gaining possession of the earth and mastery over nature. From the time of Descartes and John Locke to the present, faith in God progressively became, for a great number of men, such a faith to live by. Finally, the religious feeling shifted to the cult of man. Our forebears undertook and pursued, with infinite hopefulness, a courageous, stubborn, and bright search for a faith to live by, which was a faith in man. This faith, during some decades, seemed all-powerful and produced splendid, though brittle achievements. The blunt fact is that we have lost faith in man.

What is called today atheistic existentialism is the clearest symptom of this fact. Kierkegaard's existentialism was the anguish of faith searching for incomprehensible and unspeakable reality. Even Heidegger's existentialism searches for the mystery of being through the heartrending experience of nothingness. But atheistic existentialism, such as has been heralded in recent years by writers who are but submissive mirrors of their time, does not reflect the anguish of man confronting nothingness; it reflects and declares the longing of man for nothingness. It expresses the temptation and desire not to be any longer. Yet this is impossible. Longing for nothingness and condemned to be, man abandons himself.

Communism, which is the ultimate vicissitude of anthropocentric rationalism, declares indeed its faith in man and offers itself as the last hope of optimism. Its optimism, however, is the optimism of the titanic and coercive energies of matter and technique; its man is totally subservient to the fate of history embodied in a social group. Faith in man, yes, but in what kind of man? In a collective man who deprives the individual of the liberties of the mind and makes himself into a spurious God emerging from the evolution of matter and the antinomies of history. The real man, the human person, is sacrificed to a devouring idol of the greatness of man.

Well, does despair, then, have the last word? Are we hemmed in by a tragedy?

As a matter of fact, reason demands that we have faith in man. Let us turn from the present world of man and look at the world of nature—I mean with an unsophisticated gaze. We see that, despite the all-pervading law of struggle and conflict, nature in its depths is permeated with an abysmal, supra-individual, and inescapable peace, which is the root goodness and the universal strength of being. And man, as part of nature, has an essence which is good in itself. We see that the evolution of the cosmos is a persevering, though constantly thwarted, movement toward higher forms of life and consciousness, which achieves a final victory in the human species and is taken over, within the limits of the latter, by human liberty, and that from the age of the cave man, the slow and painful progress of mankind testifies to energies in man which make any contempt of the human race childish and presumptuous. Consider with a little love any individual whatever in the anonymous common mass of poor humanity. The better you know him, the more you discover in him hidden resources of goodness that evil has been unable to destroy. Man's difficult condition comes from the fact that he is not only a creature of nature but also one of reason and freedom—elements which are weak in him and yet are his indestructible fortitude and tokens of his abiding dignity. No failures or stains can efface his original greatness.

Yes, we see that we must have faith in man. But we cannot. Our experience keeps reason in check. The present world of man has been for us a revelation of evil; it has shattered our confidence. We have seen too many crimes for which no just revenge can compensate, too many deaths in desperation, too sordid a debasement of human nature. Our vision of man has been covered over by the unforgettable image of the bloody ghosts in extermination camps. Totalitarian craving for power, either Nazi or Communist, feeding on our moral weaknesses, has let devils loose everywhere. Everything we loved seems to have been poisoned; everything in which we trusted seems to have failed. Science and progress are turned to our own destruction. Our very being is threatened by mental and moral atomization. Our very language has been perverted: our words have become ambiguous and seem only able to convey deception. We live in Kafka's world. Where is our faith to live by?

Perhaps we have chosen the wrong road. Perhaps we would have done better to cling to a faith to live and die for, instead of seeking a faith to live by only. Ancient pagan wisdom knew that man's noblest, happiest, and most human aspect is appendant to what is supra-human, and that he can only live by what he lives for and is ready to die for, and what is better than himself. If our humanism has failed, it is perhaps because it was centered in man alone, and was utilitarian, not heroic; because it tried to relegate death and evil to oblivion, instead of facing them and overcoming them by an ascent of the soul into eternal life; because it trusted in techniques instead of in love, I mean in Gospel love.

St. Paul says that faith is the substance of things hoped for and goes on to say that it is a conviction of things not seen. Faith is an adherence to superhuman truth, an entrance into the realm of invisible and divine things; faith makes our whole life append-ant to a living Whole which is infinitely better and more lovable than our own life; faith is a meeting with a Person Who is Truth itself and Love itself, and to Whom the giving of oneself results in supreme freedom, and in Whom dying results in indestruc-tible life.

Then we live for truth, and that truth for which we live is stronger than the world. Then we live for love, and that love for which we live has made the world and will finally renew and transfigure it. Then we are free, and nothing in the world can break our faith.

And this God Who is Truth and Love has made man in His image. He has destined man to share in His own life. His Son died to save man. Despite all the catastrophes that man's failures and refusals cause, He leads man's history toward godlike fulfil-ment and transfiguration. Such is the greatness of man. Here is the rock of our faith in him.

Thus faith in man revives if it is rooted in the supra-human. Faith in man is saved by faith in God.

Human history moves in a definite direction. It depends on both natural and spiritual energies, and among all kinds of con-flicts it tends to the natural fulfilment of mankind—namely, the progressive manifestation of the essence and potentialities of man, the progressive development of the structures of his knowl-edge, his moral conscience, and his social life, mankind's progres-sive conquest of unity and freedom. And it tends also to a spiritual fulfilment which is supra-temporal and transcends his-tory, and which the Christian considers to be the kingdom of God and the revelation of the sons of God. Though inseparably intermingled, these two trends of history relate to two thoroughly distinct orders, and often the weakness of man opposes the one while furthering the other. And contrary to them, evil also devel-ops in history; so that a downward movement causes losses to increase at the same time as an upward movement causes the sap of the world to produce better fruits. In the happiest periods of history evil is at work obscurely in the bloom of our precarious gardens. In the darkest eras the good is invisibly preparing unforeseeable conquests. And good is stronger than evil. Finally the saying of the Scriptures will be fulfilled: Tell the righteous that all is well. In old Jewish apocalyptic writings it was stated that the age of the sufferings of the Messiah would be the age of his greatest victories.

In presenting his book, *On the Threshold of the Apocalypse,* to one of his readers some thirty years ago, Léon Bloy wrote on the first page: "Cher ami donnez-vous la peine d'entrer" ("Dear friend, pray walk in"). It seems that, as a matter of fact, we did walk in. Our age appears as an apocalyptic age, a liquidation of several centuries of history. We are picking the grapes of wrath. We have not finished suffering. But at the end of the crisis a new world will emerge.

Bearing these thoughts in mind, experience—that very experience which jeopardized our faith in man—is transfigured. It assumes a meaning. It is not the revelation of the absurdity of existence but of the pangs and travail of history, not the revelation of the root baseness and contemptibleness of man but of his distress laid bare when he falls from his pride, and of the trials and catastrophes through which the abiding greatness of his destiny asserts itself.

A historical reckoning such as the one we are undergoing does not take place in one day. Time is necessary to make reason able to control the formidable material means which industrial and technological revolution has put in our frail hands. Time is necessary to stir up, from the depths of human bewilderment, the moral and spiritual revolution that is incomparably more needed than any other revolution. For nothing less is required than a terrestrial triumph of Gospel inspiration in the social behavior of mankind. We do not lose hope. The renewal of civilization that we hope for, the age of integral humanism, the time when science and wisdom are to be reconciled, the advent of a fraternal commonwealth and of true human emancipation—all this we do not await on the morrow. But we await them on the day after the morrow, on the day which St. Paul announced will be, after the worst darkness, like a springtime of splendor and renovation for the world.

Every effort made in this direction will finally bear fruit. I refer not only to the spiritual struggle of those who have heard, as Henri Bergson put it, the call of the hero, and who awaken men to evangelic love, but also to the temporal struggle of all those—scientists, poets, pioneers of social justice—who give themselves to the improvement and illumination of their brothers' lives; I refer to the daily exertion of those who can know no rest as long as their brothers are in enslavement and misery. Even if the general state of the world and our stock of accumulated errors prevent such efforts from overcoming at present the evils which are streaming in from everywhere, they are preparing an era, under God, of greater dignity for man and of expanding love.

Yet even that will be but a moment in the history of a small and perishable planet. And hope goes beyond time. For finally we are waiting for the resurrection of the dead, and life eternal. Such is the faith we live for, and, because we live for it, the faith we live by.[6]

Sources

—

CHAPTER XI: THEOCENTRIC HUMANISM

All selections in this chapter are taken from Jacques Maritain's *The Range of Reason* (Charles Scribner's Sons, New York, 1952).

[1] "The Possibilities for Co-operation in a Divided World," page 178, lines 2-41; page 179, lines 1-11.

[2] "Christian Humanism," page 188, lines 20-40; page 189, lines 1-32.

[3] *Ibid.*, page 194, lines 3-41; page 195, lines 1-30.

4 "The Pluralist Principle in Democracy," page 166, lines 17-39; page 167, lines 1-26 and 35-41; page 168, lines 1-10.

5 "The Possibilities for Co-operation in a Divided World," page 183, lines 19-41; page 184, lines 1-31.

6 "A Faith To Live By," page 200, lines 1-32; pages 201-203; page 204, lines 1-27.

CHAPTER XII

REINHOLD NIEBUHR (1892–   )

If there is a single thread uniting the complex and eloquent works
that have been Niebuhr's contribution to the literature of modern
philosophy and Protestant defense, it might be termed a crusade to
combat the easy optimism of an age of reason and science by restoring the concept of original sin and the tragic human condition. In
the pages of a mass-circulation magazine, Reinhold Niebuhr is characterized as "the number one theologian of United States Protestantism." In the choicer and more revealing language of the historian
Arthur Schlesinger, Jr.: "No man has had as much influence as a
preacher in this generation; no preacher has had as much influence in
the secular world."

Niebuhr, who is now Vice President of Union Theological Seminary in New York, was born in Wright City, Missouri, on June 21,
1892. His father had emigrated to this country from Germany at the
age of seventeen, and at the time of Reinhold's birth was a pastor
of the Evangelical Synod Church in Wright City. The early death
of his father, and the consequent financial strain upon the mother,
who was faced with the education of her children, probably had
something to do with Niebuhr's attendance at Elmhurst College,
Illinois, an institution which he left, in 1910, without a degree, to
enter Eden Theological Seminary, near St. Louis. Three years later
he transferred to the Yale Divinity School, receiving his Bachelor of
Divinity degree in 1914, and his Master's of Art in 1915.

In 1915, upon his ordination into the ministry of the Evangelical
Synod of North America, Niebuhr undertook his first and only pas-
torate with the Bethel Evangelical Church in Detroit. The thirteen-
year experience in Detroit was characterized by a vigorous interest in
the labor movement, a type of radical preaching that was sympathetic

to Socialism and to the militant organizers among the automobile workers of that key city. It was common gossip that when Niebuhr left Detroit to join the faculty of Union Theological Seminary, the industrialists breathed a sigh of relief. Two years later, Niebuhr was appointed to the William E. Dodge, Jr., Professorship of Applied Christianity at Union Theological, and his connection with that institution has grown in responsibility with the years.

As early as his Detroit days, Niebuhr understood that the world crisis of our time involves the most fundamental questions of political morality. One of his early books, *Moral Man and Immoral Society*, is still a powerful statement of the requirement for a just social order before "moral man" can be expected to flourish. In *The Children of Light and the Children of Darkness*, Niebuhr attacks the moral irresponsibility of the "children of light," who, out of pure and noble intentions, fail to join issue with the complex realities of power. In this connection Niebuhr forthrightly criticized American churches and religious leaders for a brand of exhortation and advice that is both irrelevant and dangerous, and for such continual criticism Niebuhr has gained some powerful enemies in American Christian circles. On political matters Niebuhr has evidenced the kind of wisdom bereft of fanaticism that is identifiable with liberal pragmatism. Some of his later books, like *Christianity and Power Politics* and *Christian Realism and Political Problems*, and his numerous articles in journals of opinion like the *New Leader*, bear evidence to his habit of carefully weighing the realistic alternatives, and the moral consequences of political decision.

The courage and integrity that caused Niebuhr to associate with the Socialists in the decade of the thirties was demonstrated again as World War II approached, when he broke with the Socialists in June, 1940, over the issue of the European War, which he realized that the United States would have to enter, and in which, morally, it *should* intervene. Because Niebuhr believes that "Man's capacity for justice makes democracy possible; but man's inclination to injustice makes democracy necessary," he has been deeply concerned with concrete issues of foreign policy as well as national domestic policy in America. While he has resorted to a kind of extended preachment on American mistakes in his *The Irony of American History*, he strongly believes in America's capacity to define its national interests in generous terms that provide for the rights of other nations.

Niebuhr's book *The Self and the Drama of History* returns to the interest that conditioned his Gifford Lectures at Edinburgh in 1929, when he chose as his theme *The Nature and Destiny of Man*. Here his appreciation of the Hebraic component of Western civilization is eloquently stated; his continuity with the Hellenic tradition established; and a general philosophy of the self, both in its creaturely limitations and in its creative glories, is effectively set forth.

CHRISTIAN REALISM AND THE POLITICAL CRISIS
—

REINHOLD NIEBUHR

1. *The Secular Roots of Our Predicament*

The natural inclination of the convinced Christian, when viewing the tragic realities of our contemporary world, is to bear witness to the truth in Christ against the secular substitutes for the Christian faith which failed to anticipate, and which may have helped to create the tragic world in which we now live. Did they not destroy the sense of a divine sovereignty to which we are all subject? And did they not invent schemes of redemption from evil which made repentance unnecessary?

This inclination may also define our responsibility. But I doubt whether it is our primary responsibility. It is also our opportunity to bring the truth of the Word of God to bear upon the secular roots of our present predicament because our current history is actually a remarkable illustration of the way Nemesis overtakes the pride of man and how divine judgment is visited upon men and nations who exalt themselves above measure.

The liberal part of our culture thought that the Christian idea of the sinfulness of all men was outmoded. In its place it put the idea of a harmless egotism, rendered innocuous either by a prudent self-interest or by a balance of all social forces which would transmute the selfishness of all into a higher social harmony. The vanity of that idea was proved by the ever more dynamic disproportions of power in our society and the ever greater destruction of community in a technical society. Sometimes the liberal part of our culture conceived the idea of redemption through growth and development. Men suffered (so it was argued) not from sin but from impotence. But fortunately the whole historical process was itself redemptive. It translated man from impotence to power, from ignorance to intelligence, from being the victim to becoming the master of historical destiny. This illusion proved as tragic as the first one. Since the sin of man lies in the corruption of his will and not in his weakness, the possibilities of evil grow with the development of the very freedom and power which were supposed to emancipate man.

The obvious illusions of the liberal world prompted a Marxist rebellion against the whole liberal culture. In place of confidence in a simple harmony of all social forces it proclaimed confidence in a new harmony of society through a revolutionary destruction of property, thus making a social institution the root of evil in man and promising redemption through its destruction. In place of the idea of redemption through endless growth and development it promised redemption through the death of an old order and the rise of a new one. But this was not redemption through the perpetual dying to self of the Christian Gospel. It was the promise of a new life for us through the death of our foes.

The tragedy of our age has been deepened by the fact that 1) this alternative to secular liberalism proved in many respects even more illusory and erroneous, 2) the two forms of error have involved the world in a bitter civil war which rends society asunder from the national to the international community.

It proved even more erroneous because the prophets of this new religion turned into tyrannical priest-kings who, having lost all sense of the contingent character of all human interests and ideas, filled the world with the cruelty of their self-righteousness. It proved more erroneous because the doctrine of the socialization of property when raised to a doctrine of religious redemption, rather than followed pragmatically, merely combines economic and political power in the hands of one oligarchy and produces tyranny. The obvious evils and cruelties of this alternative have given the proponents of the old order good pretexts for not repenting of their own sins but to be content with calling attention to the perils of the alternative.

Perhaps it is because there is a little truth and so much error in both secular alternatives to the Christian faith that they have involved the world in such a hopeless civil war in which each side had enough truth to preserve its sense of high mission and enough error to frighten the other side with the possible consequences of its victory.[1]

2. *The Sins of the Church*

We must undoubtedly bear witness against both types of secular illusion from the standpoint of the truth which we have not of ourselves but from the Gospel. In such a witness the contemporary situation offers the Gospel truth a powerful support. We must preach the Gospel in the day in which the modern man who was so confident that he could control his own destiny is hopelessly caught in an historic fate in which the human will seems to have become completely impotent and frustrated. The vaunted virtues of each side are vices from the standpoint of the other side and sins in the sight of God. The word of the Psalmist fits our situation exactly: "The heathen have raged and the people have imagined vain things. But he who sitteth in the heavens shall laugh."

But let us not presume to laugh with God. God's derisive laughter is the justified divine judgment upon this new and yet very old pride of modern man. We must not laugh, lest we forget that His judgment is upon us, as well as upon them. We are too deeply implicated in the disaster of our day to permit ourselves more than provisional testimony against a so-called secular society. That society in both its liberal and Marxist variety came into being, partly because of the deep involvement of Christianity in the social sins of our day and in the stubbornness of the social injustices. A brief catalog of the sins of the Church proves the depth of our involvement. 1) There is no social evil, no form of injustice whether of the feudal or the capitalist order which has not been sanctified in some way or other by religious sentiment and thereby rendered more impervious to change. In a sense the word of Marx is true: "The beginning of all criticism is the criticism of religion. For it is on this ultimate level that the pretensions of men reach their most absurd form. The final sin is always committed in the name of religion." 2) A part of the Church, fearing involvement in the ambiguities of politics, has declared the problems of politics to be irrelevant to the Christian life. It has abandoned modern men in the perplexities of the modern community and has seen brotherhood destroyed in a technical society without a qualm. Usually this neutrality has not even been honestly neutral. The neutral Church is usually an ally of the established social forces. 3) A part of the Church, facing the complexities of the political order, has been content with an insufferable sentimentality. These problems would not arise, it has declared, if only men would love one another. It has insisted that the law of love is a simple possibility when every experience proves that the real problem of our existence lies in the fact that we ought to love one another, but do not. And how do we establish tolerable community in view of the fact that all men, including Christians, are inclined to take advantage of each other? Even now many Christians fatuously hope that Christian conference will speak some simple moral word which will resolve by love the tragic conflict in the world community. The most opportunistic statesman, who recognizes the complexities which this sentimentality obscures, is a publican who may enter the Kingdom of God before the Phariseeism which imagines that we can lift ourselves above the tragic moral ambiguities of our existence by a simple act of the will. 4) A part of the Church, conscious of these perplexities, has been ready to elaborate detailed schemes of justice and of law for the regulation of the political and social life of mankind, below the level of love and of grace. But it has involved itself in a graceless and inflexible legalism. It does not know that all law can easily be the instrument of sin; that inflexible propositions of justice, particularly in the rapidly shifting circumstances of modern technical development, may hinder rather than help the achievement of true justice. One contribution which Christianity certainly ought to make to the problem of political justice is to set all propositions of justice under the law of love, resolving the fruitless debate between pragmatists and legalists and creating the freedom and maneuverability necessary to achieve a tolerable accord between men and nations in ever more complex human relations. We need a pragmatic attitude toward every institution of property and of government, recognizing that none of them are as sacrosanct as some supposedly Christian or secular system of law has made them, that all of them are subject to corruption and that their abolition is also subject to corruption. This freedom need not degenerate into lawlessness, if it is held in the knowledge that "all things are yours, and ye are Christ's and Christ is God's." [2]

3. *The Christian Witness in Our Time*

We have spoken negatively. The Christian Church must bear witness against every form of pride and vainglory, whether in the secular or in the Christian culture, and be particularly intent upon our own sins lest we make Christ the judge of the other but not of ourselves. But the experience of repentance does not stand alone. It is a part of a total experience of redemption. Positively our task is to present the Gospel of redemption in Christ to nations as well as to individuals. According to our faith we are always involved in sin and in death because we try too desperately to live, to preserve our pride, to maintain our prestige. Yet it is possible to live truly if we die to self, if the vainglory of man is broken by divine judgment that life may be truly reformed by divine grace. This promise of new life is for individuals; yet who can deny its relevance for nations and empires, for civilizations and cultures also, even though these collective forms of life do not have the exact integrity of the individual soul; nor do they have as direct an access to divine judgment and grace?

The situation in the collective life of mankind today is that we have made shipwreck of our common life through the new powers and freedom which a technical civilization has placed at our disposal. The shipwreck, manifested in the misery and insecurity of the whole world, is an objective historical judgment. It is the death which has followed upon a vainglorious life of the nations. Without faith it is nothing but death. Without faith it generates the sorrow of the world, which is despair. Without faith this confusion is the mark of meaninglessness which follows the destruction of the simple systems of life's meaning which have had ourselves, our nation and our culture at its center. It is by faith in the God revealed in One who died and rose again that death can become the basis of new life, that meaninglessness turns into meaning, that judgment is experienced as grace. Our business is so to mediate the divine judgment and grace that nations, classes, states and cultures, as well as individuals, may discern the divine author of their wounds, that they may also know the possibility of a new and whole life. In a day of complacency and security the Christian Church must anticipate the judgment which is to come and declare that the day of the Lord will be darkness and not light. In the day of judgment and catastrophe the Christian Gospel has a message of hope for those who truly repent.

It is true that the human situation is such that repentance is always required even as evil always flourishes. But it is wrong to preach this Gospel *sub specie aeternitatis* as if there were no history with its time and seasons, and with its particular occasions. Nor is our preaching of any avail if we only persuade men and nations to acknowledge the original sin which infects us all but not the particular sins of which we are guilty. Not the least of our tasks is to expound a judgment and a mercy which tempers the wind to the shorn sheep. Must we not warn victorious nations that they are wrong in regarding their victory as a proof of their virtue, lest they engulf the world in a new chain of evil by their vindictiveness, which is nothing else than the fury of their self-righteousness? And is our word to the defeated nations not of a different order, reminding them that their warfare is accomplished seeing that they have received at the Lord's hand double for all their sins, and that the punishment is really at the Lord's hand even though it is not nicely proportioned to the evil committed? Must we not warn powerful and secure nations and classes that they have an idolatrous idea of their own importance and that as surely as they say, "I sit as a queen and shall never know sorrow," so surely shall "in one moment her sorrow come"? And must we not remind those who are weak and defrauded and despised that God will avenge the cruelties from which they suffer but will also not bear the cruel resentment which corrupts their hearts? Must we not say to the rich and secure classes of society that their vaunted devotion to the laws and structures of society which guarantee their privileges is tainted with self-interest; and must we not say to the poor that their dream of a propertyless society of perfect justice turns into a nightmare of new injustice because it is based only upon the recognition of the sin which the other commits and knows nothing of the sin which the poor man commits when he is no longer poor but has become a commissar? Everywhere life is delivered unto death because it is ensnared in self-delusion and practices every evasion rather than meet the true God. And everywhere the Church is caught in this dance of death because it allows the accents of national pride and of racial prejudice, the notes of self-esteem and complacency to color its message, so that the whole business of religion in our day could seem to the cynical observer (even as it must appear to the righteous God) as a vast effort to lobby in the courts of the Almighty to gain a special advantage for our cause in the divine adjudication. If the slogan that the Church should be the Church is to have a meaning other than its withdrawal from the world, must it not mean that by prayer and fasting it has at least extricated itself in some degree from its embarrassing alliances with this or that class, race and nation so that it may speak the word of God more purely, and more forthrightly to each man and nation, but also to each generation according to the peculiar needs of the person and the hour?

A new life is possible for those who die to the old self, whether nations or individuals, at any time and in any situation. But on the positive side there are also special words to be spoken to an age besides timeless words. The new life which we require collectively in our age is a community wide enough to make the world-wide interdependence of nations in a technical age sufferable; and a justice carefully enough balanced to make the dynamic forces of a technical society yield a tolerable justice rather than an alternation of intolerable anarchy and intolerable tyranny. To accomplish this purpose some of our own preconceptions must go and the same law of love which is no simple possibility for man or society must be enthroned as yet the final standard of every institution, structure and system of justice. To those who exalt freedom we must declare that freedom without community is not love but leads to man making himself his own end. To those who exalt community we must declare that no historic community deserves the final devotion of man, since his stature and structure is such that only God can be the end of his life. Against those who make the state sacrosanct we must insist that the state is always tempted to set its majesty in rebellious opposition to the divine majesty. To those who fear the extension of the state for the regulation of modern economic life we must point out that their fears are frequently prompted not by a concern for justice but by a jealous desire to maintain their own power. A tolerable community under modern conditions cannot be easily established; it can be established at all only if much of what has been regarded as absolute is recognized to be relative; and if everywhere men seek to separate the precious from the vile and sharply distinguish between their interests and the demands which God and the neighbor make upon them.[3]

4. The Affinity Between Democracy and Biblical Faith

The democratic wisdom which learns how to avoid and negate conflicting ideologies, based upon interest, may be, of course, the result of experience rather than of special Christian insights. But it cannot be denied that biblical faith (from which Judaism and Christianity are derived) is unique in offering three insights into the human situation which are indispensable to democracy. The first is that it assumes a source of authority from the standpoint of which the individual may defy the authorities of this world. ("We must obey God rather than man.") The second is an appreciation of the unique worth of the individual which makes it wrong to fit him into any political program as a mere instrument. A scientific humanism frequently offends the dignity of man, which it ostensibly extols, by regarding human beings as subject to manipulation and as mere instruments of some "socially approved" ends. It is this tendency of a scientific age which establishes its affinity with totalitarianism, and justifies the charge that a scientific humanism is harmless only because there is not a political program to give the elite, which its theories invariably presuppose, a monopoly of power. The third insight is the biblical insistence that the same radical freedom which makes man creative also makes him potentially destructive and dangerous, that the dignity of man and the misery of man therefore have the same root. This insight is the basis of all political realism in which secular theory, whether liberal or Marxist, is defective; it justifies the institutions of democracy more surely than any sentimentality about man, whether liberal or radical.[4]

5. Toward World Community

Virtually all arguments for world government rest upon the simple presupposition that the desirability of world order proves the attainability of world government. Our precarious situation is unfortunately no proof, either of the moral ability of mankind to create a world government by an act of the will, or of the political ability of such a government to integrate a world community in advance of a more gradual growth of the "social tissue" which every community requires more than government.

Most advocates of world government also assume that nations need merely follow the alleged example of the individuals of another age who are supposed to have achieved community by codifying their agreements into law and by providing an agency of some kind for law enforcement. This assumption ignores the historic fact that the mutual respect for each other's rights in particular communities is older than any code of law; and that machinery for the enforcement of law can be efficacious only when a community as a whole obeys its laws implicitly, so that coercive enforcement may be limited to a recalcitrant minority.

The fallacy of world government can be stated in two simple propositions. The first is that governments are not created by fiat (though sometimes they can be imposed by tyranny). The second is that governments have only limited efficacy in integrating a community. . . .

The fact is that even the wisest statecraft cannot create social tissue. It can cut, sew and redesign social fabric to a limited degree. But the social fabric upon which it works must be "given."

The international community is not totally lacking in social tissue; but it is very scant, compared with that of particular states. Let us briefly assess the various factors in it. Most important as a force of social cohesion in the world community is the increasing economic interdependence of peoples of the world. But it is important to contrast this economic interdependence immediately with the wide disparity in the economic strength of various nations. . . .

A second factor in the social tissue of the world community is the fear of mutual annihilation, heightened in recent years by the new dimension which atomic discoveries have given to mankind's instruments of death. We must not underestimate this fear as a social force, even as we must recognize that some culturally pluralistic communities of past history have achieved some cohesion through the minimal conviction that order is to be preferred to anarchy. But the fear of destruction in itself is less potent than the fear of specific peril from a particular foe. There is no record in history of peoples establishing a common community because they feared each other, though there are many instances when the fear of a common foe acted as the cement of cohesion.

The final and most important factor in the social tissue of the world community is a moral one. Enlightened men in all nations have some sense of obligation to their fellow-men, beyond the limits of their nation-state. There is at least an inchoate sense of obligation to the inchoate community of mankind. The desperate necessity for a more integrated world community has undoubtedly increased this sense of obligation, inculcated in the conscience of mankind since the rise of universal, rather than parochial, philosophies and religions. This common moral sense is of tremendous importance for the moral and religious life of mankind; but it does not have as much immediate political relevance as is sometimes supposed. Political cohesion requires common convictions on particular issues of justice; and these are lacking. . . .

In short, the forces which are operating to integrate the world community are limited. To call attention to this fact does not mean that all striving for a higher and wider integration of the world community is vain. That task must and will engage the conscience of mankind for ages to come. But the edifice of government which we build will be sound and useful if its height is proportionate to the strength of the materials from which it is constructed. The immediate political situation requires that we seek not only peace, but also the preservation of a civilization which we hold to be preferable to the universal tyranny with which Soviet aggression threatens us. Success in this double task is the goal; let us not be diverted from it by the pretense that there is a simple alternative.

We would, I think, have a better chance of success in our struggle against a fanatical foe if we were less sure of our purity and virtue. The pride and self-righteousness of powerful nations are a greater hazard to their success in statecraft than the machinations of their foes. If we could combine a greater degree of humility with our stubborn resolution, we might not only be more successful in holding the dyke against tyranny, but we might also gradually establish a genuine sense of community with our foe, however small. No matter how stubbornly we resist Russian pressure, we should still have a marginal sense of community with the Soviet Union, derived from our sense of being involved in a common fate of tragic proportions and from a recognition of a common guilt of mutual fear. If community in basic terms is established by various organic forces of history, it must finally be preserved by mutual forbearance and forgiveness.[5]

6. God and Man's Fate

Perhaps our generation will fail. Perhaps we lack the humility and charity for the task. There are ominous signs of our possible and even probable failure. There is the promise of a new life for men and nations in the Gospel; but there is no guarantee of historic success. There is no way of transmuting the Christian Gospel into a system of historical optimism. The final victory over man's disorder is God's and not ours; but we do have responsibility for proximate victories. Christian life without a high sense of responsibility for the health of our communities, our nations and our cultures degenerates into an intolerable other-worldliness. We can neither renounce this earthly home of ours nor yet claim that its victories and defeats give the final meaning to our existence.

Jesus wept over Jerusalem and regretted that it did not know the things that belonged to its peace. In the Old Testament we have the touching story of Abraham bargaining with God about the size of the saving remnant which would be needed to redeem the city. Would fifty or forty or thirty be required? He and the Lord finally settled for twenty. Only a small leaven is needed, only a little center of health can become the means of convalescence for a whole community. That fact measures the awful responsibility of the people of God in the world's cities of destruction.

But there is a climax in this story which is frequently disregarded. It is a terrible climax which has relevance for our own day. However small the saving remnant which God requires for the reconstruction of our communities, it was not forthcoming in Sodom and Gomorrah. Perhaps it is valid to express the surmise that the leavening minority in Sodom may have been quantitatively adequate but that its righteousness was irrelevant for saving Sodom and Gomorrah. One has the uneasy feeling that we are in that position. There is so little health in the whole of our modern civilization that one cannot find the island of order from which to proceed against disorder. Our choices have become terribly circumscribed. Must we finally choose between atomic annihilation or subjection to universal tyranny? If such a day should come we will remember that the mystery of God's sovereignty and mercy transcends the fate of empires and civilizations. He will be exalted though they perish. However, He does not desire their perdition but rather that they turn from their evil ways and live. From us He demands that we work while it is day, since the night cometh when no man can work.[6]

Sources
—

CHAPTER XII: CHRISTIAN REALISM AND THE POLITICAL CRISIS

All selections in this chapter are taken from Reinhold Niebuhr's *Christian Realism and Political Problems* (Charles Scribner's Sons, New York, 1953).

[1] Chapter VIII, "The Christian Witness in the National and Social Order," pages 105-107; and page 108, lines 1-7.

[2] *Ibid.*, page 108, lines 8-29; pages 109-110; and page 111, lines 1-4.

[3] *Ibid.*, page 111, lines 5-29; pages 112-114; and page 115, lines 1-24.

[4] Chapter VII, "Democracy, Secularism and Christianity," page 101; and page 102, lines 1-2.

[5] Chapter II, "The Illusion of World Government," page 16, line 29; page 17, lines 1-25; page 26, lines 22-26; page 27, lines 1-7 and lines 25-28; page 28, lines 1-25; page 29, lines 22-29; and page 30, lines 1-23.

[6] Chapter VIII, page 115, lines 25-29; pages 116-117.

CHAPTER XIII

SARVEPALLI RADHAKRISHNAN (1888–   )

Sir Sarvepalli Radhakrishnan, philosopher, student of comparative religion, educator, and Vice President of India, is a reminder to the modern world of the Platonic dictum that philosophy and political power should be joined for the better governance of men. This distinguished man, formerly the colleague of Gandhi and Rabindranath Tagore and now a close associate of Prime Minister Nehru, is regarded as the greatest living thinker of the East, and the foremost representative of its rich philosophical tradition. He is also thoroughly at home with the philosophic and religious traditions of the West, has taught for several years at Oxford, and is the leading spokesman today for a reconciliation of Eastern and Western values. A philosopher friend once called him "a philosophical bilinguist" whose work was to reflect upon "the spiritual wisdom of the world."

Radhakrishnan was born on September 5, 1888, and was educated at Madras Christian College. In 1911-1916 he was Assistant Professor of Philosophy at Presidency College, Madras, and then University Professor of Philosophy at Mysore, in 1918-1921. His next post was the George V Professorship of Philosophy at Calcutta University. He also held high posts in educational administration in his native country, including nine years of service as Vice Chancellor of the Benaras Hindu University. In the late 1920's he journeyed to America, to its bustling Midwestern capital city, where he was the Haskell Lecturer in Comparative Religion at the University of Chicago, and later the Hibbert Lecturer.

In consequence of his intellectual eminence, Radhakrishnan was called upon for various international political services. He was a member of the International Committee of Intellectual Co-operation with the League of Nations in Geneva in 1931-1939, and also played a valuable role in the League's successor, the United Nations. He served as Chairman of the Executive Board of UNESCO in Paris in 1948-1949. He became a member of the Indian Constituent Assembly for the period 1947–1949. In 1949 he was appointed Indian Ambassador to the Soviet Union. In 1952 he assumed his present service as Vice President of India.

In the field of educational organization, Radhakrishnan has also been a leader. He served as President of the All-Asia Education Conference at Benaras in 1930; and in 1949 he was made Chairman of the Universities Commission in the Indian Government.

Despite these multifarious political and ambassadorial functions, Radhakrishnan has somehow, out of his great vitality, found it possible to be a prolific creative scholar, with literally scores of articles, addresses, lectures, reports, and specially edited volumes to add to his many important full-length books. Among his principal works are: his magnum opus *Indian Philosophy*, a monumental two-volume work to which the author devoted some twenty years of research and writing; and two other influential books, *An Idealist View of Life* (the Hibbert Lectures) and *Eastern Religions and Western Thought*. Notable in all of Radhakrishnan's work is the spirit of his inquiries into comparative philosophy and religion, a spirit that can best be seen by the manner in which he formulates a central question: "May we not strive for a philosophy which will combine the best of European humanism and Asiatic religion, a philosophy profounder and more living than either, endowed with greater spiritual and ethical force, which will conquer the hearts of men and compel peoples to acknowledge its sway?" Since philosophy for Radhakrishnan is a way of life and a habit of pursuing the truth in order to obtain self-knowledge and moral guidance, he sees no possibility of excluding politics and international affairs from the philosopher's concern. He has said that "religion includes faith in human brotherhood, and politics is the most effective means of rendering it into visible form. Politics is but applied religion."

THE RELIGION OF THE SPIRIT AND THE WORLD'S NEED

—

SARVEPALLI RADHAKRISHNAN

1. *The Function of Philosophy*

There are tasks and responsibilities open to an Indian student of philosophic thought, living in this profoundly meaningful period of history. The prominent feature of our time is not so much the wars and the dictatorships which have disfigured it, but the impact of different cultures on one another, their interaction, and the emergence of a new civilisation based on the truths of spirit and the unity of mankind. The tragedies and catastrophes which occupy so much of the foreground of our consciousness are symbolic of the breakdown of the separatist tendencies and the movement towards the integration of national societies in a world whole. In the confusions of the contemporary scene, this fallible, long-suffering and apparently helpless generation should not overlook the great movement towards integration in which it is participating.

Through her connection with Great Britain, India is once again brought into relationship with the Western world. The interpenetration of the two great currents of human effort at such a crisis in the history of the human race is not without meaning for the future. With its profound sense of spiritual reality brooding over the world of our ordinary experience, with its lofty insights and immortal aspirations, Indian thought may perhaps wean us moderns from a too exclusive occupation with secular life or with the temporary formulations in which logical thought has too often sought to imprison spiritual aspiration. We do not seem to be mentally or spiritually prepared for the increasing intimacy into which remote peoples are drawn by the force of physical and economic circumstances. The world which has found itself as a single body is feeling for its soul. May we not prepare for the truth of the world's yet unborn soul by a free interchange of ideas and the development of a philosophy which will combine the best of European humanism and Asiatic Religion, a philosophy profounder and more living than either, endowed with greater spiritual and ethical force, which will conquer the hearts of men and compel peoples to acknowledge its sway? Such a view of the function of philosophy in modern life is born out of a necessity of thought and an Indian student may perhaps make a little contribution to the development of a world perspective in philosophy.[1]

Though I have not had a sense of vocation, a sense that I was born to do what I am now carrying out, my travels and engagements in different parts of the world for over a generation gave me a purpose in life. My one supreme interest has been to try to restore a sense of spiritual values to the millions of religiously displaced persons, who have been struggling to find precarious refuges in the emergency camps of Art and Science, of Fascism and Nazism, of Humanism and Communism. The first step to recovery is to understand the nature of the confusion of thought which absorbs the allegiance of millions of men. Among the major influences which foster a spirit of scepticism in regard to religious truth are the growth of the scientific spirit, the development of a technological civilisation, a formal or artificial religion which finds itself in conflict with an awakened social conscience, and a comparative study of religions.[2]

2. *The Decay of Religion*

Since 1500 mankind has been steadily marching towards the formation of a single society. The two wars have led to a shrinkage of space and contraction of the world. The physical unity of the world requires to sustain it a psychological oneness. The barriers of dogmatic religions are sterilising men's efforts to coordinate their forces to shape the future. Each religion is a rival

to others. There are some things which are more important than
our particularist allegiances: truth and humanity and that universal religious consciousness which is the common possession of
all human beings by virtue of their spiritual endowment. So long
as our group loyalties are strong and overridding we cannot belong to the general human society.

Religion, as it has been functioning, is unscientific and un-
social. On account of these features of traditional religion large
sections of humanity are the victims of unwilling disbelief. It is
an age of incoherence in thought and indecision in action. Our
values are blurred, our thought is confused, our aims are waver-
ing, and our future is uncertain. There are bits of knowledge here
and there but no visible pattern. W. B. Yeats refers to our condition in memorable words which we may well ponder:

> Things fall apart; the centre cannot hold.
> Mere anarchy is loosed upon the world,
> The blood-dimmed tide is loosed, and everywhere
> The ceremony of innocence is drowned;
> The best lack all conviction, while the worst
>   are full of passionate intensity.

If we are to overcome the dangers that threaten us, we must
confront them fearlessly and take the measure of their power to
injure us. The issue for religion in our day is not in regard to
doctrinal differences or ritual disagreements, but it concerns the
very existence of religion. The state of coldness or indifference
which ignores religion is more deadly than open rejection. Even
Marx looks upon religion, not as insignificant but as pernicious.
Our modern intellectuals sum up the situation thus: some think
God exists, some think not, it is impossible to tell, but it does
not matter.[3]

3. *The Need for Integration*

The mind of the world requires to be pulled together and the
present aimless stare of dementia replaced by a collective rational

purpose. We need a philosophy, a direction and a hope, if the present state of indecision is not to lead us to despair. Belief may be difficult, but the need for believing is inescapable. We are in search of a spiritual religion, that is universally valid, vital, clear-cut, one that has an understanding of the fresh sense of truth and the awakened social passion which are the prominent character-istics of the religious situation today. The severe intellectual hon-esty and the burning passion for social justice are not to be slighted. They are expressions of spiritual sincerity. Our religion must give us an energy of thought which does not try to use eva-sions with itself, which dares to be sincere, an energy of will which gives us the strength to say what we believe and do what we say. If the world is today passing through a mood of atheism, it is because a higher religion is in process of emergence. Doubt and denial of God have often proved dialectical moments in the history of religions, ways by which mankind has increased its knowledge of God and emancipated itself from imperfect con-ceptions of religion.

The opposite of religion is not irreligion but a counter-reli-gion. When the Buddha denied the Vedic gods, he did so in the name of a higher religion. When Socrates was put to death on the charge of atheism, his offence was the repudiation of an im-perfect religion. When Christians were brought into the Roman amphitheatre to undergo martyrdom for their convictions, the pagan mob shouted "The atheists to the lions." Atheism has often been the expression of the vitality of religion, its quest for reality in religion. The fact that man is unable or unwilling to acknowledge God means only that he cannot accept the ideas and beliefs about God framed by men, the false gods which obscure the living and ineffable God. Today the world is very sick, for it is passing through a crisis of the birth of a new religion. . . .[4]

4. The Roots of Religion

The tension in human nature is what makes man interesting. Without it he would not become aware of his utter nothingness, his forlornness, his insufficiency, his dependence, his weakness, his emptiness. His anguish and suffering have a dialectical necessity. The roots of religion are in this inner torment which has to be resolved. He must strive after unity with nature, with man, with himself. Only when he is victorious in his struggle does he attain human dignity. We are seekers, pilgrims on the march for the city that is to be, for we have no abiding city on earth. We must reach out beyond the frontiers of our dual, divided consciousness. We cannot remain content within an impermeable solitude of our own anguished desires. We cannot remain for ever in a state of unfulfilment. Even the lowest forms of life strive after adjustment.

The ancestors of man played an important part in this great drama of cosmic evolution, though they did not understand either the play or their part in it. Man has also to play his part, but with a knowledge of the structure and meaning of the play. By his intelligence he must comprehend the cosmic plan and by his will further it. Human progress does not depend on the slow action of physical or biological laws. It can be speeded up by our effort, if we liberate ourselves from bondage, if we escape from the life that is in part and enter into the life which is whole. The prayer of the Upanisads, "Lead me from the unreal to the real, lead me from darkness to light, lead me from death to immortality," assumes that we live in a world of fear, of care, of abandonment, of death, of nothingness, and we seek a world of being, of fearlessness, of freedom, of spirit, of eternity. We seek to transcend the finitude of human existence and gain life eternal.

Sometimes we are tempted to go back, become unthinking and unreflective, sink into the simplicity of biological existence, submerge in the elemental animal. This would be a deliberate sacrifice of our wholeness, an abandonment of the attempt to achieve integrity. We cannot reverse the process and throw away our heritage. Self-conscious man cannot become the instinctive animal. Even if he refuses to employ his intellectual consciousness he cannot get back the original integration with the environ-

ment. Memory and expectancy will interfere. Job seeks his
asylum in sleep but does not succeed. "When I say, my bed shall
comfort me, my couch shall ease my complaint, then thou scarest
me with dreams and terrifiest me through visions." We cannot
shake off our rationality. We cannot get away from the strains
of our self-consciousness. The cure for our unrest is not a relapse
into the womb of the unconscious, but a rise into creative consciousness. What we aim at is the enlightenment of the sage and
not the inexperience of the new-born babe.

We cannot cure the affliction caused by intellect, the loneliness, the insecurity and the anguish by drugs, by the myths of
religion or the dogmas of politics. These plans of escape from the
prison of our life may help a few for a little time. If we take
opium we may find a few moments beautiful and calm in contrast to the jarring world outside; but they will not last. The unscientific dogmas, the crude superstitions tell us more about the
mind of man than about the structure of reality, and cannot save
man from scepticism.

If the lonely individual clings to something outside of him, he
may gain security, but he does so at the expense of his integrity as
an individual. We may renounce freedom of inquiry and bind
our eyes from further seeking with the bandage of a final creed.
We may thus be saved from making decisions or assuming responsibility for the future. But we will be disturbed and dissatisfied at the root, for the emergence of the individual self cannot
be stifled. Happiness is in freedom, and freedom is in greatness of
spirit.

It is argued that scientific progress will destroy the feeling of
loneliness with which we regard the alien world and terminate
the inability of men to determine their own destiny.

We may grant that we can anticipate the course of natural
phenomena and even to some extent control it. But nature can
never be tamed to do man's will. Her blind caprices, her storms
and tempests, her cyclones and earthquakes will continue to shatter his work and dash his dreams. Man cannot alter the limits of

his life or his body. "Thou fool, this night shall thy soul be required of thee." Increasing knowledge of science without a corresponding growth of religious wisdom only increases our fear of death. Our scientific culture is unparalleled in human history. We have dominated the forces of nature, controlled the seas and conquered the air. We have increased production, combated disease, organised commerce, and made man master of his environment; and yet the lord of the earth cannot live in safety. He has to hide under the earth, wear gas masks. He is haunted by the fears of wars and lives in the company of uncertainties. This war-haunted, machine-driven civilisation cannot be the last word of human striving. Unless we are blind idiots or self-satisfied morons, we will know that scientific organisation is not the fulfilment of the spirit of man.[5]

5. *Fellowship, Not Fusion, of Religions*

We must move along a path which shall pass beyond all the differences of the historical past and eventually be shared in common by all mankind. Belief in exclusive claims and monopolies of religious truth has been a frequent source of pride, fanaticism and strife. The vehemence with which religions were preached and the savagery with which they were enforced are some of the disgraces of human history. Secularism and paganism point to the rivalries of religions for a proof of the futility of religion. A little less missionary ardour, a little more enlightened scepticism will do good to us all. Our attitude to other religions should be defined in the spirit of that great saying in a play of Sophocles, where Antigone says, "I was not born to share men's hatred, but their love." [6]

The world is seeking not so much a fusion of religions as a fellowship of religions, based on the realisation of the foundational character of man's religious experience. William Blake says: "As all men are alike (though infinitely various), so all Religions, as all similars, have one source." The different religions may retain their individualities, their distinctive doctrines and characteristic pieties, so long as they do not impair the sense of spiritual fellowship. The light of eternity would blind us if it came full in the face. It is broken into colours so that our eyes can make something of it. The different religious traditions clothe the one Reality in various images and their visions could embrace and fertilise each other so as to give mankind a many-sided perfection, the spiritual radiance of Hinduism, the faithful obedience of Judaism, the life of beauty of Greek Paganism, the noble compassion of Buddhism, the vision of divine love of Christianity, and the spirit of resignation to the sovereign lord of Islam. All these represent different aspects of the inward spiritual life, projections on the intellectual plane of the ineffable experiences of the human spirit.

If religion is the awareness of our real nature in God, it makes for a union of all mankind based on communion with the Eternal. It sees in all the same vast universal need it has felt in itself. The different religions take their source in the aspiration of man towards an unseen world, though the forms in which this aspiration is couched are determined by the environment and climate of thought. The unity of religions is to be found in that which is divine or universal in them and not in what is temporary and local. Where there is the spirit of truth there is unity. As in other matters, so in the sphere of religion there is room for diversity and no need for discord. To claim that any one religious tradition bears unique witness to the truth and reveals the presence of the true God is inconsistent with belief in a living God who has spoken to men "by diverse portions and in diverse manners." God is essentially self-communicative and is of ungrudging goodness, as Plato taught. There is no such thing as a faith once for all delivered to the saints. Revelation is divine-human. As God does not reveal His Being to a stone or a tree, but only to men, His revelation is attuned to the state of the human mind. The Creative Spirit is ever ready to reveal Himself to the seeking soul provided the search is genuine and the effort intense. The authority for revelation is not an Infallible book or an Infallible Church but the witness of the inner light. What is needed is not submission to an external authority but inward illumination which, of course, is tested by tradition and logic. If we reflect on the matter deeply we will perceive the unity of spiritual aspiration and endeavour underlying the varied upward paths indicated in the different world faiths. The diversity in the traditional formulations tends to diminish as we climb up the scale of spiritual perfection. All the paths of ascent lead to the mountain top. This convergent tendency and the remarkable degree of agreement in the witness of those who reach the mountain top are the strongest proof of the truth of religion.[7]

6. *Universal Religion*

The mandate of religion is that man must make the change in his own nature in order to let the divine in him manifest itself. It speaks of the death of man as we know him with all his worldly desires and the emergence of the new man. This is the teaching not only of the Upanisads and Buddhism but also of the Greek mysteries and Platonism, of the Gospels and the schools of Gnosticism. This is the wisdom to which Plotinus refers, when he says, "This doctrine is not new; it was professed from the most ancient times though without being developed explicitly; we wish only to be interpreters of the ancient sages, and to show by the evidence of Plato himself that they had the same opinions as ourselves." This is the religion which Augustine mentions in his well-known statement: "That which is called the Christian Religion existed among the Ancients, and never did not exist, from the beginning of the human race until Christ came in the flesh, at which time the true religion, which already existed, began to be called Christianity." This truth speaks to us in varying dialects across far continents and over centuries of history. Those who overlook this perennial wisdom, the eternal religion behind all religions, this *sanātana dharma*, this timeless tradition, "wisdom uncreate, the same now that it ever was, and the same to be forevermore," and cling to the outward forms and quarrel among themselves, are responsible for the civilized chaos in which we live. It is our duty to get back to this central core of religion, this fundamental wisdom which has been obscured and distorted in the course of history by dogmatic and sectarian developments.

At the level of body and mind, physique and temperament, talents and tastes, we are profoundly unlike one another; but at the deepest level of all, that of the spirit which is the true ground of our being, we are like one another. If religion is to become an effective force in human affairs, if it is to serve as the basis for the new world order, it must become more inward and more universal, a flame which cleanses our inward being and so cleanses the world. For such a religion the historical expressions of spiritual truth and the psychological idioms employed by religions to convey the universal truth cease to be rocks of offence. The barriers dividing men will break down and the reunion and integration of all, what the Russians call *sobornost*, an altogetherness in which we walk together creatively and to which we all contribute, a universal church will be established. Then will the cry of St. Joan in Bernard Shaw's epilogue to that play be fulfilled: "O God that madest this beautiful earth, when will it be ready to receive thy saints?" Then will come a time when the world will be inhabited by a race of men, with no flaw of flesh or error of mind, freed from the yoke not only of disease and privation but of lying words and of love turned into hate. When human beings grow into completeness, into that invisible world which is the kingdom of heaven, then will they manifest in the outer world the Kingdom which is within them. That day we shall cease to set forth God dogmatically or dispute about his nature but leave each man to worship God in the sanctuary of his heart, to feel after him and to possess him.

While I never felt attracted to travelling for its own sake, I have travelled a great deal and lived in places far from home, in England and France, America and Russia. For some years, I have spent long periods in England and the qualities of the English people such as their love of justice, their hatred of doctrinairism, their sympathy for the underdog, made an impression on me. All Souls College, which has provided a second home for me all these years, has given me an insight into English intellectual life with its caution and stability, confidence and adventure. Whatever one may feel about the character of the Russian Government, the people there are kindly and human and their lives are filled as anywhere else with jokes and jealousies, loves and hates. Though I have not been able to take root in any of these foreign countries, I have met many, high and low, and learned to feel the human in them. There are no fundamental differences among the peoples of the world. They have all the deep human feelings, the craving for justice above all class interests, horror of bloodshed and violence. They are working for a religion which teaches the possibility and the necessity of man's union with himself, with nature, with his fellowmen, and with the Eternal Spirit of which the visible universe is but a manifestation and upholds the emergence of a complete consciousness as the destiny of man. Our historical religions will have to transform themselves into the universal faith or they will fade away. This prospect may appear strange and unwelcome to some, but it has a truth and beauty of its own. It is working in the minds of men and will soon be a realised fact. Human unity depends not on past origins but on future goal and direction, on what we are becoming and whither we are tending. Compared with the civilisation that is now spreading over the earth's surface, thanks to science and technology, the previous civilisations were restricted in scope and resources. Scientists claim that organic life originated on this planet some 1200 million years ago, but man has come into existence on earth during the last half million years. His civilisation has been here only for the last 10,000 years. Man is yet in his infancy and has a long period ahead of him on this planet. He will work out a higher integration and produce world-minded men and women.

The eternal religion, outlined in these pages, is not irrational or unscientific, is not escapist or a-social. Its acceptance will solve many of our desperate problems and will bring peace to men of good will.

This is the personal philosophy which by different paths I have attained, a philosophy which has served me in the severest tests, in sickness and in health, in triumph and in defeat. It may not be given to us to see that the faith prevails; but it is given to us to strive that it should.[8]

Sources
—

CHAPTER XIII: THE RELIGION OF THE SPIRIT AND THE WORLD'S NEED

All selections from Radhakrishnan's essay entitled " 'The Religion of the Spirit and the World's Needs' (Fragments of a Confession)" are taken from the volume in the Library of Living Philosophers, *The Philosophy of Sarvepalli Radhakrishnan*, edited by Paul Arthur Schilpp (Tudor Publishing Company, New York, 1952).

[1] Page 7, lines 4-40.
[2] Page 14, lines 5-19.
[3] Page 24, lines 34-35; page 25, lines 1-34.
[4] Page 25, lines 35-40; page 26, lines 1-27.
[5] Page 52, lines 37-41; pages 53-54.
[6] Page 72, lines 3-15.
[7] Page 75, lines 39-41; page 76; page 77, lines 1-14.
[8] Page 80, lines 6-41; pages 81-82.

PART FOUR

SELECTIONS FROM HUMANISTIC PHILOSOPHERS

CHAPTER XIV

JEAN-PAUL SARTRE (1905–)

Sartre is by specific intent the advocate of a philosophy tempered for the crisis of our time. This world-famous French Existentialist, who has now become a professional literary man, was a professor of philosophy, a writer of plays and novels, and one of the French patriots in the Resistance movement during the occupation of France in the Second World War. Although he is the inheritor of a tradition that stems from Kierkegaard, Sartre's "leap of faith" never goes so high as to include God. He is explicitly and rationally atheistic, accepting the Dostoievskian dilemma that if God does not exist, everything is possible, and adding to it the additional implication that if God did exist it would change nothing for man. Man himself is a "useless passion," unable to comprehend his own being, forlorn, fragile, disgusted by the meaningless everything of outward existence, and the agonizing nothingness of his own unjustified and indefinable self. Thus, man is "nothing else but what he makes of himself. Such is the first principle of existentialism." With this knowledge, Sartre thinks man can become ready to commit himself to a "project"; he becomes acutely aware of his freedom to choose whatever values he will. Since man's freedom is thus rootless and absolute, it is an ambiguous state, both frightening and liberating.

Jean-Paul Sartre was born in Paris on June 21, 1905. His grandfather, on his mother's side, had been a professor of German at the Lycée Henri IV in Paris; Sartre's immediate family environment could not have been too academic in view of the fact that Sartre's father was a sailor who happened to die in Indochina when Sartre was a small child. Sartre was educated at the Lycée at St. Rochelle and the Lycée Henri IV. He obtained his higher education at the École Normale Supérieure and in 1928 took his *Agrégation de Philos-*

ophie. Sartre then became *professeur* at Laon, later at Le Havre. Shortly afterward he went to Berlin to study contemporary German philosophy. Upon his return to France, he again took up the duties of teaching, this time at the Lycée Pasteur at Neuilly. He served in the French Army, at the Maginot Line, in 1939, was captured in June, 1940, and repatriated in the spring of 1941. More teaching followed, until, in 1944, he gave it up to devote himself to his literary pursuits on a full-time basis. In the following year he visited the United States, and once home again began to edit *Les Temps Modernes*, a journal which made its first appearance in the fall of 1946.

Perhaps the most impressive document Sartre ever wrote is his eloquent testimony printed in the volume *The Republic of Silence* which was edited by A. J. Liebling some years after the close of the war. In this ultimate situation where a man either keeps faith with his fellows in the resistance, loses his life but maintains his humanity; or breaks faith, evidences the *mauvais fois* which preserves himself as an object rather than as a man, Sartre demonstrates that his brand of Existentialism and heroism can co-exist. "Thus the basic question of liberty was posed, and we were brought to the verge of the deepest knowledge that man can have of himself. For the secret of a man is not his Oedipus complex or his inferiority complex: it is the limits of his own liberty, his capacity for resisting torture and death."

Sartre's evident fascination with thorough commitment to a political movement is sometimes thought to be inconsistent with his general philosophy. A critic writes: "His love of freedom and love of firmly defined political systems are in constant conflict with one another. . . . Sartre suffers the fate of his fictional heroes who are forever unable to decide to which side they belong." Sartre has offered his considerable talents to the French Communist Party on several occasions but has, perhaps with brutal realism, been treated as though he were a Trojan horse, too costly for the apparatus of true believers.

Sartre's writings venture into the fields of metaphysics, ethics, aesthetics, and biography—in addition to his novels and plays. He has contributed many essays on political and social questions to the literary magazines of France and America. His major philosophical work is the ponderous *Being and Nothingness*, published in France in 1943, translated into English the following year. His two best plays are the short ones *The Flies* and *No Exit*. A series of novels, *The Roads to Liberty*, now number four volumes; but some students of Sartre's literary work still prefer his first small novel, invitingly entitled *Nausea* (1937). Two important essayistic discussions are *Existentialism and Humanism* (1948) and *What Is Literature?* (1947).

ATHEISTIC EXISTENTIALISM

JEAN-PAUL SARTRE

1. *Some Charges Against Existentialism*

I should like on this occasion to defend existentialism against some charges which have been brought against it.

First, it has been charged with inviting people to remain in a kind of desperate quietism because, since no solutions are possible, we should have to consider action in this world as quite impossible. We should then end up in a philosophy of contemplation; and since contemplation is a luxury, we come in the end to a bourgeois philosophy. The communists in particular have made these charges.

On the other hand, we have been charged with dwelling on human degradation, with pointing up everywhere the sordid, shady, and slimy, and neglecting the gracious and beautiful, the bright side of human nature; for example, according to Mlle. Mercier, a Catholic critic, with forgetting the smile of the child. Both sides charge us with having ignored human solidarity, with considering man as an isolated being. The communists say that the main reason for this is that we take pure subjectivity, the *Cartesian I think*, as our starting point; in other words, the moment in which man becomes fully aware of what it means to him to be an isolated being; as a result, we are unable to return to a state of solidarity with the men who are not ourselves, a state which we can never reach in the *cogito*.

From the Christian standpoint, we are charged with denying the reality and seriousness of human undertakings, since, if we reject God's commandments and the eternal verities, there no longer remains anything but pure caprice, with everyone permitted to do as he pleases and incapable, from his own point of view, of condemning the points of view and acts of others.

I shall try today to answer these different charges. Many people are going to be surprised at what is said here about humanism. We shall try to see in what sense it is to be understood. In any case, what can be said from the very beginning is that by existentialism we mean a doctrine which makes human life possible and, in addition, declares that every truth and every action implies a human setting and a human subjectivity. . . .

Actually, it is the least scandalous, the most austere of doctrines. It is intended strictly for specialists and philosophers. Yet it can be defined easily. What complicates matters is that there are two kinds of existentialist; first, those who are Christian, among whom I would include Jaspers and Gabriel Marcel, both Catholic; and on the other hand the atheistic existentialists, among whom I class Heidegger, and then the French existentialists and myself. What they have in common is that they think that existence precedes essence, or, if you prefer, that subjectivity must be the starting point.[1]

2. *Man Makes Himself*

Atheistic existentialism, which I represent, . . . states that if God does not exist, there is at least one being in whom existence precedes essence, a being who exists before he can be defined by any concept, and that this being is man, or, as Heidegger says, human reality. What is meant here by saying that existence precedes essence? It means that, first of all, man exists, turns up, appears on the scene, and, only afterwards, defines himself. If man, as the existentialist conceives him, is indefinable, it is because at first he is nothing. Only afterward will he be something, and he himself will have made what he will be. Thus, there is no human nature, since there is no God to conceive it. Not only is man what he conceives himself to be, but he is also only what he wills himself to be after this thrust toward existence.

Man is nothing else but what he makes of himself. Such is the first principle of existentialism. It is also what is called subjectivity, the name we are labeled with when charges are brought against us. But what do we mean by this, if not that man has a greater dignity than a stone or table? For we mean that man first exists, that is, that man first of all is the being who hurls himself toward a future and who is conscious of imagining himself as being in the future. Man is at the start a plan which is aware of itself, rather than a patch of moss, a piece of garbage, or a cauliflower; nothing exists prior to this plan; there is nothing in heaven; man will be what he will have planned to be. Not what he will want to be. Because by the word "will" we generally mean a conscious decision, which is subsequent to what we have already made of ourselves. I may want to belong to a political party, write a book, get married; but all that is only a manifestation of an earlier, more spontaneous choice that is called "will." But if existence really does precede essence, man is responsible for what he is. Thus, existentialism's first move is to make every man aware of what he is and to make the full responsibility of his existence rest on him. And when we say that a man is responsible for himself, we do not only mean that he is responsible for his own individuality, but that he is responsible for all men.

The word subjectivism has two meanings, and our opponents play on the two. Subjectivism means, on the one hand, that an individual chooses and makes himself; and, on the other, that it is impossible for man to transcend human subjectivity. The second of these is the essential meaning of existentialism. When we say that man chooses his own self, we mean that every one of us does likewise; but we also mean by that that in making this choice he also chooses all men. In fact, in creating the man that we want to be, there is not a single one of our acts which does not at the same time create an image of man as we think he ought to be. To choose to be this or that is to affirm at the same time the value of what we choose, because we can never choose evil. We always choose the good, and nothing can be good for us without being good for all.

If, on the other hand, existence precedes essence, and if we grant that we exist and fashion our image at one and the same time, the image is valid for everybody and for our whole age. Thus, our responsibility is much greater than we might have supposed, because it involves all mankind. If I am a workingman and choose to join a Christian trade-union rather than be a communist, and if by being a member I want to show that the best thing for man is resignation, that the kingdom of man is not of this world, I am not only involving my own case—I want to be resigned for everyone. As a result, my action has involved all humanity. To take a more individual matter, if I want to marry, to have children; even if this marriage depends solely on my own circumstances or passion or wish, I am involving all humanity in monogamy and not merely myself. Therefore, I am responsible for myself and for everyone else. I am creating a certain image of man of my own choosing. In choosing myself, I choose man.[2]

3. "Anguish" and "Despair"

This helps us understand what the actual content is of such rather grandiloquent words as anguish, forlornness, despair. As you will see, it's all quite simple.

First, what is meant by anguish? The existentialists say at once that man is anguish. What that means is this: the man who involves himself and who realizes that he is not only the person he chooses to be, but also a law-maker who is, at the same time, choosing all mankind as well as himself, can not help escape the feeling of his total and deep responsibility. Of course, there are many people who are not anxious; but we claim that they are hiding their anxiety, that they are fleeing from it. Certainly, many people believe that when they do something, they themselves are the only ones involved, and when someone says to them, "What if everyone acted that way?" they shrug their shoulders and answer, "Everyone doesn't act that way." But really, one should always ask himself, "What would happen if everybody looked at things that way?" There is no escaping this disturbing thought except by a kind of double-dealing. A man who lies and makes excuses for himself by saying "not everybody does that," is someone with an uneasy conscience, because the act of lying implies that a universal value is conferred upon the lie.

Anguish is evident even when it conceals itself. This is the anguish that Kierkegaard called the anguish of Abraham. You know the story: an angel has ordered Abraham to sacrifice his son; if it really were an angel who has come and said, "You are Abraham, you shall sacrifice your son," everything would be all right. But everyone might first wonder, "Is it really an angel, and am I really Abraham? What proof do I have?"

There was a madwoman who had hallucinations; someone used to speak to her on the telephone and give her orders. Her doctor asked her, "Who is it who talks to you?" She answered, "He says it's God." What proof did she really have that it was God? If an angel comes to me, what proof is there that it's an angel? And if I hear voices, what proof is there that they come from heaven and not from hell, or from the subconscious, or a pathological condition? What proves that they are addressed to me? What proof is there that I have been appointed to impose my choice and my conception of man on humanity? I'll never find any proof or sign to convince me of that. If a voice addresses me, it is always for me to decide that this is the angel's voice; if I consider that such an act is a good one, it is I who will choose to say that it is good rather than bad.

Now, I'm not being singled out as an Abraham, and yet at every moment I'm obliged to perform exemplary acts. For every man, everything happens as if all mankind had its eyes fixed on him and were guiding itself by what he does. And every man ought to say to himself, "Am I really the kind of man who has the right to act in such a way that humanity might guide itself by my actions?" And if he does not say that to himself, he is masking his anguish.

There is no question here of the kind of anguish which would lead to quietism, to inaction. It is a matter of a simple sort of anguish that anybody who has had responsibilities is familiar with. For example, when a military officer takes the responsibility for an attack and sends a certain number of men to death, he chooses to do so, and in the main he alone makes the choice. Doubtless, orders come from above, but they are too broad; he interprets them, and on this interpretation depend the lives of ten or fourteen or twenty men. In making a decision he can not help having a certain anguish. All leaders know this anguish. That doesn't keep them from acting; on the contrary, it is the very condition of their action. For it implies that they envisage a number of possibilities, and when they choose one, they realize that it has value only because it is chosen. We shall see that this kind of anguish, which is the kind that existentialism describes, is explained, in addition, by a direct responsibility to the other men whom it involves. It is not a curtain separating us from action, but is part of action itself.

When we speak of forlornness, a term Heidegger was fond of, we mean only that God does not exist and that we have to face all the consequences of this. . . .

The existentialist . . . thinks it very distressing that God does not exist, because all possibility of finding values in a heaven of ideas disappears along with Him; there can no longer be an *a priori* Good, since there is no infinite and perfect consciousness to think it. Nowhere is it written that the Good exists, that we must be honest, that we must not lie; because the fact is we are on a plane where there are only men. Dostoievsky said, "If God

didn't exist, everything would be possible." That is the very starting point of existentialism. Indeed, everything is permissible if
God does not exist, and as a result man is forlorn, because neither within him nor without does he find anything to cling to.
He can't start making excuses for himself.

As for despair, the term has a very simple meaning. It means
that we shall confine ourselves to reckoning only with what depends upon our will, or on the ensemble of probabilities which
make our action possible. When we want something, we always
have to reckon with probabilities. I may be counting on the ar-
rival of a friend. The friend is coming by rail or street-car; this
supposes that the train will arrive on schedule, or that the street-
car will not jump the track. I am left in the realm of possibility;
but possibilities are to be reckoned with only to the point
where my action comports with the ensemble of these possibilities, and no further. The moment the possibilities I am considering are not rigorously involved by my action, I ought to disengage
myself from them, because no God, no scheme, can adapt the
world and its possibilities to my will. When Descartes said,
"Conquer yourself rather than the world," he meant essentially
the same thing.[3]

4. *Man is Freedom*

If existence really does precede essence, there is no explaining
things away by reference to a fixed and given human nature. In
other words, there is no determinism, man is free, man is freedom. On the other hand, if God does not exist, we find no values
or commands to turn to which legitimize our conduct. So, in the
bright realm of values, we have no excuse behind us, nor justification before us. We are alone, with no excuses.

That is the idea I shall try to convey when I say that man is
condemned to be free. Condemned, because he did not create
himself, yet, in other respects is free; because, once thrown into
the world, he is responsible for everything he does.[4]

5. Commitment and Action

Given that men are free and that tomorrow they will freely decide what man will be, I can not be sure that, after my death, fellow-fighters will carry on my work to bring it to its maximum perfection. Tomorrow, after my death, some men may decide to set up Fascism, and the others may be cowardly and muddled enough to let them do it. Fascism will then be the human reality, so much the worse for us.

Actually, things will be as man will have decided they are to be. Does that mean that I should abandon myself to quietism? No. First, I should involve myself; then, act on the old saw, "Nothing ventured, nothing gained." Nor does it mean that I shouldn't belong to a party, but rather that I shall have no illusions and shall do what I can. For example, suppose I ask myself, "Will socialization, as such, ever come about?" I know nothing about it. All I know is that I'm going to do everything in my power to bring it about. Beyond that, I can't count on anything. Quietism is the attitude of people who say, "Let others do what I can't do." The doctrine I am presenting is the very opposite of quietism, since it declares, "There is no reality except in action." Moreover, it goes further, since it adds, "Man is nothing else than his plan; he exists only to the extent that he fulfills himself; he is therefore nothing else than the ensemble of his acts, nothing else than his life."

According to this, we can understand why our doctrine horrifies certain people. Because often the only way they can bear their wretchedness is to think, "Circumstances have been against me. What I've been and done doesn't show my true worth. To be sure, I've had no great love, no great friendship, but that's because I haven't met a man or woman who was worthy. The books I've written haven't been very good because I haven't had the proper leisure. I haven't had children to devote myself to because I didn't find a man with whom I could have spent my life. So there remains within me, unused and quite viable, a host of propensities, inclinations, possibilities, that one wouldn't guess from the mere series of things I've done."

Now, for the existentialist there is really no love other than one which manifests itself in a person's being in love. There is no genius other than one which is expressed in works of art; the genius of Proust is the sum of Proust's works; the genius of Racine is his series of tragedies. Outside of that, there is nothing. Why say that Racine could have written another tragedy, when he didn't write it? A man is involved in life, leaves his impress on it, and outside of that there is nothing. To be sure, this may seem a harsh thought to someone whose life hasn't been a success. But, on the other hand, it prompts people to understand that reality alone is what counts, that dreams, expectations, and hopes warrant no more than to define a man as a disappointed dream, as miscarried hopes, as vain expectations. In other words, to define him negatively and not positively. However, when we say, "You are nothing else than your life," that does not imply that the artist will be judged solely on the basis of his works of art; a thousand other things will contribute toward summing him up. What we mean is that a man is nothing else than a series of undertakings, that he is the sum, the organization, the ensemble of the relationships which make up these undertakings.

May I ask whether anyone has ever accused an artist who has painted a picture of not having drawn his inspiration from rules set up *a priori*? Has anyone ever asked, "What painting ought he to make?" It is clearly understood that there is no definite painting to be made, that the artist is engaged in the making of his painting, and that the painting to be made is precisely the painting he will have made. It is clearly understood that there are no *a priori* aesthetic values, but that there are values which appear subsequently in the coherence of the painting, in the correspondence between what the artist intended and the result. Nobody can tell what the painting of tomorrow will be like. Painting can be judged only after it has once been made. What connection does that have with ethics? We are in the same creative situation.

We never say that a work of art is arbitrary. When we speak of a canvas of Picasso, we never say that it is arbitrary; we understand quite well that he was making himself what he is at the very time he was painting, that the ensemble of his work is embodied in his life.

The same holds on the ethical plane. What art and ethics have in common is that we have creation and invention in both cases. We can not decide *a priori* what there is to be done. I think that I pointed that out quite sufficiently when I mentioned the case of the student who came to see me, and who might have applied to all the ethical systems, Kantian or otherwise, without getting any sort of guidance. He was obliged to devise his law himself. Never let it be said by us that this man—who, taking affection, individual action, and kind-heartedness toward a specific person as his ethical first principle, chooses to remain with his mother, or who, preferring to make a sacrifice, chooses to go to England—has made an arbitrary choice. Man makes himself. He isn't ready made at the start. In choosing his ethics, he makes himself, and force of circumstances is such that he can not abstain from choosing one. We define man only in relationship to involvement. It is therefore absurd to charge us with arbitrariness of choice.[5]

6. *Existentialism and Humanism*

I've been reproached for asking whether existentialism is humanistic. It's been said, "But you said in *Nausea* that the humanists were all wrong. You made fun of a certain kind of humanist. Why come back to it now?" Actually, the word humanism has two very different meanings. By humanism one can mean a theory which takes man as an end and as a higher value. Humanism in this sense can be found in Cocteau's tale *Around the World in Eighty Hours* when a character, because he is flying over some mountains in an airplane, declares, "Man is simply amazing." That means that I, who did not build the airplanes, shall personally benefit from these particular inventions, and that I, as man, shall personally consider myself responsible for, and honored by, acts of a few particular men. This would imply that we ascribe a value to man on the basis of the highest deeds of certain men. This humanism is absurd, because only the dog or the horse would be able to make such an over-all judgment about man, which they are careful not to do, at least to my knowledge.

But it cannot be granted that a man may make a judgment about man. Existentialism spares him from any such judgment. The existentialist will never consider man as an end because he is always in the making. Nor should we believe that there is a mankind to which we might set up a cult in the manner of Auguste Comte. The cult of mankind ends in the self-enclosed humanism of Comte, and, let it be said, of fascism. This kind of humanism we can do without.

But there is another meaning of humanism. Fundamentally it is this: man is constantly outside of himself; in projecting himself, in losing himself outside of himself, he makes for man's existing; and, on the other hand, it is by pursuing transcendent goals that he is able to exist; man, being this state of passing-beyond, and seizing upon things only as they bear upon this passing-beyond, is at the heart, at the center of this passing-beyond. There is no universe other than a human universe, the universe of human subjectivity. This connection between transcendency, as a constituent element of man—not in the sense that God is transcendent, but in the sense of passing beyond—and subjectivity, in the sense that man is not closed in on himself but is always present in a human universe, is what we call existentialist humanism. Humanism, because we remind man that there is no law-maker other than himself, and that in his forlornness he will decide by himself; because we point out that man will fulfill himself as man, not in turning toward himself, but in seeking outside of himself a goal which is just this liberation, just this particular fulfillment.

From these few reflections it is evident that nothing is more unjust than the objections that have been raised against us. Existentialism is nothing else than an attempt to draw all the consequences of a coherent atheistic position. It isn't trying to plunge man into despair at all. But if one calls every attitude of unbelief despair, like the Christians, then the word is not being used in its original sense. Existentialism isn't so atheistic that it wears itself out showing that God doesn't exist. Rather, it declares that even if God did exist, that would change nothing. There you've got our point of view. Not that we believe that God exists, but we think that the problem of His existence is not the issue. In this sense existentialism is optimistic, a doctrine of action, and it is plain dishonesty for Christians to make no distinction between their own despair and ours and then to call us despairing.[6]

Sources

—

CHAPTER XIV: ATHEISTIC EXISTENTIALISM

The selections are from Jean-Paul Sartre's *Existentialism* (Philosophical Library, New York, 1947).

[1] Page 11; page 12, lines 1-24; page 15, lines 11-24.

[2] Page 18, lines 4-25; page 19, lines 1-25; page 20, lines 1-25; page 21, lines 1-19.

[3] Page 21, lines 24-25; page 22, lines 1-25; page 23; page 24; page 25, lines 1-18; page 26, lines 17-25; page 27, lines 1-8; page 34, lines 21-25; page 35, lines 1-16.

[4] Page 27, lines 9-24.

[5] Page 36, lines 24-25; pages 37-38; page 39, lines 1-24; page 50, lines 3-25; page 51.

[6] Page 58, lines 12-25; pages 59-61.

CHAPTER XV

KARL R. POPPER (1902–   )

Karl Popper is one of the leading philosophers of science today. He was originally a member of the famous Vienna Circle which was the spawning ground for logical empiricism; but, unlike his colleagues, he has shown a strong interest in the history of philosophy, and in political and ethical philosophy. He is best known for his study *The Open Society and Its Enemies*, a book which has become a contemporary classic in political theory. It examines some of the principles of social reconstruction in the light of a critical review of the philosophy of politics and history. "It sketches some of the difficulties faced by a civilization which aims at humaneness and reasonableness, at equality and freedom . . . and tries thereby to contribute to our understanding of totalitarianism, and of the significance of the perennial fights against it."

Karl Popper was born in Austria in 1902, was educated at Vienna University, and has taught in England, at Canterbury University College, Christchurch, New Zealand, and at the University of London where he is now Professor of Logic and Scientific Method. His early work in scientific method, *Logik der Forschung* (Logic of Scientific Discovery), analyzed the methods of physics and proposed that the basic test of whether a theory or statement is empirical is by specifying the physical conditions under which it would be falsified.

With the rise of totalitarianism, Popper turned to examine the methods of the social sciences, and was particularly interested in establishing why the social sciences are backward. This interest led to a series of papers which concluded that it is impossible to predict the future. These papers have been published under the title *The Poverty of Historicism*. The main thread of the argument is that we cannot predict the future because human history is strongly influenced by the growth of knowledge and because it is logically impossible to predict the growth of knowledge itself. "This means that we must reject the possibility of a *theoretical history*; that is to say, of a historical social science that would correspond to *theoretical physics*."

Where the argument was purely logical before this, Popper decided it was essential to see how the historicist fallacy arose, and was led to explore critically the greatest intellectual leaders of mankind, and particularly Plato and Marx, in order to show where they failed. Having done this, Popper then published his study of *The Open Society*, which includes his refutation of the historical figures and attempts to outline the principles of democratic social reconstruction, which he has called "piecemeal social engineering" in contrast to "Utopian social engineering."

That logic is not incompatible with passionate conviction is revealed in the words that Popper selects to dedicate one of his books: "In memory of the countless men and women of all creeds or nations or races who fell victims to the fascist and communist belief in Inexorable Laws of Historical Destiny."

CRITICAL RATIONALISM
—
KARL R. POPPER

1. *The Revolt Against Reason*

Marx was a rationalist. With Socrates, and with Kant, he believed in human reason as the basis of the unity of mankind. But his doctrine that our opinions are determined by class interest hastened the decline of this belief. Like Hegel's doctrine that our ideas are determined by national interests and traditions, Marx's doctrine tended to undermine the rationalist belief in reason. Thus threatened both from the right and from the left, a rationalist attitude to social and economic questions could hardly resist when historicist prophecy and oracular irrationalism made a frontal attack on it. This is why the conflict between rationalism and irrationalism has become the most important intellectual, and perhaps even moral, issue of our time. . . .

We could say that rationalism is an attitude of readiness to listen to critical arguments and to learn from experience. It is fundamentally an attitude of admitting that '*I may be wrong and you may be right, and by an effort, we may get nearer to the truth.*' It is an attitude which does not lightly give up hope that by such means as argument and careful observation, people may reach some kind of agreement on most problems of importance. In short, the rationalist attitude, or, as I may perhaps label it, the 'attitude of reasonableness,' is very similar to the scientific attitude, to the belief that in the search for truth we need co-operation, and that, with the help of argument, we can attain something like objectivity. . . .

The fact that the rationalist attitude considers the argument rather than the person arguing is of far-reaching importance! It leads to the view that we must recognize everybody with whom we communicate as a potential source of argument and of reasonable information; it thus establishes what may be described as the 'rational unity of mankind.' . . .

The irrationalist attitude may be developed along the following lines. Though perhaps recognizing reason and scientific argument as good enough instruments with which to scratch the surface of things, or as means to serve some irrational end, the irrationalist will insist that 'human nature' is in the main not rational. Man, he holds, is more than a rational animal, and also less. In order to see that he is less, we need only consider how small is the number of men who are capable of argument; this is why, according to the irrationalist, the majority of men will always have to be tackled by an appeal to their emotions and passions rather than by an appeal to their reason. But man is also more than just a rational animal, since all that really matters in his life goes beyond reason. Even the few scientists who take reason and science seriously are bound to their rationalist attitude merely because they love it. Thus even in these rare cases, it is the emotional make-up of man and not his reason that determines his attitude. Moreover, it is his intuition, his mystical insight into the nature of things rather than his reasoning which makes a great scientist. Thus rationalism cannot offer an adequate interpretation even of the apparently rational activity of the scientist. But since the scientific field is exceptionally favourable to a rationalist interpretation, we must expect that rationalism will fail even more conspicuously when it tries to deal with other fields of human activity. And this expectation, so the irrationalist will continue his argument, proves to be quite accurate. Leaving aside the lower aspects of human nature, we may look to one of its highest, to the fact that man can be creative. It is the small creative minority of men who really matter; the men who create works of art, or of thought, or who founded religions or states; these few exceptional individuals allow us to glimpse the real greatness of man. But although these leaders of mankind know how to make use of reason for their purposes, they are never men of reason. Their roots lie deeper. Creativeness is an entirely irrational, a mystical faculty. . . .

The issue between rationalism and irrationalism is of long standing. Although Greek philosophy undoubtedly started off as a rationalist undertaking, there were streaks of mysticism even in its first beginnings. It is the yearning for the lost unity and shelter of tribalism which expresses itself in these mystical elements within a fundamentally rational approach. An open conflict between rationalism and irrationalism broke out for the first time in the middle ages, as the opposition between scholasticism and mysticism. (It is perhaps not without interest that rationalism flourished in the former Roman provinces, while men from the 'barbarian' countries were prominent among the mystics.) In the nineteenth century, when the tide of a rationalist 'materialism' was rising, irrationalists had to pay some attention to it, and to argue with it. But the tide has turned, and 'profoundly significant allusions . . . and allegories' (as Kant puts it) have become the fashion of the day. An oracular irrationalism (especially with Bergson and the majority of German philosophers and intellectuals) has established the habit of ignoring or at best deploring the existence of such an inferior being as a rationalist. To them the rationalist—or the 'materialist,' as they often say— and especially, the rationalist scientist, are the poor in spirit, pursuing soulless and largely mechanical activities, and completely unaware of the deeper problems of life and philosophy. And the rationalists usually reciprocate by dismissing irrationalism as sheer nonsense. Never before has the break been so complete.[1]

2. *The Faith in Reason*

In this issue, I am entirely on the side of rationalism. This is so much the case that even where I feel that rationalism has gone too far I still sympathize with it, holding as I do that an excess in this direction is harmless indeed as compared with an excess in the other. In my opinion, the only way in which excessive rationalism is likely to prove harmful is that it tends to undermine its own position and thus to further an irrationalist reaction. It is only this danger which induces me to examine the claims of an excessive rationalism more closely and to advocate a modest and self-critical rationalism which recognizes certain limitations. Accordingly, I shall distinguish in what follows between two rationalist positions, which I label 'critical rationalism' and 'uncritical rationalism' or 'comprehensive rationalism.'

Uncritical or comprehensive rationalism can be described as the attitude of the person who says 'I am not prepared to accept anything that cannot be defended by means of argument or experience.' We can express this also in the form of the principle that any assumption which cannot be supported either by argument or by experience is to be discarded. Now it is easy to see that this principle of an uncritical rationalism is inconsistent; for since it cannot, in its turn, be supported by argument or by experience, it implies that it should itself be discarded. . . . Uncritical rationalism is therefore logically untenable; and since a purely logical argument can show this, uncritical rationalism can be defeated by its own chosen weapon, argument. . . .

The rationalist attitude is characterized by the importance it attaches to argument and experience. But neither logical argument nor experience can establish the rationalist attitude; for only those who are ready to consider argument or experience, and who have therefore adopted this attitude already, will be impressed by them. That is to say, a rationalist attitude must be first adopted if any argument or experience is to be effective, and it cannot therefore be based upon argument or experience. (And this consideration is quite independent of the question whether or not there exist any convincing rational arguments which favour the adoption of the rationalist attitude.) We have to conclude from this that the rationalist attitude cannot possibly be based upon argument or experience, and that a comprehensive rationalism is untenable.

But this means that whoever adopts the rationalist attitude does so because without reasoning he has adopted some decision, or belief, or habit, or behaviour, which therefore in its turn must be called irrational. Whatever it may be, we can describe it as an irrational *faith in reason*. . . .

The choice before us is not simply an intellectual affair, or a matter of taste. It is a moral decision. . . . For the question whether we adopt some more or less radical form of irrationalism, or whether we adopt that minimum concession to irrationalism which I have termed 'critical rationalism,' will deeply affect our whole attitude towards other men, and towards the problems of social life. It has already been shown that rationalism is closely connected with the belief in the unity of mankind. Irrationalism which is not bound by any rules of consistency may be combined with any kind of belief, even with belief in the brotherhood of man; but the fact that it may easily be combined with a very different belief and especially with a romantic belief in the existence of an elect body in the division of men into leaders and led, into natural masters and natural slaves, shows clearly that a moral decision is involved in the choice between it and rationalism. . . .

Arguments cannot *determine* a fundamental moral decision. But this does not imply that our choice cannot be *helped* by any kind of argument whatever. On the contrary, whenever we are faced with a moral decision of a more abstract kind, it is most helpful to analyse carefully the consequences which are likely to result from the alternatives between which we have to choose. For only if we can visualize these consequences in a concrete and practical way do we really know what the decision is about; otherwise we decide blindly. . . .[2]

The nineteenth-century conflict between science and religion appears to me to be superseded. Since an 'uncritical' rationalism is inconsistent, the problem cannot be the choice between knowledge and faith, but only between two kinds of faith. The new problem is: which is the right faith and which is the wrong faith? What I have tried to show is that the choice with which we are confronted is between a faith in reason and in human individuals and a faith in the mystical faculties of man by which he is united to a collective; and that this choice is at the same time a choice between an attitude that recognizes the unity of mankind and an attitude that divides men into friends and foes, into masters and slaves.[3]

3. *Consequences of Irrationalism*

Let us examine the consequences of irrationalism. . . . The irrationalist insists that emotions and passions rather than reason are the mainsprings of human action. To the rationalist's reply that, though this may be so, we should do what we can to remedy it, and should try to make reason play as large a part as it possibly can, the irrationalist would rejoin (if he condescends to such a discussion) that this attitude is hopelessly unrealistic. For it does not consider the weakness of 'human nature,' the feeble intellectual endowment of most men and their obvious dependence upon emotions and passions.

It is my firm conviction that this irrational emphasis upon emotion and passion leads ultimately to what I can only describe as crime. One reason for this opinion is that this attitude, which is at best one of resignation towards the irrational nature of human beings, at worst one of scorn for human reason, must lead to an appeal to violence and brutal force as the ultimate arbiter in any dispute. For if a dispute arises, then this means that those more constructive emotions and passions which might in principle help to get over it, reverence, love, devotion to a common cause, etc., have shown themselves incapable of solving the problem. But if that is so, then what is left to the irrationalist except the appeal to other and less constructive emotions and passions, to fear, hatred, envy, and ultimately, to violence? This tendency is very much strengthened by another and perhaps even more important attitude which also is in my opinion inherent in irrationalism, namely, the stress on the inequality of men.

It cannot, of course, be denied that human individuals are, like all other things in our world, in very many respects very unequal. Nor can it be doubted that this inequality is of great importance and even in many respects most desirable. (The fear that the development of mass production and collectivization may react upon men by destroying their inequality or individuality is one of the nightmares of our times.) But all this simply has no bearing upon the question whether or not we should decide to treat men, especially in political issues, as equals, or as much like equals as possible; that is to say, as possessing equal rights, and equal claims to equal treatment; and it has no bearing upon the question whether we ought to construct political institutions accordingly. 'Equality before the law' is *not a fact but a political demand based upon a moral decision*; and it is quite independent of the theory—which is probably false—that 'all men are born equal.' Now I do not intend to say that the adoption of this humanitarian attitude of impartiality is a direct consequence of a decision in favour of rationalism. But a tendency towards impartiality is closely related to rationalism, and can hardly be excluded from the rationalist creed. Again, I do not intend to say that an irrationalist could not consistently adopt an equalitarian or impartial attitude; and even if he could not do so consistently, he is not bound to be consistent. But I do wish to stress the fact that the irrationalist attitude can hardly avoid becoming entangled with the attitude that is opposed to equalitarianism. This fact is connected with its emphasis upon emotions and passions; for we cannot feel the same emotions towards everybody. Emotionally, we all divide men into those who are near to us, and those who are far from us. The division of mankind into friend and foe is the obvious emotional division; and this division is recognized in the Christian commandment, 'Love thy enemies!'. Even the best Christian who really lives up to this commandment (there are not many, as is shown by the attitude of the average good Christian towards 'materialists' and 'atheists'), even he cannot feel equal love for all men. We cannot really love 'in the abstract'; we can love only those whom we know. Thus the appeal even to our best emotions, love and compassion, can only tend to divide mankind into different categories. And this will be more true if the appeal is made to lesser emotions and passions. Our 'natural' reaction will be to divide mankind into friend and foe; into those who belong to our tribe, to our emotional community, and those who stand outside it; into believers and unbelievers; into compatriots and aliens; into class comrades and class enemies; and into leaders and led. . . .[4]

4. History Has No Meaning

Is there a meaning in history?

I do not wish to enter here into the problem of the meaning of 'meaning'; I take it for granted that most people know with sufficient clarity what they mean when they speak of the 'meaning of history' or of the 'meaning of life.' And in this sense, in the sense in which the question of the meaning of history is asked, I answer: *History has no meaning.*

In order to give reasons for this opinion, I must first say something about that 'history' which people have in mind when they ask whether it has meaning. So far, I have myself spoken about 'history' as if it did not need any explanation. That is no longer possible; for I wish to make it clear that *'history' in the sense in which most people speak of it simply does not exist;* and this is at least one reason why I say that it has no meaning.

How do most people come to use the term 'history'? They learn about it in school and at the University. They read books about it. They see what is treated in the books under the name 'history of the world' or 'the history of mankind,' and they get used to looking upon it as a more or less definite series of facts. And these facts constitute, they believe, the history of mankind.

But the realm of facts is infinitely rich, and there must be selection. According to our interests, we could, for instance, write a history of art; or of language; or of feeding habits; or of typhus fever (see Zinsser's *Rats, Lice, and History*). Certainly, none of these is the history of mankind (nor all of them taken together). What people have in mind, when they speak of the history of mankind, is rather the history of the Egyptian, Babylonian, Persian, Macedonian, and Roman empires, and so on, down to our own day. In other words: They speak about a *history of mankind,* but what they mean, and what they have learned about in school, is the *history of political power.*

There is no history of mankind, there are only many histories of all kinds of aspects of human life. And one of these is the history of political power. This is elevated into the history of the world. But this, I hold, is an offence against every decent conception of mankind. It is hardly better than to treat the history of embezzlement or of robbery or of poisoning as the history of mankind; for *the history of power politics is nothing but the history of international crime and mass murder* (including, it is true, some of the attempts to suppress them). This history is taught in schools, and many of the greatest criminals are presented as heroes.

But is there really no such thing as a universal history in the sense of a concrete history of mankind? There can be none. This must be the reply of every humanitarian, I believe, and especially that of every Christian. A concrete history of mankind, if there were any, would have to be the history of all men. It would have to be the history of all human hopes, struggles, and sufferings. For there is no one man more important than any other. Clearly, this concrete history cannot be written. We must make abstractions, we must neglect, select. But with this we arrive at the many histories; and among them, at that history of international crime and mass murder which has been advertised as the history of mankind.

But why has just the history of power been selected, and not, for example, that of poetry? There are several reasons. One is that power affects us all, and poetry only a few. Another is that men are inclined to worship power. But there can be no doubt that the worship of power is one of the worst kinds of human idolatries, a relic of the time of the cage, of human servitude. The worship of power is born of fear, an emotion which is rightly despised. A third reason why power politics has been made the core of 'history' is that those in power wanted to be worshipped and could enforce their wishes. Many historians wrote under the supervision of the generals and the dictators.

I know that these views will meet with the strongest opposition, especially from some apologists for Christianity; for although there is hardly anything in the New Testament to support this view, it is often considered a Christian dogma that God reveals Himself in history; that history has meaning; and that its meaning is the purpose of God. Historicism is thus held to be a necessary element of religion. But I do not admit this. I contend that this view is pure idolatry and superstition, not only from the point of view of a rationalist or humanist but from the Christian point of view itself. . . .

I do not deny that it is as justifiable to interpret history from a Christian point of view as it is to interpret it from any other point of view; and it should certainly be emphasized, for example, how much of our Western aims and ends, humanitarianism, freedom, equality, we owe to the influence of Christianity. But at the same time, the only rational as well as the only Christian attitude even towards the history of freedom is that we are ourselves responsible for it, in the same sense in which we are responsible for what we make of our lives, and that only our conscience can judge us, not our worldly success. The theory that God reveals Himself and His judgment in history is indistinguishable from the theory that worldly success is the ultimate judge and justification of our actions; it comes to the same thing as the doctrine that history will judge, that is to say, that future might is right; it is the same as what I have called 'moral futurism.' To maintain that God reveals Himself in what is usually called 'history,' in the history of international crime and of mass murder, is indeed blasphemy; for what really happens within the realm of human lives is hardly ever touched upon by this cruel and at the same time childish affair. The life of the forgotten, of the unknown individual man; his sorrows and his joys, his suffering and death, this is the real content of human experience down the ages. If that could be told by history, then I should certainly not say that it is blasphemy to see the finger of God in it. But such a history does not and cannot exist. . . . [5]

5. We Can Give History a Meaning

History has no meaning, I contend. But this contention does not imply that all we can do about it is to look aghast at the history of political power, or that we must look on it as a cruel joke. For we can interpret it, with an eye to those problems of power politics whose solution we choose to attempt in our time. We can interpret the history of power politics from the point of view of our fight for the open society, for a rule of reason, for justice, freedom, equality, and for the control of international crime. Although history has no ends, we can impose these ends of ours upon it; and *although history has no meaning, we can give it a meaning.* . . .

Neither nature nor history can tell us what we ought to do. Facts, whether those of nature or those of history, cannot make the decision for us, they cannot determine the ends we are going to choose. It is we who introduce purpose and meaning into nature and into history. Men are not equal; but we can decide to fight for equality. Human institutions such as the state are not rational, but we can decide to fight to make them more rational. We ourselves and our ordinary language are, on the whole, emotional rather than rational; but we can try to become a little more rational, and we can train ourselves to use our language as an instrument not of self-expression (as our romantic educationists would say) but of rational communication. History itself—I mean the history of power politics, of course, not the non-existent story of the development of mankind—has no end nor meaning, but we can decide to give it both. We can make it our fight for the open society and against its antagonists (who, when in a corner, always protest their humanitarian sentiments, in accordance with Pareto's advice); and we can interpret it accordingly. Ultimately, we may say the same about the 'meaning of life.' It is up to us to decide what shall be our purpose in life, to determine our ends.

This dualism of facts and decisions is, I believe, fundamental. Facts as such have no meaning; they can gain it only through our decisions. Historicism is only one of many attempts to get over this dualism; it is born of fear, for it shrinks from realizing that we bear the ultimate responsibility even for the standards we choose. But such an attempt seems to me to represent precisely what is usually described as superstition. For it assumes that we can reap where we have not sown; it tries to persuade us that if we merely fall into step with history everything will and must go right, and that no fundamental decision on our part is required; it tries to shift our responsibility on to history, and thereby on to the play of demoniac powers beyond ourselves; it tries to base our actions upon the hidden intentions of these powers, which can be revealed to us only in mystical inspirations and intuitions; and it thus puts these actions and decisions on the moral level of one who, inspired by horoscopes and dreams, chooses his lucky number in a lottery. Like gambling, historicism is born of our despair in the rationality and responsibility of our actions. It is a debased hope and a debased faith, an attempt to replace the hope and the faith that springs from our moral enthusiasm and the contempt for success by a certainty that springs from a pseudo-science; a pseudo-science of the stars, or of 'human nature,' or of historical destiny.

Historicism, I assert, is not only rationally untenable, it is also in conflict with any religion that teaches the importance of conscience. For such a religion must agree with the rationalist attitude towards history in its emphasis on our supreme responsibility for our actions, and for their repercussions upon the course of history. True, we need hope; to act, to live without hope goes beyond our strength. But we do *not* need more, and we must not be given more. We do not need certainty. Religion, in particular, should not be a substitute for dreams and wish fulfilment; it should resemble neither the holding of a ticket in a lottery, nor the holding of a policy in an insurance company. The historicist element in religion is an element of idolatry, of superstition.

This emphasis upon the dualism of facts and decisions determines also our attitude towards such ideas as 'progress.' If we think that history progresses, or that we are bound to progress, then we commit the same mistake as those who believe that history has a meaning that can be discovered in it and need not be given to it. For to progress is to move towards some kind of end, towards an end which exists for us as human beings. 'History' cannot do that; only we, the human individuals, can do it; we can do it by defending and strengthening those democratic institutions upon which freedom, and with it progress, depends. And we shall do it much better as we become more fully aware of the fact that progress rests with us, with our watchfulness, with our efforts, with the clarity of our conception of our ends, and with the realism of their choice.

Instead of posing as prophets we must become the makers of our fate. We must learn to do things as well as we can, and to look out for our mistakes. And when we have dropped the idea that the history of power will be our judge, when we have given up worrying whether or not history will justify us, then one day perhaps we may succeed in getting power under control. In this way we may even justify history, in our turn. It badly needs such justification.[6]

Sources

—

CHAPTER XV: CRITICAL RATIONALISM

All selections are from K. R. Popper's *The Open Society and Its Enemies* (Princeton University Press, Princeton, 1950).

[1] Page 410, lines 1-11; page 411, lines 1-15 and 32-36; page 413, lines 33-40; page 414; page 415, lines 1-17.

[2] Page 415, lines 18-30; page 416, lines 20-38; page 417, lines 23-37; page 418, lines 2-10.

[3] Page 431, lines 14-24.

[4] Page 419, lines 17-40; page 420.

[5] Page 453, lines 4-40; page 454, lines 1-39; page 455, lines 9-30.

[6] Page 46, lines 39-40; pages 461-463.

CHAPTER XVI

BERTRAND RUSSELL (1872–   )

Bertrand Russell has exercised an almost hypnotic sway over the Anglo-American philosophical world for half a century. This is partly because of his ability to write like a lucid angel who yet dares to borrow incisive wit from Satanic sources; but more because of his monumental contribution to mathematical philosophy in the famous three-volume *Principia Mathematica* which he wrote with Alfred North Whitehead. With the appearance of these volumes in 1910–1913, Russell won the fame which yielded him an audience for his subsequent work. That work, apart from his sustained interest in mathematics and symbolic logic, has been in the fields of theory of knowledge, and in social philosophy. An odd but true fact about this lighthearted yet brilliant philosopher is that at the same time that his books are being closely studied by professional colleagues and graduate students, his paperback reprints on subjects like marriage, education, and morals may nestle side by side with wax-wrapped sandwiches in the lunch kits of day laborers, to be resorted to with pleasure as the sandwich is consumed. In the mid-thirties, when Russell was scheduled for one of his public lectures in New York at Mecca Temple, traffic would be tied up for blocks around as the huge audiences prepared to enter the feast of sparkling learning.

In 1950 Lord Russell became the third philosopher to receive the Nobel Prize for literature "in recognition of his many-sided and significant authorship, in which he has constantly figured as a defender of humanity and freedom of thought." The citation accurately points to one irreducible element in Russell's nontechnical philosophical writings, from the early days of his famous essay "The Free Man's Worship" to his BBC broadcast on the occasion of his eightieth birthday, and to the books on ethical and political subjects

276

which continue to issue from his pen. For while Russell is often in error on positions he assumes, and while he has engaged in stormy and obdurate controversies with the passion of a political rebel, he has managed always to remind men of those traditions of civility and justice that distinguish the liberal spirit in Western civilization from the times of Pericles to our own day.

Russell has written, in his inimitable way, of his own life: "My mother having died when I was two years old, and my father when I was three, I was brought up in the house of my grandfather, Lord John Russell, afterwards Earl Russell. Of my parents, Lord and Lady Amberley, I was told almost nothing—so little that I vaguely sensed a dark mystery. It was not until I was twenty-one that I came to know the main outlines of my parents' lives and opinions. I then found, with a sense of bewilderment, that I had gone through almost exactly the same mental and emotional development as my father had." What Russell is referring to principally is that his father was expected, from family tradition, to assume a political career but that his irreverent temperament and freethinking beliefs were found unsuitable for political success. His father and mother were both friends and disciples of John Stuart Mill, and both refused to compromise with the propriety demanded of good Victorians. Russell continues: "My father wished my brother and me to be brought up as free thinkers, and appointed two free thinkers as our guardians. The Court of Chancery, however, at the request of my grandparents, set aside the will, and I enjoyed the benefits of a Christian upbringing." In one sense, the last comment may be taken as ironic, since Russell as a young man would write a pamphlet called "Why I Am Not a Christian." In another sense, the reverence for life, for love, for tolerance, and moral integrity that are supposedly the fruits of such an upbringing were served by Russell throughout his career.

Russell's intellectual output has been enormous, a partial bibliography of his books and articles running to well over forty printed pages. In this Promethean production there are at least fifty books that represent Russell's principal works. Many will recognize as old, familiar friends the following titles: *The Problems of Philosophy* (1912); *Our Knowledge of the External World* (1914); *Mysticism and Logic and Other Essays* (1918); *Roads to Freedom* (1918); *Introduction to Mathematical Philosophy* (1919); *The Practice and*

Theory of Bolshevism (1920); *The Analysis of Mind* (1921); *The Analysis of Matter* (1927); *Sceptical Essays* (1928); *Marriage and Morals* (1929); *The Scientific Outlook* (1931); *Education and the Social Order* (1932); *Freedom and Organization, 1814–1914* (1934) *Power: A New Social Analysis* (1938); *An Inquiry into Meaning and Truth* (1940); *A History of Western Philosophy* (1945); *New Hope for a Changing World* (1951); *Human Society in Ethics and Politic* (1955). And the list is open-ended.

It would be surprising if, in this vigorous and high-powered intellectual journey, there would be no changes, even indeed some inconsistencies, repudiations, contradictions. Academic lectures on Russell' "position" in philosophy always suffer from the danger of characterizing the subject at the very time that he may be writing a book that will explode his previous stand. Again, Russell's own comment is appropriate: "I am not myself in any degree ashamed of having changed my opinions. What physicist who was already active in 1900 would dream of boasting that his opinions had not changed during the last half century: . . . but philosophy in the minds of many is assimilated rather to theology than to science. A theologician proclaims eternal truths, the creeds remain unchanged since the Council of Nicaea. Where nobody knows anything, there is no point in changing your mind."

Russell's interest in history and politics has been serious, although characterized by the same volatility and reversals observable in his philosophy of knowledge. A pacifist in World War I, imprisoned for six months; an interventionist before World War II when he saw the rise of totalitarianism; he has become in the last few years a leader in a world-wide campaign to prevent the manufacture of hydrogen bombs by powers other than the U.S. and U.S.S.R., and to compel both the U.S. and U.S.S.R. to renounce and destroy nuclear weapons under international control. In one of his statements, Russell said that if he were forced to choose between a Communist world and the extinction of the human race in nuclear war, he would choose the first; and he accompanied this statement by the dangerous advice that if the U.S.S.R. did not agree to controlled disarmament, the British and American democracies should proceed with unilateral nuclear disarmament themselves. A serious debate ensued between Russell and Sidney Hook in the pages of *The New Leader* (1958), a debate

hich is still one of the most valuable discussions of the ultimate
alues of freedom and survival in contemporary literature.

HILOSOPHIC RATIONALITY FOR A CHANGING WORLD

BERTRAND RUSSELL

Perplexities of Our Time

The present time is one in which the prevailing mood is a
eeling of impotent perplexity. We see ourselves drifting towards
war that hardly anyone desires—a war that, as we all know,
lust bring disaster to the great majority of mankind. But like a
abbit fascinated by a snake, we stare at the peril without know-
ig what to do to avert it. We tell each other horror stories of
tom bombs and hydrogen bombs, of cities exterminated, of
ussian hordes, of famine and ferocity everywhere. But al-
lough our reason tells us we ought to shudder at such a
rospect, there is another part of us that enjoys it, and so we have
o firm will to avert misfortune, and there is a deep division in
ur souls between the sane and the insane parts. In quiet times
ie insane parts can slumber throughout the day and wake only
t night. But in times like ours they invade our waking time as
ell, and all rational thinking becomes pale and divorced from
ie will. Our lives become balanced on a sharp edge of hypothesis
-if there is to be a war one way of life is reasonable; if not, an-
ther. To the great majority of mankind such a hypothetical
xistence is intolerably uncomfortable, and in practice they
lopt one hypothesis or the other, but without complete convic-
on. A youth who finds scholastic education boring will say to
imself: "Why bother? I shall be killed in battle before long." . . .

Parents wonder whether the sacrifices called for by their chil-
ren's upbringing are worth while since they are likely to prove

futile. Those who are lucky enough to possess capital are apt to spend it on riotous living, since they foresee a catastrophic depreciation in which it would become worthless. In this way uncertainty balks the impulse to every irksome effort, and generates a tone of frivolous misery mistakenly thought to be pleasure, which turns outward and becomes hatred of those who are felt to be its cause. Through this hatred it brings daily nearer the catastrophe which it dreads. The nations seem caught in a tragic fate, as though, like characters in a Greek drama, they were blinded by some offended god. Bewildered by mental fog, they march towards the precipice while they imagine that they are marching away from it.[1]

There is . . . in the use of the atom-bomb and the hydrogen bomb a new danger, a danger which is not only new in kind but greater in degree than any that has existed in previous wars. We do not quite know what may be the effects of letting loose great floods of radioactivity. There are those—among them Einstein—who think that the result may be the extinction of all life on our planet. Short of that, it may easily happen that large fertile regions become infertile and uninhabitable, and that the populations of considerable areas are wiped out. I do not say that this will happen if atomic energy is employed in war; no one knows yet whether it will happen or not. But there is a risk that it may happen, and if it does repentance will come too late.

There is an oscillation in warfare between the strength of the attack and the strength of the defense. The happy ages are those in which the defense is strong; the unhappy, those in which the attack has the advantage. There is always a danger in our scientific age that at some moment the attack may acquire a really disastrous advantage. Bacteriological warfare, for example, may exterminate the enemy, but would be very likely to exterminate at the same time those who had inaugurated it. On the whole increase of scientific skill makes war more dangerous, even if at any given moment it does not make it more deadly.

Apart from mortality, there are other respects in which mod

ern war is worse than most wars of former times. Owing to the increased productivity of labor, it is possible to set aside a greater part of the population for the business of mutual slaughter, and the dislocation of daily life is greater in a modern world war than in most of the wars of former times. Fear of atomic bombs has made it irrational for populations to live in great cities. . . . In the pleasant and comfortable wars of the eighteenth and nineteenth centuries, it was chiefly the combatants who suffered; now the suffering falls increasingly upon civilians. I am an old man, and I can remember a time when it was not thought quite the thing to make war on women and children; but that happy age is past.

For all these reasons, war is a greater menace now than it was formerly. The prevention of war has become necessary if civilized life is to continue, perhaps if any kind of life is to continue. This matter is so imperative that we must not shrink from new forms of political thought or from the realization of new problems which could formerly be ignored, if not with impunity, at any rate without ultimate disaster.[2]

2. World Government

War may be avoided by makeshifts and expedients and subtle diplomacy for a time, but precariously; and so long as our present political system continues, it must be taken as nearly certain that great wars will occur from time to time. This will inevitably happen so long as there are different sovereign States, each with its own armed forces, and each the unfettered judge of its own rights in any dispute. There is only one way in which the world can be made safe from war, and that is the creation of a single world-wide authority, possessing a monopoly of all the more serious weapons.

If a world Government is to prevent serious wars, there are certain minimum powers that it must possess. First and foremost, it must have a monopoly of all the major weapons of war, and adequate armed forces for their employment. Whatever steps may be necessary must be taken to ensure that the armed forces will in all circumstances be loyal to the central Government. The world Government should proclaim certain rules for the employment of its armed forces. The most important of these should be that, in any dispute between two States, each must submit to the decision of the world Government. Any employment of force by any State against any other shall constitute it a public enemy, and shall bring punishment by the armed forces of the world Government. These are the essential powers if the preservation of peace is to be possible. Given these, others will follow. There will be need of bodies to perform legislative and judicial functions. These will develop naturally if the military conditions are fulfilled; the difficult and vital point is the placing of irresistible force in the hands of the central authority.

The central Government may be democratic or totalitarian; it may owe its origin to consent or to conquest; it may be the national Government of a State which has achieved world conquest, or it may be an authority in which each State, or alternatively, each human being, has equal rights. For my part I believe that, if it is constituted, it will be on a basis of consent in some regions and conquest in others. In a world war between two groups of nations, it may be that the victorious group will disarm the defeated group and proceed to govern the world by means of unifying institutions developed during the war. Gradually the defeated nations could be admitted to partnership as war hostility cooled. I do not believe that the human race has sufficient statesmanship or capacity for mutual forbearance to establish a world Government on a basis of consent alone. That is why I think that an element of force will be needed in its establishment and in its preservation through the early years of its existence.

But although force may be necessary at first in some parts of the world, there will be no stability and no possibility of a liberal and democratic system unless certain great causes of conflict cease to be operative. I am not thinking of the day-to-day conflicts that at present characterize the cold war, nor of the see-saw of power politics. What I am thinking of are matters in which, as things stand, there is a genuine clash between the interests of one part of the world and the interests of another. I am thinking of matters regarded as so important that each side would sooner fight than yield. For instance: shall Southeast Asia continue to be overcrowded, or shall Australia and South America cease to be white men's countries? Such really difficult causes of conflict center round three problems: population, race and creed. . . .

The conclusion to which we are driven by the facts . . . is that, while great wars cannot be avoided until there is a world Government, a world Government cannot be stable until every important country has a nearly stationary population. As this is very far from being the case at present, our conclusion may seem depressing. But there is another side to it which is by no means depressing. In former days most children died in infancy, mortality in adult life was very high, and in every country the great majority of the population endured abject poverty. Now certain nations have succeeded in preserving the lives of the overwhelming majority of infants, in enormously lowering the adult death-rate, and in nearly eliminating abject poverty. All this would have been impossible but for the fall in the birth-rate. Other nations, where disease and abject poverty are still the rule, could achieve the same level of well-being by adopting the same methods. There is therefore a new hope for mankind. The hope cannot be realized unless the causes of present evils are understood. But it is the hope that needs to be emphasized. Modern man is master of his fate. What he suffers, he suffers because he is stupid or wicked, not because it is nature's decree. Happiness is his if he will adopt the means that lie ready to his hands.[3]

3. The Value of Intelligence

Hatred of intelligence is one of the great dangers of the modern world, because with each new advance in technique intelligence becomes more necessary. . . . Progress in industrial technique depends upon inventors. Progress in war depends upon atomic physicists, not one of whom would have won the respect of his "manly" contemporaries. Wisdom in international affairs requires knowledge of geography, an acquaintance with the habits of various nations, and a capacity for seeing how the world looks from a point of view that is not your own, none of which can be obtained without intelligence. Our great democracies still tend to think that a stupid man is more likely to be honest than a clever man, and our politicians take advantage of this prejudice by pretending to be even more stupid than nature made them.

This popular fear of intelligence is one of the great dangers of our times, and like the other prejudices of which I have been speaking, it is a matter primarily for the schools. If teachers and educational authorities had more understanding of the sort of person the modern world needs, they could within a generation produce an outlook that would transform the world. But their ideal of character is an old-fashioned one. They admire most the sort of character which would give a man leadership in a gang of pirates, and if you say that commerce is a different thing from piracy, they think you soft and hope you are mistaken. All this is due to the persistence of old martial ideas that have descended to us from earlier ages. These ideas, I repeat, were appropriate to an age of unavoidable scarcity, but are not applicable to our own times, when whatever scarcity still exists is due to human stupidity and to nothing else. Although this is the case, most of us still prefer passion to intelligence, we like to have our feelings roused, we like to cheer and boo, we like to admire and we like to hate, we like to see things in black and white. Our whole mental apparatus is that which is appropriate to sending us rushing into battle with hoarse war-cries.

Consider the application of such a mentality to international banking, and you will not be surprised by the great depression which it produced whilst it reigned unchecked, nor by the belief of the Nazis that the depression could be curbed if only enough

Jews were exterminated, nor by the Russian belief that we should all be rich if all the rich men were liquidated. None of these mistakes would have been made by men in whom intelligence was capable of controlling passion, none of them would have been made by men who understood that when different groups have different interests it is because of unwise passions and not because of any physical fact.

The world is facing a prospective disaster, and is asking itself in a bewildered way why there seems no escape from a tragic fate that no one desires. The fundamental reason is that we have not adapted our mentality to our technique. We still allow ourselves ways of thinking and feeling that were appropriate in a technically simpler age. If we are to live happily with a modern technique—and it is possible for modern technique to bring a far higher level of happiness than was formerly possible—we must banish certain ideas and substitute certain others. For love of domination we must substitute equality; for love of victory we must substitute justice; for brutality we must substitute intelligence; for competition we must substitute co-operation. We must learn to think of the human race as one family, and further our common interests by the intelligent use of natural resources, marching together towards prosperity, not separately towards death and destruction. The mental change required is difficult, and will not be achieved in a moment, but if the need is recognized by educators, and if the young are brought up as citizens of this world and not of a bygone world of predatory warriors, the change can be achieved within a generation, so that we may hope to save at least a portion of mankind from the universal destruction with which we are threatened by the pursuit of obsolete ideas.[4]

4. *The Conflict Between the West and the Soviet World*

There is only too much reason to fear that Western civilization, if not the whole world, is likely in the near future to go through a period of immense sorrow and suffering and pain—a period during which, if we are not careful to remember them, the things that we are attempting to preserve may be forgotten in bitterness and poverty and disorder. Courage, hope and unshakable conviction will be necessary if we are to emerge from the dark time spiritually undamaged. It is worth while, before the actual danger is upon us, to collect our thoughts, to marshal our hopes and to plant in our hearts a firm belief in our ideals. . . .

Two very different conceptions of human life are struggling for mastery of the world. In the West we see man's greatness in the individual life. A great society for us is one which is composed of individuals who, as far as is humanly possible, are happy, free and creative. We do not think that individuals should be alike. We conceive society as like an orchestra, in which the different performers have different parts to play and different instruments upon which to perform, and in which co-operation results from a conscious common purpose. We believe that each individual should have his proper pride. He should have his personal conscience and his personal aims, which he should be free to develop except where they can be shown to cause injury to others. We attach importance to the diminution of suffering and poverty, to the increase of knowledge and the production of beauty and art. The State for us is a convenience, not an object of worship.

The Russian Government has a different conception of the ends of life. The individual is thought to be of no importance; he is expendable. What is important is the State, which is regarded as something almost divine and having a welfare of its own not consisting in the welfare of citizens. This view, which Marx took over from Hegel, is fundamentally opposed to the Christian ethic, which in the West is accepted by free-thinkers as much as by Christians. In the Soviet world human dignity counts for nothing. It is thought right and proper that men should be groveling slaves, bowing down before the semi-divine beings who embody the greatness of the State. When a man betrays his dearest friend and causes him, as a penalty for a moment's indiscretion, to vanish into the mysterious horror of a Siberian labor camp; when a schoolchild, as the result of indoctrination by his teacher, causes his parents to be condemned to death; when a man of exceptional courage, after struggling against evils, is tried, convicted, and abjectly confesses that he has sinned in opposing the Moloch power of the authorities, neither the betrayal nor the confession brings any sense of shame to the perpetrator, for has he not been engaged in the service of his divinity?

It is this conception that we have to fight, a conception which, to my mind and to that of most men who appreciate what the Western world stands for, would, if it prevailed, take everything out of life that gives it value, leaving nothing but a regimented collection of groveling animals. I cannot imagine a greater or more profound cause for which to fight. But if we are to win a victory—not only on the battlefield but in the hearts of men and in the institutions that they support—we must be clear in our own minds as to what it is that we value, and we must, like Boethius, fortify our courage against the threat of adversity.

While Russia underestimates the individual, there are those in the West who unduly magnify the separateness of separate persons. No man's ego should be enclosed in granite walls: its boundaries should be translucent. The first step in wisdom, as well as in morality, is to open the windows of the ego as wide as possible. Most people find little difficulty in including their children within the compass of their desires. In slightly lesser degree they include their friends, and, in time of danger, their country. Very many men feel that what hurts their country hurts them. In 1940 I knew Frenchmen living prosperously in America who suffered from the fall of France almost as they would have suffered from the loss of a leg. But it is not enough to enlarge our sympathies to embrace our own country. If the world is ever to have peace it will be necessary to learn to embrace the whole human race in the same kind of sympathy which we now feel toward our compatriots. And if we are to retain calm and sanity in difficult times, it is a great help if the furniture of our minds contains past and future ages.

Few things are more purifying to our conception of values than to contemplate the gradual rise of man from his obscure and difficult beginnings to his present eminence. Man, . . . when he first emerged, was a rare and hunted species, not so fleet as the deer, not so nimble as the monkey, unable to defend himself against wild beasts, without the protection of warm fur against rain and cold, living precariously upon the food that he could gather, without weapons, without domestic animals, without agriculture.

The one advantage that he possessed—intelligence—in the end gave him security. He learned the use of fire, of bows and arrows, of language, of domestic animals and, at last, of agriculture. He learned to co-operate in communities, to build great palaces and pyramids, to explore the world in all directions, and, at last, to cope with disease and poverty. He studied the stars, he invented geometry, and he learned to substitute machines for muscles in necessary labor. Some of the most important of these advances are very recent and are as yet confined to Western nations.

We of the Western world, faced with Communism's hostile criticism have been too modest and too defensive in our attitude. Throughout the long ages since life began, to repeat what was said earlier, the mechanism of evolution has involved cruel suffering, endless struggle for bare subsistence, and in the end, in most cases, death by starvation. This is the law in the animal kingdom, and it remained until the present century the law among human beings also. Now, at last, certain nations have discovered how to prevent abject poverty, how to prevent the pain and sorrow and waste of useless births condemned to premature death, and how to substitute intelligence and care for the blind ruthlessness of nature.

The nations that have made this discovery are trustees for the future of mankind. They must have the courage of their new way of life and not allow themselves to be bemused or bewildered by

he slogans of the semi-civilized. We have a right to hopes that
ire rational, that can be itemized and set forth in statistics. If we
illow ourselves to be robbed of these hopes for the sake of irra-
ional dreams, we shall be traitors to the human race.[5]

The Western world has achieved, not completely but to a
considerable extent, a way of life having certain merits that are
iew in human history. It has nearly eliminated poverty. It has
:ut down illness and death to a degree that a hundred years ago
would have seemed fantastic. It has spread education through-
iut the population, and it has achieved a quite new degree of
iarmony between freedom and order. These are not things which
Asia, if it becomes quickly independent, can hope to achieve.
We, in the West, aware of the appalling poverty of Southeast
Asia, and convinced that this poverty is a propaganda weapon in
the hands of the Russians, have begun to think for the first time
that something ought to be done to raise the standard of life in
these regions. But their habits and our beliefs between them
make the task, for the present, a hopeless one. Every increase of
production, instead of raising the standard of life, is quickly
swallowed up by an increase in population. Eastern populations
do not know how to prevent this, and Western bigots prevent
those who understand the problem from spreading the necessary
information. What is bad in the West is easily spread: our rest-
lessness, our militarism, our fanaticism, and our ruthless belief in
mechanism. But what is best in the West—the spirit of free
inquiry, the understanding of the conditions of general prosperity, and emancipation from superstition—these things powerful forces in the West prevent the East from acquiring. So long
as this continues, Eastern populations will remain on the verge
of destitution, and in proportion as they become powerful, they
will become destructive through envy. In this they will, of course,
have the help of Russia, unless and until Russia is either defeated
or liberalized.[6]

5. *The Ethic of Happiness*

I have been speaking hitherto of public perplexities, but it is
not these alone which trouble the Western mind. Traditional
systems of dogma and traditional codes of conduct have not the
hold that they formerly had. Men and women are often in genu
ine doubt as to what is right and what is wrong, and even as to
whether right and wrong are anything more than ancient super
stitions. When they try to decide such questions for themselves
they find them too difficult. They cannot discover any clear pur
pose that they ought to pursue or any clear principle by which
they should be guided. Stable societies may have principles that,
to the outsider, seem absurd. But so long as the societies remain
stable their principles are subjectively adequate. That is to say
they are accepted by almost everybody unquestioningly, and they
make the rules of conduct as clear and precise as those of the
minuet or the heroic couplet. Modern life, in the West, is not at
all like a minuet or a heroic couplet. It is like free verse which
only the poet can distinguish from prose. Two great systems of
dogma lie in wait for the modern man when his spirit is weary: I
mean the system of Rome and the system of Moscow. Neither of
these gives scope for the free mind, which is at once the glory and
the torment of Western man. It is the torment only because of
growing pains. The free man, full grown, shall be full of joy and
vigor and mental health, but in the meantime he suffers.

Not only publicly, but privately also, the world has need of
ways of thinking and feeling which are adapted to what we
know, to what we can believe, and what we feel ourselves compelled to disbelieve. There are ways of feeling that are traditional
and that have all the prestige of the past and weighty authority,
and that yet are not adapted to the world in which we live, where
new techniques have made some new virtues necessary and some
old virtues unnecessary. The Hebrew prophets, surrounded by
hostile nations, and determined that their race should not be
assimilated by Gentile conquerors, developed a fierce doctrine in

which the leading conception was sin. The Gentiles sinned always and in all their ways, but the Jews, alas, were only too apt to fall into sin themselves. When they did so they were defeated in battle and had to weep by the waters of Babylon. It is this pattern which has inspired moralists ever since. The virtuous man has been conceived as one who, though continually surrounded by temptation, though passionately prompted to sin, nevertheless, by almost superhuman strength of will, succeeds in walking along the straight and narrow path, looking meanwhile disdainfully to the right and left at those inferior beings who have loitered to pluck flowers by the way. In this conception, virtue is difficult, negative, and arid. It is constrictive and suspicious of happiness. It is persuaded that our natural impulses are bad and that society can only be held together by means of rigid prohibitions. I do not wish to pretend that society can hold together if people murder and steal. What I do say is, that the kind of man whom I should wish to see in the world is one who will have no impulse to murder, who will abstain from murder not because it is prohibited but because his thoughts and feelings carry him away from impulses of destruction. The whole conception of sin has, as it were, gone dead, so far, at least, as conscious thought and feeling are concerned. Most people have not thought out any other system of ethics, and have not, perhaps, theoretically rejected the old system. But it has lost its hold on them. They do not murder or steal as a rule, because it would not be to their interest to do so, but one cannot say as much for their obedience to the Seventh Commandment. They have, in fact, no wish to conform to the ancient pattern. The Publican thanks God that he is not as this Pharisee, and imagines that in so doing he has caught the point of the parable. It does not occur to him that feeling superior is what is reprehended, and that whether it is the Publican or the Pharisee who feels superior is an unimportant detail.

I should wish to persuade those to whom traditional morals have gone dead, and who yet feel the need of some serious purpose over and above momentary pleasure, that there is a way of thinking and feeling which is not difficult for those who have not been trained in its opposite, and which is not one of self-restraint, negation and condemnation. The good life, as I conceive it, is a happy life. I do not mean that if you are good you will be happy; I mean that if you are happy you will be good. Unhappiness is deeply implanted in the souls of most of us. How many people we all know who go through life apparently gay, and who yet are perpetually in search of intoxication whether of the Bacchic kind or some other. The happy man does not desire intoxication. Nor does he envy his neighbor and therefore hate him. He can live the life of impulse like a child, because happiness makes his impulses fruitful and not destructive. There are many men and women who imagine themselves emancipated from the shackles of ancient codes but who, in fact, are emancipated only in the upper layers of their minds. Below these layers lies the sense of guilt crouching like a wild beast waiting for moments of weakness or inattention, and growling venomous angers which rise to the surface in strange distorted forms. Such people have the worst of both worlds. The feeling of guilt makes real happiness impossible for them, but the conscious rejection of old codes of behavior makes them act perpetually in ways that feed the maw of the ancient beast beneath. A way of life cannot be successful so long as it is a mere intellectual conviction. It must be deeply felt, deeply believed, dominant even in dreams. I do not think that the best kind of life is possible in our day for those who, below the level of consciousness, are still obsessed by the load of sin. It is obvious that there are things that had better not be done, but I do not think the best way to avoid the doing of such things is to label them sin and represent them as almost irresistibly attractive. And so I should wish to offer to the world something scarcely to be called an ethic, at any rate in the old acceptation of that word, but something which, nonetheless, will save men from moral perplexity and from remorse and from condemnation of others. What I should put in the place of an ethic in the old sense is encouragement and opportunity for all the impulses that are creative and expansive. I should do everything possible to liberate men from fear, not only conscious fears, but the old imprisoned primeval terrors that we brought with us out of the jungle. I should make it clear, not merely as an intellectual proposition, but as something that the heart spontaneously believes, that it is not by making others suffer that we shall achieve our own happiness, but that happiness and the means to happiness depend upon harmony with other men. When all this is not only understood but deeply felt, it will be easy to live in a way that brings happiness equally to ourselves and to others. If men could think and feel in this way, not only their personal problems, but all the problems of world politics, even the most abstruse and difficult, would melt away. Suddenly, as when the mist dissolves from a mountain top, the landscape would be visible and the way would be clear. It is only necessary to open the doors of our hearts and minds to let the imprisoned demons escape and the beauty of the world take possession.[7]

6. *Love and Fortitude*

If bad times lie ahead of us we should remember while they last the slow march of man, checkered in the past by devastations and retrogressions, but always resuming the movement toward progress. Spinoza, who was one of the wisest of men and who lived consistently in accordance with his own wisdom, advised men to view passing events "under the aspect of eternity." Those who can learn to do this will find a painful present much more bearable than it would otherwise be. They can see it as a passing moment—a discord to be resolved, a tunnel to be traversed. The small child who has hurt himself weeps as if the world contained nothing but sorrow, because his mind is confined to the present. A man who has learned wisdom from Spinoza can see even a lifetime of suffering as a passing moment in the life of humanity. And the human race itself, from its obscure beginning to its unknown end, is only a minute episode in the life of the universe.

What may be happening elsewhere we do not know, but it is improbable that the universe contains nothing better than ourselves. With increase of wisdom our thoughts acquire a wider scope both in space and in time. The child lives in the minute, the boy in the day, the instinctive man in the year. The man imbued with history lives in the epoch. Spinoza would have us live not in the minute, the day, the year or the epoch, but in eternity. Those who learn to do this will find that it takes away the frantic quality of misfortune and prevents the trend towards madness that comes with overwhelming disaster. Spinoza spent the last day of his life telling cheerful anecdotes to his host. He had written: "A free man thinks of death least of all things, and his wisdom is a meditation not of death but of life." And he carried out this precept when it came to his own death.

I do not mean that the man who is freed from the tyranny of unwisdom will be destitute of emotion—on the contrary, he will feel friendship, benevolence and compassion in a higher degree than the man who has not emancipated himself from personal anxieties. His ego will not be a wall between him and the rest of mankind. He will feel, like Buddha, that he cannot be completely happy while anybody is miserable. He will feel pain—a wider and more diffused pain than that of the egoist—but he will not find the pain unendurable. He will not be driven by it to invent comfortable fairy tales which assure him that the sufferings of others are illusory. He will not lose poise and self-control. Like Milton's Satan he will say:

> The mind is its own place, and in itself
> Can make a Heav'n of Hell, a Hell of Heav'n.

Above all, he will remember that each generation is trustee to future generations of the mental and moral treasure that man has accumulated through the ages. It is easy to forget the glory of man. When King Lear is going mad he meets Edgar, who pretends to be mad and wears only a blanket. King Lear moralizes: "Unaccommodated, man is no more but such a poor, bare, forked animal as thou art."

This is half of the truth. The other half is uttered by Hamlet:

What a piece of work is man! how noble in reason! how infinite in faculty! In form and moving how express and admirable! in action how like an angel! in apprehension how like a god!

Soviet man, crawling on his knees to betray his friends and family to slow butchery, is hardly worthy of Hamlet's words, but it is possible to be worthy of them. It is possible for every one of us. Every one of us can enlarge his mind, release his imagination and spread wide his affection and benevolence. And it is those who do this whom ultimately mankind reveres. The East reveres Buddha, the West reveres Christ. Both taught love as the secret of wisdom. The earthly life of Christ was contemporary with that of the Emperor Tiberius, who spent his life in cruelty and disgusting debauchery. Tiberius had pomp and power: in his day millions trembled at his nod. But he is forgotten except by historians.

Those who live nobly, even if in their day they live obscurely, need not fear that they will have lived in vain. Something radiates from their lives, some light that shows the way to their friends, their neighbors, perhaps to long future ages. I find many men nowadays oppressed with a sense of impotence, with the feeling that in the vastness of modern societies there is nothing of importance that the individual can do. This is a mistake. The individual, if he is filled with love of mankind, with breadth of vision, with courage and with endurance, can do a great deal.

As geological time goes, it is but a moment since the human race began, and only the twinkling of an eye since the arts of civilization were first invented. In spite of some alarmists, it is hardly likely that our species will completely exterminate itself. And so long as man continues to exist, we may be pretty sure that, whatever he may suffer for a time, and whatever brightness may be eclipsed, he will emerge sooner or later, perhaps strengthened and reinvigorated by a period of mental sleep. The universe is vast and men are but tiny specks on an insignificant planet. But the more we realize our minuteness and our impotence in the face of cosmic forces, the more astonishing becomes what human beings have achieved.

It is to the possible achievements of man that our ultimate loyalty is due, and in that thought the brief troubles of our unquiet epoch become endurable. Much wisdom remains to be learned, and if it is only to be learned through adversity, we must endeavor to endure adversity with what fortitude we can command. But if we can acquire wisdom soon enough, adversity may not be necessary and the future of man may be happier than any part of his past.[8]

There are certain things that our age needs, and certain things that it should avoid. It needs compassion and a wish that mankind should be happy; it needs the desire for knowledge and the determination to eschew pleasant myths; it needs, above all, courageous hope and the impulse to creativeness. The things that it must avoid, and that have brought it to the brink of catastrophe, are cruelty, envy, greed, competitiveness, search for irrational subjective certainty, and what Freudians call the death wish.

The root of the matter is a very simple and old-fashioned thing, a thing so simple that I am almost ashamed to mention it, for fear of the derisive smile with which wise cynics will greet my words. The thing I mean—please forgive me for mentioning it—is love, Christian love, or compassion. If you feel this, you have a motive for existence, a guide in action, a reason for courage, an imperative necessity for intellectual honesty. If you feel this, you have all that anybody should need in the way of religion. Although you may not find happiness, you will never know the deep despair of those whose life is aimless and void of purpose; for there is always something that you can do to diminish the awful sum of human misery.[9]

7. *Philosophic Rationality*

When I was young I hoped to find religious satisfaction in philosophy. . . . I have always ardently desired to find some justification for the emotions inspired by certain things that seemed to stand outside human life and to deserve feelings of awe. I am thinking in part of very obvious things, such as the starry heavens and a stormy sea on a rocky coast; in part of the vastness of the scientific universe, both in space and time, as compared to the life of mankind; in part of the edifice of impersonal truth, especially truth which, like that of mathematics, does not merely describe the world that happens to exist. Those who attempt to make a religion of humanism, which recognizes nothing greater than man, do not satisfy my emotions. And yet I am unable to believe that, in the world as known, there is anything that I can value outside human beings, and, to a much lesser extent, animals. Not the starry heavens, but their effects on human percipients, have excellence; to admire the universe for its size is slavish and absurd; impersonal non-human truth appears to be a delusion. And so my intellect goes with the humanists, though my emotions violently rebel. In this respect, the "consolations of philosophy" are not for me.

In more purely intellectual ways, on the contrary, I have found as much satisfaction in philosophy as any one could reasonably have expected. Many matters which, when I was young, baffled me by the vagueness of all that had been said about them, are now amenable to an exact technique, which makes possible the kind of progress that is customary in science. Where definite knowledge is unattainable, it is sometimes possible to prove that it is unattainable, and it is usually possible to formulate a variety of exact hypotheses, all compatible with the existing evidence. Those philosophers who have adopted the methods derived from logical analysis can argue with each other, not in the old aimless way, but cooperatively, so that both sides can concur as to the outcome. . . .[10] They confess frankly that the human intellect is unable to find conclusive answers to many questions of profound importance to mankind, but they refuse to believe that there is some "higher" way of knowing, by which we can discover truths hidden from science and the intellect. For this renunciation they have been rewarded by the discovery that many questions, formerly obscured by the fog of metaphysics, can be answered with precision, and by objective methods which introduce nothing of the philosopher's temperament except the desire to understand. Take such questions as: What is number? What are space and time? What is mind, and what is matter? I do not say that we can here and now give definitive answers to all these ancient questions, but I do say that a method has been discovered by which, as in science, we can make successive approximations to the truth, in which each new stage results from an improvement, not a rejection, of what has gone before.

In the welter of conflicting fanaticisms, one of the few unifying forces is scientific truthfulness, by which I mean the habit of basing our beliefs upon observations and inferences as impersonal, and as much divested of local and temperamental bias, as is possible for human beings. To have insisted upon the introduction of this virtue into philosophy, and to have invented a powerful method by which it can be rendered fruitful, are the chief merits of the philosophical school of which I am a member. The habit of careful veracity acquired in the practice of this philosophical method can be extended to the whole sphere of human activity, producing, wherever it exists, a lessening of fanaticism with an increasing capacity of sympathy and mutual understanding. In abandoning a part of its dogmatic pretensions, philosophy does not cease to suggest and inspire a way of life.[11]

All this is new during my lifetime. . . . This extension of the sphere of reason to new provinces is something that I value very highly. Philosophic rationality may be choked in the shocks of war and the welter of new persecuting superstitions, but one may hope that it will not be lost utterly or for more than a few centuries. In this respect, my philosophic life has been a happy one.[12]

Sources

—

CHAPTER XVI: PHILOSOPHIC RATIONALITY FOR A CHANGING WORLD

The selections from Bertrand Russell are drawn principally from his recent book *New Hopes for a Changing World* (Simon and Schuster, 1951), denoted as "N." The remaining selections are taken from *The Impact of Science on Society* (Simon and Schuster, 1951), denoted as "I"; *The Philosophy of Bertrand Russell* (Northwestern University, 1944) denoted as "P"; and *A History of Western Philosophy* (Simon and Schuster, 1945), denoted as "H."

[1] N, page 3; page 4, lines 1 and 5-18.
[2] N, page 91, lines 15-34; page 92, lines 1-27.
[3] N, page 92, lines 28-34; page 93; page 94, lines 1-19; page 95, lines 6-28.
[4] N, page 158, lines 13-34; page 159; page 160, lines 1-15.
[5] N, page 179, lines 12-22; page 181, lines 11-34; page 182; page 183; page 184, lines 1-13.
[6] N, page 6, lines 23-34; page 7, lines 1-18.
[7] N, page 8, lines 9-34; page 9; page 10; page 11, lines 1-31.
[8] N, page 184, lines 14-34; page 185; page 186; page 187, lines 1-11.
[9] I, page 91, lines 24-32; page 92, lines 1-12.
[10] P, page 19, lines 21, 26-37; page 20, lines 1-20.
[11] H, page 835, lines 27-38; page 836.
[12] P, page 20, line 20, lines 22-27.

CHAPTER XVII

SIDNEY HOOK (1902–   )

It is a mistake for any bright student who is not a philosophy "major" to wander into a class given by Professor Hook, for he is likely to change his subject to philosophy before the warning bell has sounded on the first lecture. Sidney Hook, who is one of the leading naturalist philosophers in the United States, possesses an enviable flair for the drama of ideas, and combines in his discourse learned but crystal-clear analysis, wit, and psychological insight. These several qualities are not always present in the philosophical temperament.

Sidney Hook was born in New York City on December 20, 1902. He spent his childhood in Brooklyn where he attended the local public schools. At the City College of New York, he studied philosophy with Morris Raphael Cohen. He entered Columbia University's Graduate School in 1923, where he came under the lasting influence of John Dewey. In 1924 Hook was a University Scholar; in 1926–1927 he was awarded one of the coveted University Fellowships in Philosophy. At the end of that year, he received his Ph.D., and the following year, on a Guggenheim Fellowship, studied in Berlin, Munich, and at the Marx-Engels Institute in Moscow. When he returned to the United States he began his long-lasting teaching connection with New York University, entering as an instructor of philosophy at Washington Square College in 1927, becoming Assistant Professor in 1932, Associate Professor and Chairman of the Department in 1933, and Professor a few years thereafter. In 1947 New York University Graduate School appointed him Head of the Department of Philosophy and in 1948, Chairman of the Division of Philosophy and Psychology. For many years while fulfilling these duties, Hook lectured to large audiences at the New School for Social Research on Contemporary Philosophy, Ethics, and Social Philosophy.

Sidney Hook's career has been unusually active and broad in its interests. He has written important books and articles in philosophy, educational theory, social criticism, the philosophy of history, and the politics of democracy. An early interest in Hegel and Marx issued in two books, *Toward the Understanding of Karl Marx* (1933), which has been called "the best presentation of the social philosophy of Karl Marx in the English language," and *From Hegel to Marx* (1936). Hook's interest in Marxism, however, was giving way in the 1930's to a deeper interest in the American pragmatic tradition and particularly in Dewey's Instrumentalism. A close friendship existed between the aging philosopher and the young colleague, and Hook worked closely with Dewey on many of his manuscripts in these and later years. In 1939, when Dewey was entering his eightieth year, Hook published *John Dewey: An Intellectual Portrait*, which remains to this day the best statement of Dewey's leading ideas. A collection of essays on political philosophy, *Reason, Social Myths and Democracy* appeared in 1940; and in 1943, *The Hero in History*, for which Hook was awarded the Butler Silver Medal in April, 1945, by Columbia University. The citation called the book "an important contribution to the recent attempts to interpret history from the point of view of American naturalism and experimentalism." Hook's next major book was *Education for Modern Man* (1946), a spirited defense of liberal educational philosophy in America at a time when the salesmanship of the "Great Books" and St. John's College program was in its ascendancy.

Hook's current efforts have been to establish the vitality of liberalism in its opposition to Communism. Two recent books are: *Heresy Yes—Conspiracy No* (1953), a study of cultural freedom in the United States that took issue with doctrinaire liberalism to advocate a "tough-minded" approach to the problem of Communism; and *Common Sense and the Fifth Amendment* (1957), a study of the "self-incrimination" clause, written, the author said, from the standpoint of "unreconstructed liberalism which recognizes the primacy of morality to law, and the centrality of intelligence in morality." After many years of writing and teaching the essential principles of independent thought and inquiry, Hook saw the need to form an organization for the defense of intellectual freedom against the ceaseless deceptions and inroads on democracy that issued from

Communist and Communist-sympathized sources. The Committee for Cultural Freedom, with Sidney Hook as its first Chairman, was founded, and now has nine "national Communities" affiliated with the American Committee.

NATURALISM AND DEMOCRACY
—

SIDNEY HOOK

1. *The Failure of Nerve*

In the famous third chapter of his *Four Stages of Greek Religion* Gilbert Murray characterizes the period from 300 B.C. through the first century of the Christian era as marked by a "failure of nerve." This failure of nerve exhibited itself in "a rise of asceticism, of mysticism, in a sense, of pessimism; a loss of self-confidence, of hope in this life and of faith in normal human efforts; a despair of patient inquiry, a cry for infallible revelation; an indifference to the welfare of the state, a conversion of the soul to God."

A survey of the cultural tendencies of our times shows many signs pointing to a new failure of nerve in Western civilization. The revival of the doctrine of the original depravity of human nature; prophecies of doom for Western culture, no matter who wins the war or peace; the search for a center of value that transcends human interest; the mystical apotheosis of "the leader"; contempt for all social programs and philosophies, because of the obvious failure of some of them; violent attacks against secularism; posturing about the cultivation of spiritual purity; a concern with mystery rather than problems and the belief that myth and mysteries are modes of knowledge—these are only some of the secondary evidences of the new failure of nerve.

The primary evidence of the new failure of nerve is to be

found in an attitude which accompanies all the movements and views listed in the previous paragraph and many others as well. It exhibits itself as a loss of confidence in scientific method and in varied quests for a "knowledge" and "truth" which are uniquely different from those won by the processes of scientific inquiry. Often, with no great regard for consistency, these uniquely different truths are regarded as "superior" to the common garden variety of science and good sense. This distrust of scientific method is often concealed by statements to the effect that science, of course, has a certain validity in its proper place and sphere, that only the pretensions of scientific philosophy—naturalism, empiricism, positivism—are being criticized. Yet it is not to the actual procedures of scientific inquiry that such critics go to correct this or that formulation of scientific philosophy; rather do they invoke the claims of some rival method to give us knowledge of what is beyond the competence of scientific method. Occasionally they boldly assert that their substitute method gives a more reliable and complete knowledge even of the matters that the sciences report. What an eloquent revelation is contained in Reinhold Niebuhr's words, "Science which is only science cannot be scientifically accurate."

Distrust of scientific method is transformed into open hostility whenever some privileged "private" truth pleads for exemption from the tests set up to safeguard the intelligence from illusion. The pleas for exemption take many forms. They are rarely direct and above board. Usually they are presented as corollaries of special *theories* of knowledge, being, or experience. There are some who interpret science and discursive knowledge generally as merely a method of confirming what we *already* know, in a dim but sure way, by other modes of experience. If the methods of scientific inquiry do not yield this confirmation, they are held to be at fault; some other way must be found of validating and communicating primal wisdom. Others maintain that scientific method can give us only partial truths, which become less partial, not by subjecting them to more careful scientific scrutiny, but by incorporating them into a theological or metaphysical system. Still others openly declare it to be axiomatic that every experience, every feeling and motion, directly reports a truth that cannot be warranted and does not need to be warranted by experiment or inference.

These, bluntly put, are gateways to intellectual and moral irresponsibility. But of the view that every mode of experience gives direct authentic knowledge it would, perhaps, be more accurate to say that it carries us far beyond the gateways. For frequently it is a defense of willful obscurantism. It starts from the assumption that *every* experience gives us an authentic report of the objective world instead of material for judgment. It makes our viscera an organ of knowledge. It justifies every passionate prejudice by asserting that if only we feel deeply enough about anything, our feeling must declare some truth about the object which provokes it that is just as legitimate as the considered judgment which discovers the root of the feeling in a personal aberration. After all, is it not the case that every heresy-hunting bigot and hallucinated fanatic is convinced that there is a truth in the feelings, visions, and passions that run riot within him? Hitler is not the only one for whom questions of evidence are incidental when they are not dismissed as impertinent. If the voice of feeling cannot be mistaken, every difference would be an invitation to battle, every insane mind could set itself up as a prophet. It is not only as a defense against the marginally sane that we need the safeguards of critical, scientific method. Every vested interest in social life, every inequitable privilege, every "truth" promulgated as a national, class, or racial truth likewise denies the competence of scientific inquiry to evaluate its claims. Nor are our own normal selves free from the tendency to mistake intensity of the feeling or conviction with which beliefs are held as indubitable evidence of their validity.

Sometimes the demand that the revelations of feeling, intuition, and emotion meet scientific canons of evidence is rejected as an arbitrary legislative decree concerning what visions are permissible and what may or may not exist. The complaint is made that such a demand impoverishes the imaginative resources and chokes off the vision, without which there is no growth or new knowledge, but at most a blind fooling with canons and methods. As far as seeing visions and winning new truths are concerned, such an interpretation is nothing short of grotesque. The essential point, where the question of knowledge or truth arises, is whether we have seen a vision or been a victim of a delusion; or, to avoid the appearance of question-begging, whether we have beheld a trustworthy or untrustworthy vision. Some people claim to see things that we know are not there. If seeing were believing, men could be perpetually duped.

The intelligent demand for evidence need not paralyze the pioneers of truth who catch glimpses of what may until then be undreamed of. For the sciences themselves do not demand complete or exact confirmation of an hypothesis to begin with, but only enough to institute further inquiries; and the history of science is sufficient evidence that the discipline of its method, far from being a bar against the discovery of new truths, is a positive aid in acquiring them. As for decreeing what does or can *exist*, there is nothing in scientific method that *forbids* anything to exist. It concerns itself only with the responsibility of the assertions that proclaim the existence of anything. It does not jeer at the mystical swoon of rapture; it only denies the mystic's retrospective cognitive claims for which no evidence is offered except the fact of the trance.

Scientific method does not entail any metaphysical theory of existence, and certainly not metaphysical materialism. The attack upon scientific method, in order to be free to believe whatever voice speaks to us, is really a flight from responsibility. This is the dominant characteristic of the failure of nerve.[1]

2. *Naturalism and Religion*

Despite the variety of specific doctrines which naturalists have professed from Democritus to Dewey, what unites them all is the wholehearted acceptance of scientific method as the only reliable way of reaching truths about the world of nature, society, and man. The differences between naturalists in the history of thought can easily be explained in terms of (1) varying historical conceptions of what fields and problems are amenable to scientific treatment and (2) progressive refinements in the methods of inquiry themselves. All their differences can in principle be resolved by appealing to the *method* to which they give common allegiance, except for those temperamental differences of emphasis and selective bias which no naturalist claims to be an avenue to truth. The least common denominator of all historic naturalisms, therefore, is not so much a set of specific doctrines as the method of scientific or rational empiricism.

Naturalism is opposed to all known forms of supernaturalism, not because it rules out a priori what may or may not exist, but because no plausible evidence has been found to warrant belief in the entities and powers to which supernatural status has been attributed. The existence of God, immortality, disembodied spirits, cosmic purpose and design, as these have been customarily interpreted by the great institutional religions, are denied by naturalists for the same generic reasons that they deny the existence of fairies, elves, and leprechauns. There are other conceptions of God, to be sure, and provided they are not self-contradictory in meaning, the naturalist is prepared in principle to consider their claims to validity. All he asks is that the conception be sufficiently definite to make possible specific inferences of the determinate conditions—the *how, when,* and *where* of His operation. The trouble with most conceptions of God which differ from the conventional ones is that either they are so vague that no one can tell what they mean or else they designate something in experience for which a perfectly suitable term already exists.[2]

The revival of religion to-day is not due to the discovery of new arguments or evidence for supernaturalism or a profounder analysis of the logic of religious belief. This is apparent in the fact that among intellectuals it is not rational theology but mystical theology, not the principle of objectivity but of subjectivity, not the clear, if defective, arguments of Aquinas but the record of the tormented inner experience of Augustine, Pascal, Kierkegaard which are found most appealing. To the extent that evidence is introduced it is drawn from feeling, the feeling of awe and sublimity, of holiness and humility, dogmatically interpreted as indisputable intimations of divinity. Reason is short-circuited by the assumption that there is a non-propositional truth about the nature of things, obscurely grasped in every intense experience. The religious renaissance of our time is really part of the more inclusive movement of irrationalism in modern thought. . . .

For what these God-seeking intellectuals are looking for is not so much a theology but a theodicy, not merely, or even primarily, truth but justification and comfort.

Here is located the perennial and most powerful source of religious belief, not only for these intellectuals but for most men, especially in times of social crisis but also in periods of personal crisis. Naturalism as a philosophy is sufficient to gratify all the legitimate needs of the understanding without yielding to the conceit that human intelligence is omnipotent and that all problems will be solved. But in recognizing the reality of the evil and the horrible in human experience, in accepting the finitude not only of man but of every other creature and power, in refusing to swallow the crude or subtle efforts to picture the cosmic order as a moral order, it cannot provide the consolation which the tender-minded must have, if they are to find their existence meaningful and tolerable. It is not that the believer lacks the tough-mindedness to recognize the existence of evil, but that, if he is not to choke to death on it like Ivan Karamazov, he must blunt its sharp edge and learn to believe on no rational grounds that it fulfils a "higher" purpose he does not see.

An intelligent naturalism, no matter how Promethean, will recognize that in addition to the suffering that flows from social inequalities and injustice, there are major experiences of frustration, grief, and loss from which sensitive human beings cannot escape. In the best of societies death may be conquered, but not tragedy. It is not the poor we will always have with us, but the "Underground Man." Scientific knowledge increases human power at the same time as it brings home to us the fundamental precariousness of human existence. Bertrand Russell to the contrary, the growth of science does not make for cosmic impiety or a decline in intellectual humility. Why should the world appear less wonderful or awesome if some day we step from one planet to another, synthesize protoplasm, or lift the darkness from the minds of the insane?

A seasoned naturalism is not Utopian. It realizes that knowledge and wisdom do not guarantee happiness, that they can do little or nothing to lessen the pangs of the mediocre, of the ugly, of those bereft of love or friendship. It cannot promise total security, even when it understands the needs of those who seek it.

Max Weber somewhere suggests that the great religions are interpretations of the world which try to make sense of the meaningless suffering in human life. Although this is not the whole story, I believe it does express something essential in the attitude of the religious person for whom suffering *must* have a meaning and no good cause ever goes down to final defeat. It is true that some naturalists have been shallow optimists—something easily remediable in the light of more knowledge—but such a charge is peculiarly malapropos coming from religious believers whose emotional compulsions have led them to accept optimism on the vastest scale imaginable.

There are some reluctant naturalists with a hankering for the genteel tradition who blame the "new failure of nerve" on the philosophy of naturalism because it does not offer an adequate analysis of the alienation of the modern intellectual and his moral predicaments. How unwarranted such a view is becomes apparent when we reflect upon the fact that philosophical naturalism has never been so far removed from the crudities of reductive materialism as to-day. It leaves unexplained why the modern intellectual in search of salvation evinces such an obvious distaste towards the very attempt at scientific explanation in history and psychology, and why he substitutes for it not a more rigorous theoretical scheme, but, as his enthusiasm for Toynbee shows, extravagant myth. His dissatisfaction is not intellectual but emotional. The critics who are homesick for gentility look to naturalism to provide a faith to live by equivalent to religious faith. This is precisely what naturalism cannot do if it is honest to the facts of experience. They forget that religious faith cannot be separated from religious belief or dogma, and ultimately from the question of truth. Otherwise we have a serious fooling or a discussion in religious terms of ethical or aesthetic subject matter.

Pruned of its sentimentalism, there is a deep insight in Feuerbach's philosophy of religion according to which the secret of theology is (philosophical) anthropology. What Marx did was not to renounce this insight but to show that the emotional needs of which religion was both an expression and gratification could not be dissociated from their cultural matrix. He overstated his position, and some who imagine themselves his followers have made a grotesquerie of it.

So long as religion is freed from authoritarian institutional forms, and conceived in personal terms, so long as its overbeliefs are a source of innocent joy, a way of overcoming cosmic loneliness, a discipline of living with pain and evil, otherwise unendurable and irremediable, so long as what functions as a vital illusion or poetic myth is not represented as a public truth to whose existence the once-born are blind, so long as religion does not paralyze the desire and the will to struggle against unnecessary cruelties of experience, it seems to me to fall in an area of choice in which rational criticism may be suspended. In this sense, a man's personal religion justifies itself to him in the way his love does. Why should he want to make a public cult of it? And why should we want him to prove that the object of his love is the most lovely creature in the world? Nonetheless, it still remains true that as a set of cognitive beliefs, religion is a speculative hypothesis of an extremely low order of probability.[3]

3. *Philosophy of Democracy*

At the present juncture of world history it is true that what is most precious in human experience is threatened on a global scale not by authoritarian religions, which have been chastened by their sufferings at the hands of their secular rivals, but by the fearful expansion of Stalinism and its total and absolute terror. What we need as a rallying cry is freedom, not salvation. A man can choose to save his soul and count the world well lost for it: and one man's salvation is another's superstition. A sure way to lose the struggle for a democratic world is to permit the Pope to take the lead in a crusade against Bolshevism. The struggle of the unfettered intelligence against institutional orthodoxy must continue despite the fact that conflicting orthodoxies, in the interest of their own religious freedom, find themselves allied for the moment against the super-orthodoxy that will brook no dissent, not even that of silence.

Just as it is fatal to conduct the international struggle against Stalinism in the name of capitalism—Stalinism can more easily come to terms with moribund capitalism than with democratic socialism—so with the slogans of the parochial religions of the West which the majority of mankind does not accept. What can unite Christian and non-Christian alike in a common struggle for freedom is only the pluralistic philosophy of democracy.[4]

By democracy as a way of life we mean a way of organizing human relationships which embodies a certain complex of moral ideals. . . . We are all acquainted with situations in which we say that a political democracy has traduced its own ideals. Whenever we criticize existing states which conform to the political definition of democracy on the ground that they are not democratic enough; whenever we point out that Athenian democracy was limited only to free men or that in some parts of the American

South it is limited only to white men, or that in some countries it is limited only to men, we are invoking a broader principle of democracy as a controlling reference in our judgments of comparison. This principle is an ethical one.

What is this principle of ethical democracy? It is the principle of equality—an equality, not of status or origin, but of opportunity, relevant functions, and social participation. . . . *Why should we treat individuals of unequal talents and endowments as persons who are equally entitled to relevant consideration and care?* Short of a treatise, I can state only the reasons, without amplification of the concrete needs of the social situation which democracy seeks to meet and the institutional practices by which it must meet them.

1. This method of treating human beings is more successful than any other in evoking a maximum of creative, voluntary effort from all members of the community. Properly implemented, it gives all persons a stake in the community and elicits a maximum of intelligent loyalty.

2. It enlarges the scope of our experience by enabling us to acquire insight into the needs, drives, and aspirations of others. Learning to understand how life is organized by other centers of experience is both a challenge and a discipline for our imagination. In aiding the growth of others, we aid our own growth.

3. The willingness to understand another man's point of view without necessarily surrendering to it makes it more likely that different points of view may negotiate their differences and learn to live peacefully with one another. A democratic community cannot be free from strife in a world where inequalities will always exist, but its ethics, when intelligently acted upon, makes more likely the diminution of strife or its transference to socially harmless forms than is the case when its principle of equality is denied. The consequences are less toadying, less fear, and less duplicity in the equalitarian community than there are in the non-equalitarian society.

4. In nurturing the capacities of each individual so that they

may come to their greatest fulfillment we can best share our existing stores of truth and beauty and uncover new dimensions in these realms. How can anyone dedicated to the values of science and art consistently oppose a policy which maximizes the possibility of the discovery and widest dispersion of scientific truths and artistic meanings?

5. Regard for the potentialities of all individuals makes for less cruelty of man toward man, especially where cruelty is the result of blindness to, or ignorance of, the needs of others. A community organized along democratic lines is guilty of cruelty only at those points where it has failed to live up to its own ideals. A totalitarian community is systematically insensitive to the personal needs not only of members of the outlawed scapegoat group but also of the majority of its subjects who are excluded from policy-making discussions. At best, there is no way of determining these personal needs except by the interpretation of the dictator and his experts who act on the fateful dogma that they know the true interests of their subjects better than the subjects themselves. At worst, the dictator assumes not only that he speaks for his subjects but that in some mystic way he feels and thinks for them too. Despite the great limitations—limitations from the point of view of their own ideals—under which the nineteenth- and twentieth-century democracies of the Western world suffered, I think it is indisputable, on the evidence, that by and large their social life, in so far as this was the consequence of policy, displayed less cruelty than the social life of any other historical period.

6. Reasonableness of conclusions, where attitudes and interests conflict, depends upon the degree of mutual consultation and free intellectual communication between the principals involved. The democratic way of life makes possible the widest forms of mutual consultation and communication. Conclusions reached by these processes have a quality that can never be found where conclusions are imposed by force or authority—even if they are our own.[5]

4. The Moral Function of Intelligence

If the good is defined in relation to human need or interest (or preference, desire, satisfaction)—if, in other words, the nature of morals is conceived as having any relation to human nature—then every statement about the good or better in any situation has a descriptive meaning, and in principle is decidable in reference to the needs and interests involved. The nature of human nature, and most particularly the presence of shared interests in a shared experience, or the possibility of such shared interest, becomes relevant at every point. Whether, as Dewey claims, there exists "a psychological uniformity of human nature with respect to basic *needs* . . . and of certain conditions which must be met in order that any form of human association must be maintained" . . . is an empirical question to which the answer is difficult but not inaccessible to study. Since we know that men are not always aware of what their interests are, and that their interests (or attitudes) often change in the light of the knowledge of their causes and consequences, and since intelligence is also natural to man, in situations of conflict we use the method of intelligence to negotiate differences by seeking a more inclusive interest to enable us either to live with our differences, to mitigate them or to transcend them, and thus convert value conflicts into compatible value differences. This is the constructive moral function of intelligence, which to be effective must be given institutional form—educational, economic, political.

No one who soberly looks at history would wish to assert that all disagreements among human beings must yield to negotiation through intelligence, that we can be certain that men *are* sufficiently alike to work out ways of becoming more alike, or sufficiently alike to agree about the permissible limits of being different. The unwillingness to use intelligence where there is a possibility of using it, does not gainsay the fact that if it had been used, certain shared interests might have been—sometimes we can say *would* have been—discovered.

It is important to point out, however, that it is easy to exaggerate the non-negotiable differences among men, and to convert by theoretical fiat the occasions of disagreement into irresolvable ultimate differences of value attitudes. Most disagreements among men . . . are about focal aims, major or lesser, and not about allegedly ultimate values concerning which in Western culture, at any rate, most human beings *profess* to agree, to a point where Franco speaks of the "brotherhood of man under God" and Stalin speaks of "freedom." . . .

That man has intelligence is as much a fact about his nature as that he has needs and desires which he seeks to satisfy. And since the successful satisfaction of these needs depends upon the knowledge of all sorts of conditions and consequences, there is no problem about justifying the use of intelligence to the extent that any man has it. He has a natural interest in intelligence because the prospering of all his other interests depends upon it

Reflection on the social nature of the self, the success of experimental methods in the natural sciences, the costs and ineffectiveness of other methods in human affairs carries us a long way in justifying the use of intelligence in settling *conflicts* between groups and classes.[8]

5. *The Meaning of Liberalism Today*

What makes analysis of the meaning of liberalism more than an academic exercise is the challenge of the Communist movement, which invokes the freedoms that prevail in a liberal society in order to destroy it. Many proposals have been made to cope with this problem. All of them must face the question of whether, in advocating such measures, the principles of liberalism are themselves being consistently applied or compromised.

It is easier to say what liberalism is not than what it is. It is not identical with the belief in laissez faire or free enterprise in economics. . . . Nor is liberalism the philosophy of invariable compromise, nor the comforting notion that it is always possible to find a middle ground. . . .

From this it follows that although liberalism is naturally pacific, it is not pacifist. It does not make a fetish of "sweet reasonableness" in the face of aggression, and it is aware that appeasement may be a greater provocation to armed conflict than a judicious show of force as an index of ability to resist. The history of Allied relations with Hitler is indisputable evidence on this point.

Finally, liberalism cannot be identified with the traditional belief in specific, absolute or inalienable rights, since every such right is in fact evaluated in terms of its consequences for society and is therefore subject to modification. One right limits another, and the final adjudication of the conflict of rights is made in the reflective light of the total situation, or of that set of rationally preferred freedoms whose existence may entail the temporary abridgement of any one freedom. To say that we cannot preserve our freedoms by sacrificing them is an empty piece of rhetoric, because a *particular* freedom must sometimes be sacrificed to preserve other freedoms.

The most comprehensive and adequate definition in positive terms of the meaning of liberalism, from Socrates to John Dewey, is suggested by the memorable words of Justice Holmes. It is the belief "in the free trade of ideas—that the test of truth is the power of thought to get itself accepted in the competition of the market." This is not a program of action nor a philosophical theory of truth, but an attitude or temper of mind towards all programs. Liberals may disagree among themselves about everything else; but all of them have this faith in common. It is a faith which marks off liberal from totalitarian culture. Any action which restricts the freedom of ideas to develop or circulate is illiberal.

There are at least two presuppositions of this belief in the free market of ideas. . . .

The first is that the free expression and circulation of ideas may be checked wherever their likely effects constitute a clear and present danger to public peace or the security of the country.

This is a specific application of the principle that no right is absolute when it endangers rights of equal or greater validity. In ordinary affairs, this is a commonplace. The right to inquire is innocent, but not when it leads someone to experiment on a human being to determine how long he can survive torture. The right to free speech is precious, but not when it blasts a reputation by libelous accusation. Truth is sacred, but a person who revealed it knowing that it would be used to destroy his country is a traitor. . . .

The second presupposition of the liberal's faith in the free market of ideas is that the competition will be honestly and openly conducted. For unless there are certain rules, so to speak of honest competition, analogous to those which hold in other domains of testing and inquiry, freedom of choice is an illusion. If the market is rigged by money, power or fraud, what gets accepted is anything but the truth. If ability to withstand honest competition is not a sufficient condition of truth it is at least a necessary one. From the point of view of the liberal, it is not doctrines "fraught with death" which he fears, for his faith in intelligence is such that he is confident that in the open and honest exchange of opinion the majority of men will choose life, not death, and that if they choose death they deserve their fate. Men cannot be compelled to remain free, any more than they can be compelled to love one another. What the liberal fears is the systematic corruption of the free market of ideas by activities which make intelligent choice impossible. In short, what he fears is not heresy but conspiracy.

The failure to recognize the distinction between heresy and conspiracy is fatal to a liberal civilization, for the inescapable consequence of their identification is either self-destruction when heresies are punished as conspiracies, or destruction at the hands of their enemies, when conspiracies are tolerated as heresies.

A heresy is a set of unpopular ideas or opinions on matters of grave concern to the community. The right to profess publicly a heresy of any character, on any theme, is an essential element of a liberal society. The liberal stands ready to defend the honest heretic no matter what his views against any attempt to curb him. It is enough that the heretic pays the price of unpopularity which he cannot avoid. In some respects each of us is a heretic, but a liberal society can impose no official orthodoxies of *belief*, disagreement with which entails loss of liberty or life.

A conspiracy, as distinct from a heresy, is a secret or underground movement which seeks to attain its ends not by normal political or educational processes but by playing outside the rules of the game. Because it undermines the conditions which are required in order that doctrines may freely compete for acceptance, because where successful it ruthlessly destroys all heretics and dissenters, a conspiracy cannot be tolerated without self-stultification in a liberal society. . . .

Liberalism in the twentieth century must toughen its fibre, for it is engaged in a fight on many different fronts. It must defend the free market in ideas against the racists, the professional patrioteers, and those spokesmen of the status quo who would freeze the existing inequalities of opportunity and economic power by choking off criticism. It must also be defended against those agents and apologists of Communist totalitarianism who, instead of honestly defending their heresies, resort to conspiratorial methods of anonymity and other techniques of fifth columnists. . . .

Realistic liberalism recognizes that to survive we must solve many hard problems, and that they can be solved only by intelligence, and not by pious rhetoric. Our greatest danger is not fear of ideas but *absence* of ideas—specific ideas, addressed to concrete problems, here and now, problems of such complexity that only the ignorant can claim to know all the answers to them.

Finally, liberalism today conceives life not in terms of bare survival or of peace at any price, but in the light of ideas and ideals without which a life worthy of man cannot be attained.[7]

6. *The Faith of a Naturalist*

That the cosmic home of man limits his power, if not his dreams, is, of course, true. It is a perennial source of his humility before the intractabilities of things and the transient character of what he builds. But it is also true that this limitation is the source of his opportunities and a necessary condition for all achievement. From these truths we cannot infer that nature is the guarantor of man's ideals, certainly not of the democratic ideal. But neither is it the enemy of human ideals. Man's friends and enemies are other men. To forget this is to go from natural piety to superstition. . . . Democracy needs no cosmic support other than the *chance* to make good. That chance it has, because man is part of nature. To ask for more is unreasonable, even if it is not unworthy. The way in which man acts upon his chances is additional evidence of the objective possibilities and novelties of existence. In so far as he is caught up in the flux of things, the intelligent democratic man honestly confronts the potentialities of existence, its futurities, its openness, its indeterminateness. He is free from the romantic madness which would seek to outlaw the truths of science and of the quaint conceit, permissible only as poetry, that nature is a democratic republic. He takes the world as science describes it. He employs his knowledge of the world to increase man's power over things, to decrease man's power over man, and to enlarge the fellowship of free and equal persons striving to achieve a more just and happier society.[8]

Sources

CHAPTER XVII: NATURALISM AND DEMOCRACY

The selections from Sidney Hook are taken from his book, HERESY, YES—CONSPIRACY, NO (The John Day Company, New York, 1953), denoted here as "H": and from his articles, "Naturalism and Democracy," in NATURAL-

ISM AND THE HUMAN SPIRIT (edited by Y. Krikorian, Columbia University Press, New York, 1944), denoted as "N"; "The Desirable and the Emotive in Dewey's Ethics" in JOHN DEWEY: PHILOSOPHER OF SCIENCE AND FREEDOM (edited by S. Hook, The Dial Press, New York, 1950), denoted as "D"; and "Religion and the Intellectuals" in *Partisan Review* (New York, March, 1950), denoted as "P".

[1] N, pages 40-42; page 32, lines 1-4.

[2] *Ibid.*, page 45, lines 1-30.

[3] P, page 226, lines 6-20; pages 228-229; page 230, lines 1-12.

[4] *Ibid.*, page 231, lines 18-38.

[5] N, page 56, lines 34-36; page 49, lines 3-15; page 57, lines 28-38; page 58; page 59, lines 1-9.

[6] D, page 213, lines 7-36; page 214, lines 1-14; page 215, lines 27-36; page 216, lines 1-2.

[7] H, page 18, lines 6-15 and 28-30; page 19, lines 7-34; page 20, lines 1-4 and 8-19; page 21, lines 9-35; page 22, lines 1-14; page 35, lines 20-29; page 36, lines 11-19.

[8] N, page 64, lines 5-28.

CHAPTER XVIII

KARL JASPERS (1883–   )

Karl Jaspers is one of the founders of German Existentialism. After professional training in medicine and a successful career in psychiatry, he turned to philosophy and established himself as the leading Professor of Philosophy in Germany. In 1937 he was dismissed from his Professorship at the University of Heidelberg by the Nazis because his wife was Jewish. Forbidden to teach or publish, Jaspers lived in retirement from 1937 to 1945, when the American Army of Occupation arrived and truly liberated the Jaspers from the perpetual threat of destruction under which they had existed. Jaspers was much sought after for advice by the American authorities and soon was reinstated at Heidelberg as Rektor (President) of the University. Since 1948 he has been Professor of Philosophy at the University of Basel, Switzerland.

In 1950 Jaspers announced that he prefers to be considered "a philosopher of reason" rather than a "philosopher of existence," because the task of philosophy in our times is to further the cause of reason as opposed to the antireason and all fanaticisms and exclusive supposedly "final" systems of thought. Jaspers has always maintained that existentialism rests on awareness that our existence proper is founded upon something that transcends it, a characteristic human striving beyond itself, and that reason completes the nature of that striving. In Jaspers' words: "We know that we are all at the mercy of events outside our control. But within this destiny to which we are bound to submit, man wants to try, nevertheless, in his own power of decision, to live a life of Reason, to experience selfhood and meaning with the aid of Reason." Jaspers confesses that while reason had been present as a value in all of his earlier writings, he was instigated to work out the elaboration, even the glorification, of reason, by the

320

"realities of National Socialism in Germany." But Jaspers is also prepared to admit that his faith, nonecclesiastical but biblical in metaphysical origin, is the supporting element in his thinking.

Jaspers has produced a sizable corpus of writings, and used the years
of his retirement for reflection and writing. He writes: "When in
1938 a young friend said to me: Why are you writing, it can never
be published anyway, and one day all of your manuscripts will be
burned, I replied playfully: One never knows, I enjoy writing; what
I am thinking becomes clearer in the process; and finally, in case the
overthrow should occur someday, I do not wish to stand there with
empty hands."

His earliest work, first printed in 1913 and revised in 1919, *Psy-
chologie der Weltanschauungen*, marks the transition in his interest
from psychology to philosophy, and describes the attitudes and world
views in which the mental life of the individual takes place, the mental frames which represent "what is ultimate and complete in man,
both subjectively as experience, power and conviction, and objectively
as the formed world of objects." His most systematic work, in three
volumes, is his *Philosophie*, published in Germany in 1932. A monumental study of existentialist logic, *Philosophische Logik*, appeared
in 1947. But Jaspers is widely known to English-reading circles by his
wide-ranging philosophical essays, such as *Existentialism and Humanism*, *Reason and Anti-Reason in Our Time*, *The Perennial Scope of
Philosophy*, and *The Origin and Goal of History*.

Karl Jaspers was born in Oldenburg, Germany, on February 23,
1883, of an upper-class "conservative-liberal" family. Now, in his mid-
seventies, he reflects on "Age": "Having become aged the thinker
feels himself less than ever at the end. Kant said: when we are precisely so far along that we can truly begin, then we must withdraw
and leave the matter again in the hands of a beginner. . . . But the
expansive power of reason is not enclosed in the biological circle of
life. One may get into the mood—paradoxical for old age—that, by
virtue of one's spiritual experiences, the vision opens to new distances."

A NEW HUMANISM
—
KARL JASPERS

1. *An Era of Radical Change*

We all of us are aware that our era has altered the course of history more radically than any other era known to us. It seems comparable to the unknown age in which the first fire was kindled, in which tools were invented, in which the earliest states were established. The new facts are: modern technology with its consequences for man's working methods and for society,—the unity of the globe created by modern communications, which have made the earth smaller than for example the *orbis terrarum* of Roman days,—the absolute limit represented by the smallness of our planet—the antinomies of freedom and effective action, personality and mass, world order and imperium—the crucial importance of the increased population, transformed from nations into masses, seemingly enabled to understand and participate in developments, but actually transformed into slaves to be made use of—the breakdown of all past ideals of order and the need for finding a new human order to save us from mounting chaos—the questionableness of all traditional values, which must prove themselves or be changed—and further: the concrete political situation, determined by the world powers, the United States and Russia—an internally torn Europe, diminishing in size and thus far unable to find itself—the awakening of the vast masses of Asia, on their way to becoming crucial factors of political power.

The course of events has led us from an era of bourgeois contentment, progress, education, which pointed to the historical past as proof that it had achieved security, into an age of devastating wars, mass death and mass murder (accompanied by an inexhaustible generation of new masses), of the most terrible sense of menace, an age in which humanity is being extinguished and chaotic disintegration seems to be the master of all things.

Is all this a spiritual revolution, or is it an essentially external process, arising from technology and its consequences?—A catastrophe and an immense, as yet unclear possibility, something which will be merely destructive until man awakens and becomes able to react to it, until, instead of unconsciously renouncing, he discovers himself amid the utterly new conditions of his existence?

The picture of the future is more uncertain and unclear, but perhaps both more promising and more hopeless than ever before. If I am aware of the task of humanity, not with regard to the immediate requirements of existence, but with regard to eternal truth, I must inquire concerning the state of philosophy. What should philosophy do in the present world situation?

Today there is a de facto nihilism in numerous forms. Men have appeared, who seem to have abandoned all inwardness, for whom nothing seems to have any value, who stagger through a world of accident from moment to moment, who die with indifference and kill with indifference,—but who seem to live in intoxicating quantitative conceptions, in blind interchangeable fanaticisms, driven by elemental, irrational, overpowering and yet quickly passing emotions, and ultimately by the instinctual urge for the pleasure of the moment.

If we listen to the words that are uttered amid this tumult, they seem like a veiled preparation for death. Mass education has made men blind and thoughtless, capable of everything in their drunkenness, until finally they accept death and killing, mass death in mechanized warfare as a matter of course.

But the most lucid philosophy also aims at enabling man to face death. Philosophy seeks to find a basis on which death is to be sure not intellectually accepted, but borne in the turmoil of suffering, not with stoicism, but with a loving and confident imperturbability.[1]

2. The Present Mission of Philosophy

There is a widespread public opinion which looks on philosophy as at least superfluous; for philosophy is held to be blind to the present, its forces and movements. What is the use of philosophy? it is asked. Philosophy does not help. Plato was unable to help the Greeks, he didn't save them from going under, in fact he contributed indirectly to their decline.

All negations of philosophy originate in something outside of philosophy, either in some definite content of faith that might be endangered by philosophy, or in practical aims for which philosophy is useless, or in a nihilism that rejects everything, and hence also philosophy, as worthless.

But in philosophical effort something takes place that is not seen by all those who reject it: in it man rediscovers his primal source. In this sense, philosophy is absolute and without aim. It can neither be justified through something else, nor on the basis of utility for any purpose. It is not a girder to support us or a straw to grasp at. No one can have philosophy at his disposal. No one can use it as a means.

We venture to assert that philosophy cannot cease as long as men are living. Philosophy upholds the aspiration to attain the meaning of life beyond all worldly purposes,—to make manifest the meaning that embraces all these purposes,—cutting in a sense across life to fulfill this meaning by actual realization,—to serve the future by our own actuality,—never to debase man or a man to the level of a mere instrument.

The aim of philosophy is at all times to achieve the *independence* of man as an individual. This he gains by establishing a relation to authentic being. He gains independence of everything that happens in the world by the depth of his attachment to transcendence. What Lao Tse found in the Tao, Socrates in the divine mission and in knowledge, Jeremiah in Yahweh who revealed himself to him, what Boethius, Bruno, Spinoza knew: that was what made them independent. This philosophical independence must be confused neither with the sovereign arbitrariness of libertinism, nor with the vital energy that defies death.

At all times the task is marked by this *contradiction:* independence is to be found in aloofness from the world, in renunciation and solitude—or in the world itself, through the world, participating in the world, but without succumbing to it. Then the philosopher, who desires his freedom only with the freedom of others, his life only in communication with men, is what the fool called Confucius: "That is the man who knows it's impossible and yet carries on"—a truth applying to the finite knowledge that absolutizes its phenomenality, but a truth that does not shake the profounder truth of philosophical faith.

Philosophy addresses itself to the individual. In every world, in every situation philosophical endeavor throws the individual back upon himself. For only he who is himself—and can prove himself in solitude—can truly enter into communication.

Now, can we, within these enduring tasks of philosophy which I have formulated, say something of its present mission?

We have heard that faith in reason is at an end. The great step taken in the twentieth century, it is said, is the falling away from the *logos,* the idea of a world order. Some exult in the consciousness that life has been liberated—others castigate this great betrayal of the mind, this catastrophe that must lead to the destruction of humanity.

On this point it can be said that the step in question implies an element of truth, because it destroyed the self-assurance of an intelligence forsaken by reason, unmasked the illusion of a world harmony, ended our reliance in the rule of law and in laws as such. These were high-sounding words behind which was hidden the sordidness of a life that was disclosed by psychoanalysis. This psychotherapeutic movement broadened into a pseudophilosophy which took its partial truth from its relation to and dependence on a corrupt age.

When all this is sloughed off, the root lies bare. The root is the primal source from which we grew and which we had forgotten in the tangle of opinions, habits, ideological formulas.

Today our task is to find in existence itself a new foundation for reason. That is the urgent task in the spiritual situation defined by Kierkegaard and Nietzsche, Pascal and Dostoyevsky.

Its fulfillment cannot consist in the restoration of what has been. Today it would seem to imply the following elements:

1. We seek peace of mind by keeping ourselves constantly alert.

2. We pass through nihilism to the assimilation of our tradition.

3. We seek the purity of the sciences as a premise for the truth of our philosophy.

4. Reason becomes a boundless desire for communication.[2]

3. *Peace of Mind*

Peace of mind is the aim of philosophical thought.

Amid the greatest devastation, we should like to be certain of what remains, for that is everlasting.—In distress we reflect upon our primal source.—Amid the threat of death, we seek a thought that will make us steadfast.

Even today philosophy can give us what Parmenides knew when he built a shrine to the god in thanksgiving for the peace of mind that had come to him through philosophy. But today there is so much complacency.

It is a terrifying fact that today, despite all the upheaval and devastation, we are still in danger of living and thinking as though nothing really important had happened. It is as though a great misfortune had merely disturbed the good life of us poor victims, but as though life might now be continued in the old way. It is as though nothing had happened. Fearful or helpless or enraged at the moment, we accuse others. Anyone who feels in this way is still caught in snares that make possible only a delusive peace of mind. This peace must be transformed into unpeace. For the great danger is that what has happened may pass, considered as nothing but a great misfortune, without anything happening to us men as men, without our hearing the voice of transcendence, without our attaining to any insight and acting with insight. A tremendous decrease in clear awareness would then cause us to sink into a narrowed existence.[3]

4. *From Nihilism to Tradition*

If we refuse to be complacent, it means that nihilism is actual as a possibility of our own experience. We know the decay of valid norms, we know how precarious the world becomes when no faith, no collective self-consciousness commands adherence. A few men had such experience even in Nietzsche's time, some have had it since 1933, others more recently, but today there is scarcely a thoughtful man who has not had it. Perhaps we are now coming to the point at which we are ready to hear the message conveyed by all historical epochs of cultural breakdown, the call of their thinkers. Nihilism, as intellectual movement and as historical experience, becomes a transition to a profounder assimilation of historic tradition. From an early time, nihilism has not only been the road to the primal source—nihilism is as old as philosophy—but also the acid in which the gold of truth must be proved.

From the beginning there has been something irreplaceable in philosophy. Through all the change in human circumstances and the tasks of practical life, through all the progress of the sciences, all the development of the categories and methods of thought, it is forever concerned with apprehending the one eternal truth under new conditions, with new methods and perhaps with greater possibilities of clarity.

It is our task today, amid the most extreme nihilism, to ascertain this truth once more. This presupposes that we assimilate our tradition: it is not enough that we know it externally, that we merely contemplate it; we must possess it inwardly as our very own.

To achieve this, philosophy proper must, among other things, reject the idea of progress, which is sound for the sciences and the implements of philosophy. The advocates of this idea falsely believed that what comes later must supplant what comes earlier, as inferior, as merely a step to further progress, as having only historical interest. In this conception the new as such is mistaken for the true. Through the discovery of this novelty, one feels oneself to be at the summit of history. This was the basic attitude of many philosophers of past centuries. Over and over again they believed that they had transcended the whole past by means of something utterly new, and that thereby the time had finally come to inaugurate the true philosophy. . . .

To tear oneself away from the historical fundament in favor of something new, to make use of history as a quarry, from which to take material for arbitrary interpretations, that is a road that leads into the abyss of nihilism. . . . But . . . nilihism will, by a painful operation, bring us back to the authentic truth.

Out of nihilism there was born a new fundamental approach which teaches us to take a different view of the history of philosophy. Three thousand years of the history of philosophy become as a single present. The diverse philosophical structures contain within themselves the one truth. Hegel was the first who strove to understand the unity of this thought, but he still looked on everything that had gone before as a preliminary stage and partial truth leading up to his own philosophy. But the essential thing is that we assimilate the philosophical attainments of every epoch by remaining in constantly renewed communication with the great achievements of the past, looking upon them not as transcended but as actual.

If we succeed in establishing a loving contact with all philosophical thought, then we know that our present form of philosophy also stems from the primal source, we know how indispensable is the universal tradition, the memory without which we would sink into the nothingness of a mere moment without past and future. In our temporal transience we know the actuality and simultaneity of essential truth, of the *philosophia perennis* which at all times effaces time.[4]

5. Modern Science and Philosophy

The premise of the technology that is revolutionizing our lives is modern science. But the effects of this science extend much farther. This science represents a profound turning point in the history of mankind, but unlike technology, it is fully known only to few men, and even fewer actively participate in it, whereas the mass of mankind goes on living in pre-scientific forms of thought and makes use of the results of science as formerly primitive peoples made use of European top hats, Prince Alberts and glass beads.

After the crude beginnings made by men of earlier epochs, particularly the Greeks, it has been the modern era, since the end of the Middle Ages, that first applied really unlimited inquiry, accompanied by boundless self-criticism, to everything that happens and can happen in the world.

Science proceeds methodically, it postulates universal acceptance, and in so far as this is the case, it does in fact obtain unanimous consent; it is critically aware of its methods, it systematically verifies the whole of its inventory at all times, it is never finished, but lives in a state of progress whose goal is unforeseeable. Whatever is manifested in the world, science makes into its object. It sharpens and clarifies our consciousness of the existent, and it provides the premises for the practical realization of goals that it does not prescribe, but which in turn become an object of its inquiry.

Science is a necessary precondition of philosophy. But the spiritual situation that has arisen as a result of science has presented philosophy with difficult new tasks. Former epochs were not as clearly aware of the urgency of these tasks as we are.

1. Science must be made absolutely *pure*. For in practical operation and average thinking, it is shot through with nonscientific assertions and attitudes. Pure and strict science in its applica-

tion to the whole sphere of the existent has been magnificently achieved by individual scientists, but on the whole our spiritual life is far removed from it.

2. *Superstitious belief in science* must be exposed to the light of day. In our era of restless unbelief, men have snatched at science as a supposedly firm foundation, set their faith in so-called scientific findings, blindly subjected themselves to supposed experts, believed that the world as a whole could be put in order by scientific planning, expected science to provide life aims, which science can never offer,—and expected a knowledge of being as a whole, which is beyond the scope of science.

3. *Philosophy itself must be methodically re-clarified.* It is science in the age-old and enduring sense of methodical thought, but it is not science in the pure modern sense of an inquiry into things, leading to universally valid, cogent knowledge, identical for all.

The fallacious identification of philosophy and science by Descartes, a misconception in keeping with the spirit of these last centuries, has made science into supposedly total knowledge and has ruined philosophy.

Today the purity of philosophy must be gained along with the purity of science. The two are inseparable, but they are not the same thing; philosophy is neither a specialized science along with others, nor a crowning science resulting from the others, nor a foundation-laying science by which the others are secured.

Philosophy is bound to science and thinks in the medium of all sciences. Without the purity of scientific truth, the truth of philosophy is inaccessible.

Science has its own realm and is guided by philosophical ideas which grow up in all the sciences, though they themselves can never be scientifically justified.

The modern aspiration for consciousness of truth has become possible only on the basis of the sciences of the last century, but it has not yet been achieved. The work required for its realization is among the most urgent needs of the present historical moment.

In opposition to the disintegration of science into unrelated specialties, in opposition to the scientific superstition of the masses, in opposition to the superficiality brought upon philosophy by the confusion of science and philosophy,—scientific research and philosophy must join hands to guide us on the path of authentic truth.[5]

6. *Faith in Boundless Communication*

Through the secure validity of a common principle that permeated all everyday life, there was, almost until the present time, a cohesion among men which rarely permitted communication to become a special problem. People could content themselves with the saying: we can pray together, but not talk together. Today, when we can not even pray together, we are at length becoming fully aware that humanity implies unreserved communication among men.

Manifested being is fragmented by the multiplicity of our sources of faith, and of the historical form of our communities, each with its own special background. The only things we have identically in common are science and technology as reflected in the general categories of the understanding. These however are united only in an abstract, universal consciousness; in practice they serve both as weapons and media of communication.

Everything real in man is historical. But historicity means also multiple historicity. Hence the postulates of true communication are:

1. to become concerned with the historically different without becoming untrue to one's own historicity—

2. to reveal the relativity of scientific truth, while fully recognizing its just claims—

3. to abandon the claim of faith to exclusivity because of the breach of communication it implies, yet without losing the absoluteness of one's own fundament—

4. to take up the inevitable struggle with the historically different, but to sublimate the battle in the loving battle, in communication through the truth that develops when men act in common, not as abstract individuals—

5. to orient ourselves toward the depths that are disclosed only with the division into manifold historicities, to one of which I belong, but which all concern me and which all together guide me to that source.

Philosophical faith is inseparable from complete openness to communication. For authentic truth arises only where faiths meet in the presence of the Comprehensive. Hence it is true that only believers can realize communication.—On the other hand, untruth grows out of the fixation of contents of faith that merely repel one another. Hence it is impossible to talk with fanatics. Philosophical faith sees deviltry in every compulsion to break off communication and in every desire to break off communication.

This philosophical faith in communication has been called utopian. Its critics argue that men are not so. They are moved by their passions, their will to power, their competing practical interests. Communication nearly always fails, and most certainly fails with the mass of men. The best solution, according to this view, is to subordinate men to conventions and laws, which serve to veil the general indiscipline and villainy, both of which exclude communication. To expect too much of men is the best way to ruin them.

In answer to this we may say:

1. Men are not as they are; they themselves remain question and task: all total judgments concerning them say more than we can know.

2. Communication in every form is so much a part of man as man in the very depth of his being, that it must always remain possible and one can never know how far it will go.

3. The will to boundless communication is not a program but the very essence of philosophical faith—and from it stem the

particular purposes and methods of communication at all its levels.

4. Boundless openness to communication is not the consequence of any knowledge, it is the decision to follow a human road. The idea of communication is not utopia, but faith. Each man is confronted with the question whether he strives toward it, whether he believes in it, not as in something other-worldly, but as in something utterly actual: whether he believes in our potentiality really to live together, to speak together, through this togetherness to find our way to the truth, and hereby finally to become authentically ourselves.[6]

7. *The Present as the Turning-Point of the Ages*

Today, for the first time, there is a real unity of mankind which consists in the fact that nothing essential can happen anywhere that does not concern all. In this situation the technological revolution effected by the Europeans through science and discoveries is merely the material basis and precipitating cause of the spiritual catastrophe. . . .

Out of this experience of our historical situation as the turning-point of the ages, our gaze returns again and again. To the question: have such radical metamorphoses taken place before? our answer was: we know nothing of the event of the Promethean Age, when man first came into possession of his world through tools, fire and speech. But within history the greatest turning-point was the Axial Period . . . .[7] [This is] the period around 500 B.C., in the spiritual process that occurred between 800 and 200 B.C. It is there that we meet with the most deepcut dividing line in history. Man, as we know him today, came into being. . . .

The most extraordinary events are concentrated in this period. Confucius and Lao-tse were living in China, all the schools of Chinese philosophy came into being, including those of Mo-ti, Chuang-tse, Lieh-tsu and a host of others; India produced the Upanishads and Buddha and, like China, ran the whole gamut of philosophical possibilities down to scepticism, to materialism, sophism and nihilism; in Iran Zarathustra taught a challenging view of the world as a struggle between good and evil; in Palestine the prophets made their appearance, from Elijah, by way of Isaiah and Jeremiah to Deutero-Isaiah; Greece witnessed the appearance of Homer, of the philosophers—Parmenides, Heraclitus and Plato—of the tragedians, Thucydides and Archimedes. Everything implied by these names developed during these few centuries almost simultaneously in China, India, and the West, without any one of these regions knowing of the others.

What is new about this age, in all three areas of the world, is that man becomes conscious of Being as a whole, of himself and his limitations. He experiences the terror of the world and his own powerlessness. He asks radical questions. Face to face with the void he strives for liberation and redemption. By consciously recognising his limits he sets himself the highest goals. He experiences absoluteness in the depths of selfhood and in the lucidity of transcendence.[8]

If we have now entered into a new radical metamorphosis of humanity, this is no repetition of the Axial Period, but a happening that is different to its very roots.

First of all *outwardly*. Our Age of Technology is not merely relatively universal, like the events in those three mutually independent worlds of the Axial Period, but absolutely universal, because it is planetary. It is not a process that is mutually related in meaning, yet separate in fact; it is a single whole in continual mutual intercourse. Today it is taking place with consciousness of universality. It is bound to bring a different decision concerning humanity from the one that was reached then. For whereas all previous periods of crucial change were local and susceptible of being supplemented by other happenings, in other places, in other worlds, so that even if they failed the possibility of the salvation of man by other movements was left open, what is happening now is absolutely decisive. There is no longer anything outside it.

Inwardly, however, something manifestly quite different from

the Axial Period is involved. Then the plenitude, now the emptiness. If we become aware of the turning-point, we know that we
are only in the preparatory stage. The present age is one of real
technological and political remoulding, not yet of eternal spiritual creations. We may more readily liken ourselves, with our
grandiose scientific discoveries and technological inventions, to
the epoch of the invention of tools and weapons, of the first use
of domestic animals and horses, than with the age of Confucius,
Buddha and Socrates. The fact that we are tackling the high task
of reconstructing humanity from its origin, that we sense the fateful question as to how we can, in faith, become specifically human beings, is, however, evinced in the current tendency, which
is becoming increasingly strong, to look back toward our origin.
The deep matrix from which we sprang, the specific reality which
was concealed by the veil of secondary cultural constructions,
turns of phrase, conventions and institutions, is to become articulate once more. In this process of self-understanding through the
knowledge of whence we come the mirror of the great Axial
Period of humanity will perhaps, once more, prove one of the
essential assurances.[9]

8. *Future Possibilities: World Empire or World Order*

All the phenomena of the present have the appearance of a
preparatory struggle for the points of departure of the final battle
for the planetary order. Contemporary world politics are seeking
a basis for the ultimate settlement, whether this is to be reached
by military or peaceful means. Until this has been achieved, all
conditions and power relationships are temporary. . . .

The question is, along what path will the unitary world order
be attained. It might take place along the desperate road of force,
as, in the words of Bismarck, the unity of Germany could be
achieved only by 'blood and iron.' Or it might take place
through an order arising by negotiation out of maturing understanding in mutuality, in the same way as, in the eighteenth century, the States of North America found their way to union at

the cost of abrogating an essential part of their particular sovereignty in favour of the sovereignty of the whole.

The shape of the order would, in the first case, be the static peace of despotism, in the second case, a peaceful community of all subject to transmutation in perennial democratic unrest and self-rectification. Reducing the possibilities to a simple antithesis, therefore, the issue is between the path to world empire or the path to world order.

World empire. This is world peace through a single power, which coerces all from one point on the earth. It maintains itself by the use of force. It moulds the levelled masses by terror and total planning. A uniform world view is forced upon all, in simple outlines, by propaganda. Censorship and direction of spiritual activity compel the latter to play its part in the plan of the moment, which may be modified at any time.

World order. This is unity without unifying force other than that afforded by common decision in negotiation. Orders agreed upon can only be altered along the legally fixed path by new decisions. The supremacy of this procedure and of majority decisions has been accepted in common; it guarantees the common rights of all, which also protect those who are for the time being in a minority; these rights remain an order of mankind in movement and self-rectification.

. . . World order, with the abolition of absolute sovereignty, would mean the abolition of the old concept of the State in favour of mankind. The outcome would not be a World State (that would be a world empire), but an order, perennially reestablished in negotiation and decision, of States governing themselves within legally restricted domains: an all-embracing federalism.[10]

9. *The Faith of the Future*

If it be deemed improbable that a world order will develop without unity of faith, I venture to assert the reverse. The universality of a world order obligatory to all (in contrast to a world empire) is possible *only* when the multiple contents of faith remain free in their historical communication, without the unity of an objective, universally valid doctrinal content. The common element of all faith in relation to world order can only be that everyone desires the ordering of the foundations of existence, in a world community in which he has room to evolve with the peaceful means of the spirit.

... There is in us an insufficiency, something resembling waiting, resembling readiness. Philosophy is incomplete and must remain aware of the fact, if it is not to slip into fallacy. We are wandering in the obscurity of the future, on guard against the enemies of truth, incapable of relinquishing our own thinking nescience in obedience to an imposed knowledge—but above all ready to hear and see when fulfilling symbols and profound thoughts once more illumine the path of life.

In this process, philosophising will in any case accomplish an essential task. It will repay us thoughtfully to resist the absurdities, falsifications and perversions, the claim to exclusive possession of historical truth, and blind intolerance. Philosophy leads us along the road to the point at which love acquires its depth in real communication. Then in this love, through the success of communication, the truth that links us together will be disclosed to those who are most remote in the diversity of their historical origin.

Today individuals are palpable. He who would like to live in the unclosed and unorganised and unorganisable community of authentic human beings—in what used to be called the invisible Church—does in fact live today as an individual in alliance with individuals scattered over the face of the earth, an alliance that survives every disaster, a dependability that is not fixed by any pact or specific imperative. He lives in complete insufficiency, but in a communal insufficiency, and obdurately seeks with others the right road within this world and not outside it. These individuals meet one another, exhort and encourage one another. They repudiate the modern combination of eccentric faith contents with the practice of a nihilistic realism. They know that the task imposed upon man is to realise in this world that which is possible to man, and that this possibility is not a single and solitary one. But every individual must know where he stands and for what he will work. It is as though everyone were charged by the Deity to work and live for boundless openness, authentic reason, truth and love and fidelity, without the recourse to force that is typical of the States and Churches in which we have to live and whose insufficiency we should like to oppose.[11]

10. *What Remains Essentially Valuable?*

What remains essential in view of the possible speedy end of everything we love?—What are the criteria that still hold good when the end of everything is approaching?

It seems to us to be beneath human dignity to waver between a destructive fear—which inhibits all activity—and a self-forgetful and blinkered ease in which old habits of thought continue, in which the intellectual life is no longer directed by Eros but an aimless thoughtless busyness is its only content, and work is done solely for the sake of work, regardless of the cause it ultimately serves.

The task of Reason in the face of this menace is to endure the tension, to do what is essential, to submit its daily life to the illuminated criteria, indefatigably to continue an activity that is inevitably only possible on a long-term basis. No one knows whether it will lead to success, or whether failure is its true meaning and end. But in an apparently hopeless situation Reason will never lose all hope. All those who work in the world of the mind must say to themselves: So long as I remain alive in the midst of terrible events, I intend to be prepared, to the best of my ability. I am trying to build up a life of inner activity with a goal that was set by my good genius, that is not wholly clear but is clear in respect to the step that has to be taken today under the actual conditions of my life.

It is our duty to fill the present time with a content. Time is not given us to neglect. Only in a fully lived present can there be a meaning for the future. Without our planning, the fact that we do what we can in the present makes the future possible.

But if the knowable realities of human life tempt us to doubt Reason, then taking our criterion from these realities, we may rather say: it is a miracle that philosophy continues its way through history, that it has never completely disappeared since it first came on the scene, that there is a power of self-preservation in Reason which is realised repeatedly as freedom. Reason is like an open secret that can become known to anyone at any time; it is the quiet space into which everyone can enter through his own thought.[12]

Sources
—

CHAPTER XVIII: A NEW HUMANISM

The selections from Karl Jaspers are taken from three recent books: *The Perennial Scope of Philosophy* (Philosophical Library, New York, 1949), denoted here as "P"; *The Origin and Goal of History* (Yale University Press, New Haven, 1953), denoted as "O"; and *Reason and Anti-Reason in Our Time* (Yale University Press, New Haven, 1952), denoted as "R."

[1] P, "The Philosophy of the Future": page 158, lines 9-29; page 159; page 160, lines 1-27.

[2] *Ibid.*, page 164, line 29; page 165; page 166, lines 15-29; page 167; page 168, lines 1-27.

[3] *Ibid.*, page 169, lines 2-29; page 170, lines 1-2.

[4] *Ibid.*, page 173; page 174, lines 1-19; page 175, lines 20-24; page 176, lines 1-28.

[5] *Ibid.*, page 177, lines 2-29; page 178; page 179; page 180, lines 1-2.

[6] *Ibid.*, page 180, lines 5-28; page 181; page 182; page 183, lines 1-4.

[7] O, "The Present Situation of the World": page 139, lines 21-26 and 34-40.

[8] O, "The Axial Period": page 1, lines 29-32; page 2, lines 1-23.

[9] O, "The Present Situation of the World": page 139, lines 41-46; page 140, lines 1-33.

[10] O, "The Future": page 196, lines 9-14 and 22-43; page 197, lines 1-8 and 43-44; page 198, lines 1-5.

[11] O, *ibid.*, page 227, lines 15-24 and 33-44; page 228, lines 1-26.

[12] R, page 90, lines 23-26; pages 91-92.

PHILOSOPHY FOR OUR TIME

CHAPTER XIX

REASON AND VALUES

The Philosophical Perspectives

The philosophical perspectives that have been presented are philosophies of freedom, of faith in the human person. All the writers share a common concern over the fate of man in our time. They agree that there is a profound and unique crisis, profound because it may end in the death of our civilization, unique because it threatens human existence itself. Even if the balance of mutual terror can be delicately maintained between the great thermonuclear and intercontinental powers to prevent a total war, the human aspects of our existence would still be imperiled. The tremendous technical and political forces which are now sweeping the world may mechanize or enslave man if they do not kill him. Whereas past philosophy could project the universality of reason and the humanity of all men in an abstract way, the philosophy of our day must be more concrete to deal with these matters. For we have seen reason used for evil, to defeat, dehumanize, and destroy man. And we have been forced to recognize the diverse types, conditions, and aspirations of men over a world made indivisible by technology, though still deeply divided in many important ways. The imperious issue confronting us today is whether reason can employ the new political and technological means to promote the ends of the human person, his existence, and his freedom. This theme runs through all the different philosophies that have been presented.

Differences exist in the treatment of this theme, owing to

differences of emphasis, mode of expression, and cultural background. Forster, Silone, and Sartre naturally respond to the immediate qualitative and aesthetic components of personal
existence, but with overtones that are unmistakably English,
Italian, or French. Einstein, Russell, and Hook tend to give
greater importance to the more social aspects of a liberating life
of reason, yet again with characteristic accents that recall the
differences of German-American, English, and American culture. Buber, Maritain, and Niebuhr differ from both these groups
by their preoccupation with religion, and among themselves by
the different faiths they adhere to, as well as by the fact that they
are German-Israeli, French, and American respectively. Many
other differences coexist with similarities: for example, both
Silone and Einstein, after taking quite different routes in their
lives and thought, both arrive at some sort of belief in anti-
Nazism and Socialism—but Silone, who had known international
Communism at firsthand, could put not an iota of trust in Soviet
Russia, whereas Einstein, whose approach had always been paci-
fistic, idealistic, and peripheral to his central study, in his last
years tended to put more trust in its protestations of peace and
to think the United States was more culpable (because then
more powerful) in the cold war which prevailed. Or, one other
example only, both Sartre and Jaspers are in some sense identified as "Existentialists," but the French philosopher is an atheist
and the German philosopher a transcendentalist.

2. *Philosophy and Religion*

There is one most important difference, however, among these
philosophers that should be explored. It is the difference between
those philosophers who accept religion in one of its organized
forms as fundamental and those who can not accept organized
religion on philosophical grounds. Although both groups give
primacy to the human person as the bearer of values, and recognize reason as a distinctive mark of humanity, they disagree on
the role of reason and the grounds for values. Simply put, the

former group contends that revelation gives a "higher" truth than reason and that values ultimately derive their validity from the relationship between man and God. The other group holds that no limits should be placed on the scope of human reason and that values can only be given warrant by the use of reason. From this difference flows a basic variation in accounting for the origin and nature of the crisis. The first group believes that the crisis arises from man's unbelief and the arrogance of reason that puts itself in place of God, while the other group sees it as due to man's failure to exercise his reason in his personal and social relations. Because this split goes to the heart of the issues presented in the book, and the philosophical defense of freedom, it should be examined in some detail.

The first position is the classic religious thesis about the relations between values and reason. This view holds that values cannot be given warrant by reason, because reasoning is ultimately about experience of facts and things and discriminates relationships between means and consequences in the external world. Values, on the other hand, always involve some reference to the human person and thus are concerned, not simply with things or means, but with human ends. Proponents of this view also urge that human ends are of the greatest import to man and that there is a "higher" type of knowledge which is anchored in the relation of man to God or Reality. Only this relationship gives warrant, validity, truth, to our personal values and to the politics of freedom. According to this view, it is the presumed ultimacy of science as the only valid form of knowledge that has led to the secularization of modern life, to the technical depersonalization of man, and to that mechanization of the state in our time which has burdened history with its concentration camps, secret police, and political purges. If we are to avoid the mass man and the mass state, it is asserted that we must return to the Hebrew-Greek-Christian tradition and find the absolute ground for the politics of freedom in unconditioned Being or God.

It would be a mistake to consider these views as quaintly old-fashioned or as merely irrational reactions to the crisis. They are gaining new support and influence not only from those who are brought up in a particular church but also among many who allowed their faith to languish or who never had any faith. This growing support is partly a reaction to the position taken by some of the leading spokesmen for the scientific tradition who reject values as having no grounds in reason. Such an attitude is deeply unsatisfying to all who believe that there is a real difference between a preference for coffee over tea and a preference for freedom over slavery. The proponents of the religious view have shown a concern for many of the primary values that move men, the integrity and dignity of the human person, that each person is an end of infinite worth and never simply a statistic. In a world which has become more mechanized, they have continued to bind up the wounds of the afflicted and have brought fellowship to lost souls in a rootless community. They have recognized the prevalence of evil and warned that *human* progress cannot be equated with the multiplication of material things. They have claimed that the Judaeo-Christian tradition underlies, even though often unacknowledged, the moral values associated with secular humanism and liberalism. Finally, they would maintain that the Socratic mission of caring for the soul has been practically abdicated by others, and that therefore the philosophic quest and the pastoral mission are one in modern practice.

The key philosophical issue in this position is the claim that science can treat only of the relations between means and ends, and that reason must be equated with science. If this be true, then human ends cannot be appraised by reason. Yet this is accepted as true by a wide public, partly because of the influence of two schools of philosophical thought—Historical Materialism and Logical Empiricism. Since they are not represented by selections in this volume, further comment is useful.

3. *Philosophy and Science—Historical Materialism*

Historical Materialism, as we saw in Chapter I, is the Marxist philosophy of history. Marx claimed to have found historical laws of motion that are on a theoretical par with the Newtonian laws of motion. The discovery of these laws makes prediction possible and history a science, he thought. The underlying causation of all history arises from the growth of technology and the universality of class struggle. Human action is not really a choice guided by personal ideals, but a necessary consequence of the underlying cause.

In appraising this Marxist position two elements should be discriminated. First, Marx treated moral values as ideological class prejudices. What is considered good is ultimately identified with whether it protects or promotes the position of one's class. But Marx himself was initially moved by a protest against the cruelties of English capitalism and the vision of a free society consequent on the socialization of large-scale technology. Implicit in this personal position is the judgment that freedom is a human value of an ultimate sort, that whatever promotes human freedom is an instrumental good, and that the ultimate instrument is the unhampered growth of technology. Marx somehow assumed that the growth of productivity would in fact lighten man's burden and improve the human condition by permitting greater equality in the disposition of goods, and richer opportunities for life, liberty, and the pursuit of happiness. Clearly, the judgment that freedom is a human value, without which Marx's work loses its basic motivation, is not itself a class prejudice, but an ethical claim, and thus could only have warrant on grounds other than the alleged laws of motion.

Second, Marx makes the growth of technology critical in historical change, but fails to account for *its* growth in history! Growth in technology has always been consequent on growth in knowledge, whether theoretical or practical. Before the rise of modern science, most of the changes were associated with technical innovations due to factors that were largely of a random sort, and thus could not be predicted. Changes in technology since the rise of modern science have also been associated with the growth in basic theory, and no one can predict when such changes in basic theory will take place. Thus, Marx rests his case for prediction in history on ultimately unpredictable factors. With this disappears not only historical inevitability but also the rejection of the human role. For the growth in knowledge, whether pure or practical, always results from the work of a person who has somehow decided not to accept established beliefs or practices and has decided to see whether he can effect a change in them. This makes the unpredictable changes in knowledge dependent on the unpredictable activities of individual human beings. They, by their innovations, bring about some important changes in history and thus serve as creative agents in an otherwise impersonal motion.

The tragic irony of the Marxist position is that its logic has been used against Marx's original ideal of human freedom. The Russian and Chinese Communist rulers have pushed the logic to its extreme by their program of accelerating heavy industry at the cost of human freedom and human lives. Furthermore, the fact that Marx's writings could have such a tremendous influence on modern history would appear to refute the judgment that the human person has no creative role to play in history. The rejection of a creative role and of the personal ideals that may move human beings results in reducing man to the level of a creature. Most important of all, this subordination of human ends to technical means favors a moral climate in which power becomes the supreme good.

4. *Philosophy and Science—Logical Empiricism*

Where Historical Materialism has focused on science as technology and power, the Logical Empiricists have focused on the logical analysis of scientific theory and language. This group is represented in the work of Rudolf Carnap, Hans Reichenbach,

Herbert Feigl, A. J. Ayer, and Charles Stevenson. Among these men there are more or less heated philosophic differences, but there is a consensus that scientific language alone can describe and explain aspects of reality. The kind of truth we find in empirical science is "synthetic" truth, imparting information based upon experience. The truth of logic, in contrast, is "analytic," flowing from definitions or meanings in various implicative relationships. As for ethical language, they claim that it *describes* nothing. Ethical judgments merely indicate personal feelings or attitudes. As a consequence, persuasion and imperative rhetoric are all that moral discourse can provide. By these means, or by parallel emotions and attitudes, values may be shared by other persons. Differences in belief can be resolved by recourse to empirical observation, whereas differences in attitudes can be resolved only by persuasion or by force. Whatever reasoning may appear in discussions about ethical matters can only be an attempt to show what the facts are. All else is rhetorical persuasion that wears the appearance of reasoning but cannot yield up the reality. The equation of a belief-sentence with an attitude-sentence would, from this point of view, commit the "naturalist fallacy."

Those who accept this position claim to have inherited the traditions and disciplines of modern science, to have analyzed the features that make science successful, and to have explained its most novel, up-to-date developments, with the latest instruments of logic and in a comprehensive way, so that one can see the interrelations, the unity of science itself. There is no doubt that such a doctrine is compelling to those minds that want to reject any philosophy that is inconsistent with modern science. It is compelling, first, because it is positive in its attitude; it affirms the obvious success of science as an achievement of human intelligence that goes beyond what is normally accepted by the scientific specialist. Second, because it uses the latest developments of contemporary mathematical logic to account for successful inquiry. Third, even its negative view involving the rejection of religion and traditional philosophy and ethics as so much brave, and at best, expressive nonsense is attractive to those who want to feel that there is a sound, scientific basis for such rejection, without the need for embracing other views. This attraction for young minds must not be overlooked, the feeling of being free to abandon the traditions of the past while charting a course that is open and subject to verification, like science itself. Indeed one should not overlook the prestige value of science in a civilization whose distinctive feature is the central fact of science.

Once one gets beyond the general tenets of logical empiricism, the position becomes paradoxical in three major ways. First, the empiricist roots of the position seem to get lost in quicksand because it is impossible to stipulate by formal means just how to specify synthetic truth. Originally, synthetic truth was apparently certified by direct comparison with experience or by reducing any such truth to another that can be directly compared with experience. But just what is this process of direct comparison with experience? If it involves the direct report of sense data, then what reports can truly be said to have this character; what, indeed, are to be considered sense data, and what is the actual form of any sense-data sentence? Further, if the status of such sense data provides indubitable deliverances of experience, then what becomes of the sharp distinction between the certainty of logical truths and the lack of certainty of synthetic truths? And, finally, if the certification of synthetic truth is only theoretically required as a matter of principle, then when does one perform the reduction in fact, when does one exhibit the genuine credentials of a synthetic truth? The fact is that a scientific statement itself is never directly comparable with experience. For the most part, it is not *about* direct experience, but about physical objects or events. Consequently, the testing of a factual proposition involves hypotheses or inferences which normally preclude any direct and conclusive confrontation of it with what it is about. I might observe that one of the reasons that later positivism and logical analysis have moved away from this position is the evident absurdity of a view that would make it necessary to reject most of the propositions of science, which cannot be confirmed in this manner. Instead, it is quite accurate to say that a proposition can *never* be confirmed directly, because it involves predictions about the future, and the number of derivable predictions is unlimited.

Second, the logical components of logical empiricism now seem to be less a matter of logic and more a matter of pragmatic human choice. This shift is due mainly to developments in the two sciences which have been taken as paragons of science itself, pure mathematics and mathematical physics. In the former case, the mathematician Godel has proved that mathematics contains insoluble logical problems and therefore can never be formalized in any complete system. As a consequence, mathematics is recognized as an essentially human activity like every other, though dealing with formal matters, because it can never reach rock bottom and can never be a finished completed structure. In the case of mathematical physics, Heisenberg's Principle of Indeterminacy has shown that there are real limits to precise measurement and exact prediction in the quantum domain, while Bohr's Principle of Complementarity has shown that such apparently contradictory theories as the wave and the corpuscular theories of the nature of light must both be accepted in practice if we are to take account of different physical aspects of light. As a consequence, the Aristotelian logical principle of noncontradiction, that either proposition A or non-A is true, and not both, is shown to have certain practical limitations. We are thus led back to the grounds of common sense and ordinary gross experience even in the most developed sciences. The upshot is that we must take account of the human observer, and human choice under conditions of practical control to explain the success of the scientific enterprise itself.

This brings us to the logical empiricist rejection of ethics and values as so much pure poetry or personal preference. If we inquire why ethical judgments cannot be rationally tested, we may find the answer in preoccupation with only one type of judgment which employs terms like "good," "ought," and so on. The logical empiricists have been concerned primarily with emotive statements which serve as linguistic signs of our likings and dislikings. Such statements express immediate enjoyments as experiences which are merely had, and no argument can alter the fact of such havings. This is the basic theme of the emotive theory of the meaning of ethical terms, which equates all ethical judgments with emotive sentences in the imperative form. Such an equation fails to recognize the actual complexity of human conduct and the diversity of ethical judgments. The fallacy of logical empiricism in its interpretation of values can be summed up as mistaking one actual use of ethical terms for what are, in fact, plural uses. And when the different uses of ethical terms are analyzed, it would appear that the emotive theory ignores the most important uses which men have employed as inclusive principles to guide their personal and political decisions.

Since the crisis of our time presents us with many unprecedented challenges that call for complex decisions, we must make judgments about our own and other people's political behavior, about available means and preferred human ends. The widespread belief in a gap between reason and values has encouraged some neglect of inquiry in certain areas into what are, in fact, desirable consequences of political action. Professional activity has tended to center on values as data to be measured by various methods of opinion, attitude, and content analysis. Such work requires another sort of inquiry if the values of freedom are to receive maximal support. It is true that the logical empiricists have been for freedom and have promoted democratic attitudes in matters of political and social inquiry. But when democratic attitudes are assumed in a reflex fashion, or taken to be only a group prejudice, they are considerably weakened. In short, they are deprived of any status as warranted values. Those who lack a full awareness of why democracy is really preferable to any alternative set of political values are not likely to examine policy issues in terms of the consequences they entail for well-being.

They are more disposed to envisage policy issues solely in terms of human pressures and prejudices. In this disposition, a weakened adherence to the politics of freedom is more likely to produce advisers on political decisions who concentrate on implementing the attitudes of those in power or of those who are making a bid for power. The result is that political science tends to lose its position as a vital source of information about politics and political wisdom, in appraising the objectives of public policy.

5. *Philosophy and Human Reason*

In this very brief analysis of two powerful schools of "scientific philosophy," it would appear that the religious contention that reason is identical with scientific inquiry, and thus can never appraise human ends, accords with a large body of philosophic, if not scientific, opinion. Therefore, if the matters that have the greatest import to man, such as the values of freedom, are to be given any warrant other than revelation, a different view of reason and values is required. This is the general theme of the naturalist and humanist philosophers who are presented in this book. About a generation ago the naturalist position, as represented by Santayana and Dewey, was a dominant influence in American philosophy; but in the intervening period it has been under determined attack by the religious philosophers from one quarter and the analytic philosophers from another. The recognition of this situation, reinforced by a widespread feeling among outsiders who survey technical philosophy in its various formal and linguistic proportions today, has nourished the impression that value theory has reached a dead end. In such a climate it is not difficult to understand the reluctance of American political scientists to advance an articulate defense of their democratic values and why they turn, instead, to extensive empirical research or the practical advocacy of policies they consider desirable—without theoretical justification for their chosen "ends." For these reasons, an outline of some basic features of this position deserves attention.

The key element in the position is that certain types of ethical judgment arise in situations of human conduct which are justified by recourse to evidence, reasoning, and interpersonal validation. These judgments are about things and activities which, under specified conditions, will be found to provide satisfaction or to promote well-being. They differ from purely emotive judgments that report the act of desiring or being satisfied, inasmuch as warranted ethical judgments are *appraisals* that something is desirable or genuinely satisfactory. They are, in short, valuations made in the light of deliberation concerning probable consequences and comparative worth, and based on experience. And they differ from moral rules or conventions which prescribe what must be done under certain conditions to win group approval or to avoid group censure. For warranted ethical judgments may involve the deliberate rejection of moral rules because they sometimes conflict one with another, or result in undue hardship, or obstruct recurring human inclinations, or heighten social tensions, or even, finally, because they have been rendered obsolete.

For the simplest initial example: When we tell a child, "It is bad to eat too much candy," we are predicting certain consequences (short- and long-range) of a disagreeable sort. We are distinguishing between the child's act of desiring, which is a sign of his physical or emotive preference, and what is in fact bad for him. There are, of course, more serious judgments involving the well-being of children, judgments indicated by the knowledge we may have of how to provide favorable conditions for a child's safety and self-development, and how to avoid the kind of setting and training that feeds anxiety and insecurity. Another illustration carries us to judgments involving matters of public policy, judgments that are advocated on grounds of promoting social well-being or avoiding social dangers. It is in this spirit that we find little disagreement about the need for policies which will prevent severe depression or tyrannies or wars—because these are social conditions which are normally judged to be bad. This is not to imply that the "hard" cases and bitter choices of personal life are absent on a social level; they are, of course, compounded and often mammoth as they rise up before the most enlightened minds and benevolent hearts. Nevertheless, it is of great importance, in this view, to recognize that the nature of decisions on public policy is continuous with the basic decisions we make about our children or the care of ourselves. The great and overriding human objectives of well-being are roughly what informed common sense would lead us to think they are, whether for the infant, the developing self, or the society that will crush its human members.

Ethical inquiry, so conceived, begins with specific problems of choice and decision-making and provides determinate clues as to values or ends capable of terminating those problems. These values are warranted by the character of the methods employed in reaching them, and they typically involve a process of constant intersubjective comparison, free criticism, theoretically the ideal of unlimited, open-ended inquiry. The result of such inquiry in practice is not a body of final knowledge or the discovery of absolute goods, but values which are assured of better warrant than those resulting from unreflective immediate experience, or from the high reaches of authority. Thus, values are relative to human experience of a particular sort—continuous, sustained, directed, intersubjective inquiry regarding the conditions for well-being. Like factual propositions, it is claimed these ethical valuations are judgments about observable and repeatable phases of experience, more exactly those phases in which men discriminate satisfaction and well-being. Like factual judgments, they are based, not on personal whim or group authority, but on evidence which is subject to interpersonal validation. These experiences judged in ethical propositions are observable in normal (relatively effective) living, which is, of course, not possible without considerable intersubjective support. They are also observable through the accumulative reports of the social sciences—

especially psychology, economics, and politics. Finally, as in scientific inquiry, we establish limited working hypotheses which predict that certain kinds of human behavior and political organization will, in the light of past experience, be conducive to human satisfaction, or will further the realization of social well-being.

It is this naturalistic use of the term "good" which makes sense of our ordinary concern in problems of human conduct, in which we attempt to make a reasonable choice among alternatives. This usage makes sense of certain professional concerns—like those of the doctor for the physical health of his patient, and of the psychiatrist for his patient's mental health; the economist for the economic health of society, and the political scientist for the politics of freedom. Contemporary naturalists also claim that this usage is in accord with the key concepts of some of the most illustrious moral philosophers in Western history. One example is Aristotle's treatment of eudaemonia as that activity of man involving the exercise of human faculties and capacities that provide well-being. Another example is Hume's view that "everything which contributes to the happiness of society, recommends itself directly to our approbation and good will. Here is a principle which accounts, in great part, for the origin of morality." A further example is the emphasis given to the principle of the greatest happiness, in the work of Bentham, Mill, and Sidgwick, in both ethical theory and political inquiry. The outstanding modern example is Dewey's analysis of the good as the desirable. His intent is to distinguish the desirable from what is in fact desired, at a given time and place, but to relate it to what would generally be desired by those reflecting on its consequences. It is argued that what is common to all the philosophers cited is their belief that the fundamental usage of ethical terms goes beyond a purely emotive level by calling for deliberation on consequences; and they all agree in rejecting superempirical sources and sanctions for moral rules, which they believe require the context of human experience to supply the evidence for the warranted generalizations of moral judgments. All alike find basic value in the growth, development, and fulfillment of man, and are therefore led to stress the role of shared experience and intelligence in establishing what is in fact good for the human person and the state.

The essential requirement of this conception of ethical inquiry is that it conform to the basic rule that governs all scientific inquiry, a rule which Charles Sanders Peirce gave classic formulation in his words: "Do not block the way of inquiry." In short, they contend that there are no limits, no aspects of experience that *cannot* be made the proper subject of human investigation or reason.

This closes the analysis of the basic issues of reason and values raised by the philosophers presented in this book. It is for the reader to continue to reflect on the grounds for the different positions argued by some of the most brilliant philosophical men of our time who have taken seriously the grave concerns of modern man.

CHAPTER XX

TOWARD A COMMON FAITH

1. Toward Civilization

We are at the end, and it is only proper to look for some summing up—a summation that should involve both an accounting of what we can learn from the major contemporary philosophies for a time of crisis and what we ourselves can honestly espouse and hope for. I think it is important and useful for this purpose to distinguish two parts or aspects of any adequate philosophy for our times—first, a personal philosophy in the direct and immediate sense of its relation to one's own life and one's own happiness; and, second, a more general, political, social, economic side which recognizes that we live as persons in a world which engages us in problems of general human significance. In making this distinction I do not mean to imply that they are wholly separable problems, but I want to emphasize that we do not go far without understanding that there is a sound distinction.

We have seen that the common position of the authors in this book involves a defense of values of civilization, and an analysis of the conditions, costs, and limitations of civilization. Civilization is a perilous adventure of co-operative intelligence. It is perilous because it is a human affair, and the quality of both co-operation and intelligence can affect the outcome. Co-operation stresses the necessity for communal activity of some sort—the trust, good will, workable arrangements for getting things done; there is no magic about co-operation, and its forms, conditions, limits change with other changes in the human condition.

Intelligence stresses the reflective appraisal of means and consequences. Co-operation is not a fixed organic form, but a cultural product of cumulative human effort. Intelligence is not an abstracted reason, but an organization of feelings, emotion, and reason. It is, when most effective, a co-operative activity, but it is always the quality of an individual awareness.

The history of man makes technology clearly a paramount fact. Changes and developments of technology mean more control over nature. Those in the West, or those who still speak for the older traditions of Oriental thought, who would reject all such means, and purify themselves by denying even instrumental value, cannot provide an effective workable philosophy for a world community that is being slowly born out of those technological and associated efforts of man. This is part of the significance of the rise of the underdeveloped countries—the joint acceptance of technological power and of spiritual efforts. But where a wholesale acceptance of technique has meant production and economic power as the values that solve all human problems, the rejection of means tends to lead to the poverty, not only of the body but also of the human mind and spirit.

On the other hand, it is not true that modern science creates once for all the need for one world, in a completely political sense, and for equal economic distribution. It is not true that we have solved the economic problem and the technical problem, and that what defeat us are our social institutions and our values. This is a crisis of civilization, not because of one thing, the Bomb, but because even if there were no Bomb the problems of our society at all levels—personal, social, political, economic, and spiritual—come into conflict and are involved in total reconstruction. We cannot solve the economic problem on the theory that there is plenty which is made scarce by the market mechanisms and sovereign powers. The underdeveloped and nonwhite parts of the world, which are two-thirds of the present population, cannot have their requirements simply met, either by a program of vast aid from the developed countries or by themselves. The gap between their aspirations and their resources is real. For similar reasons, we just cannot organize a world government the way the United States was organized. And therefore to make the success of such a government the condition for a future of mankind is, at present, an illusion.

The Bomb provides a dramatic and critical symbol for the crisis of our civilization, but it does not involve either death or the millennium. This is to take the symbol for what it symbolizes. Man, throughout his history, has tried to fulfill his humanity both by developing the powers of the person and of the community. This has involved the use of his reason, applied to the development of tools and technology and applied to the better organization of his social and political life. It is true that never before has there been a technological development which has involved so much power to destroy a great part of human society, the part that takes itself to be the world. It is true that never before have many men so clearly realized their common destiny as involving measures to achieve political arrangements which permit men the world over to pursue their diverse interests. It is true that many men have keener sense of the existence and difference of existing cultures, and of the span of man's career on the earth. Previous crises did not involve as large a part of the earth, as great a number of people, as many cultures, or the feeling of such total world destruction. The problems raised by the crises of our time demand the recognition of a principle of what might be called "strategic decisions." We cannot wholly undo the past; we must recognize the pressures that flow from world population, modern technology, giant states. A philosophy which would deny any of these cannot be adequate.

Within the conditions consistent with a protracted cold war, we can try to become more responsible persons and as part of this development try to work out arrangements which advance man's career in science, in art, in ethical attitudes. What our thinkers show us is the recognition of the need for a solution of the tension between human intelligence, embodied in critical science, and human values, embodied in programs of social organization and ethical faiths. On this level, we find agreement between Radhakrishnan, whom one might take superficially as the spokesman for the mystic East, and Einstein, whom one might take superficially as the spokesman for the materialistic West. One wants science to enrich human life and the other wants human ends to guide science; but they are both concerned with the good life and the good society, and they both see the practical possibilities of its developing from this time of crisis. Radhakrishnan sees it, in strategic terms, simply as the necessity of recognizing the role of the East in any future that we can foresee, and that the East, strategically, requires not only the techniques of the West, but the vision that welds together human ends and scientific means. Einstein sees it strategically as the practical requirements that flow from advanced atomic developments that will destroy man if he does not come to agree that science is a value only when it is guided toward just human ends. All the other philosophers fall somewhere between these extremes, with different accents, to propound this common faith.

2. *Toward the Person*

One of the characteristic features of the most compelling and attractive philosophies of our time is their personal aspect, after philosophy passed through a period in which the personal element was almost wholly neglected. I believe that many Western intellectuals have come to their present faith after minimizing the personal and stressing purely social-economic dogmas. Marxism, in one form or another, was attractive bait for many people in the thirties. It appeared to explain scientifically, on a vast historical scale which embraced apparently the entire human race over time and over the globe, why crisis was inevitable, why wars, revolutions, depressions, fascism, and so on, had come to dominate contemporary history. It also appeared to provide a way out, a fatherland on the one hand, and a religion for the alienated on the other. Here was a kind of personal and therefore ethical allegiance which was more commanding because the doctrine required that one should lose one's soul to find oneself a willing servant in a transcendent cause. Thus, Marxian dialectics and apologetics appeared to provide a personal ethos by requiring the denial of personality, as a "bourgeois" excrescence.

But this God has truly failed. Its failure is partly due to its incorrect analysis of social, economic, and political factors in contemporary society and partly because there is no substitute for a personal commitment, a philosophy that recognizes personal needs and the human element in the individual person as well as in social affairs. Indeed, it is, in a basic sense, the caricature of man that accounts for the failure of Marxism to explain society. We as individuals are not cogs in any economic machine; we are not molecules in a great wave of the future. We are individuals who are purposive. We choose and value; and our joint choices and values, both as shared and as opposed, make our future.

We have come to learn, through history, psychoanalysis, and anthropology, as well as and most importantly through personal experience, that there are factors that make for happiness as well as conditions that obstruct it. Life under most conditions is valued by practically all men. Life is almost, if not quite, the closest approximation to an absolute value. It is this that is reflected in religious and ethical commandments and in democratic theory—that life is an inalienable or, if one prefers, a sacred right. Persons are human beings, and human beings, whether in primitive societies, in backward colonial areas, in the Soviet Union or in the United States, have recognizable needs and satisfactions. The primary point is that there are legitimate activities and experiences which are both human and pleasurable and that these activities are not to be denied and should not be thwarted simply because there are overwhelming critical issues facing modern man. Only a neurotic person would be compelled to deny the satisfactions and pleasures that are available as long as life itself continues, even though it should be possible, under sound and rational and well-meaning social arrangements, to multiply these moments and give them greater security.

This wisdom of trying to find what happiness one can flows from the realistic appreciation that the danger of our times is not the same as pessimism that flees from reason and creates despair. After all, threats of atomic war caused prophets of doom to oversell their case at several points in the recent past. We were told that the Marshall Program of European Recovery would force the Russians to march; then NATO; then the European Army. Perhaps they merely got their dates mixed? Is war "inevitable"? It is not, although these are grave risks which we can only avoid through the patient practice of vision fortified by courage, and intelligence rooted in common human ideals.

Thus, troubles and crisis in the contemporary world do not deny the possibility of living reasonably while we live. What is necessary for that? Socratic self-knowledge; and enough knowledge of the world to comprehend what alternatives are open to one and which are favorable to one's true interests. In addition, we need the capacity for laughter. In this connection, it should be recalled that Aristotle first defined the person as the animal capable of laughter. This further implies the ability to laugh at oneself and to enrich the purely personal fate by the outgoing identification with what is best in mankind. Such an enlightened personal philosophy provided consolation on notable occasions to men caught in ultimate human predicament. Its distinctive endowment is to permit man to stand alone if need be.

3. Toward Freedom

But we need not stand alone: Machiavelli's advisory observation that "Where men's lives and fortunes are at stake they are not all insane" might be brought to bear upon the quest for freedom. It is a prime responsibility for anyone who is concerned to defend human freedom to stipulate the essential conditions without which we have an unfree, nondemocratic society. I believe the formulation of a theory of republican government which specifies these essential conditions is the significance of the work of Jefferson and Madison, two philosopher-statesmen in the American political tradition. They indicated certain minimal conditions of freedom, those by which we may test whether a given society is free and the extent to which it is free. They picked four—equality of consideration under the law; majority consent for the government; freedom for all citizens to inquire; and freedom to choose, subject to the other conditions.

The first essential test, equal treatment under the law, is the principle of justice, and involves a society that is structured, with some degree of order and recognized "liberties." This is a precondition for the other conditions of freedom, since it is the adherence to this principle that provides reasonable security of life. As an explicit declaration, one can equate it roughly to the famous Thirty-ninth Article of Magna Carta which, of course, provides that "No free man shall be taken or imprisoned . . . or in any way destroyed . . . except by the lawful judgment of his peers or the law of the land." In the intervening history of seven hundred years, the common civil rights associated with this principle add to the basic stipulation that the law is no respecter of persons, the prohibitions against arbitrary arrest, detention, or exile; the right to fair trial before an impartial tribunal; and freedom from arbitrary interference with one's privacy, home, or family. Violation of this first condition is characteristic of modern totalitarianism, and in itself definitive of political slavery—where the rule of force can resort to mass murder, arbitrary imprisonment, and the invasion of every privacy without fear that the destruction worked on a man will involve the possibility of redress under equal and impartial law. Thus, the function of this first condition is to give political significance to "the right to life."

The second condition, the consent of the governed, under some standard approximating majority rule, provides for the freedom to influence the equal and impartial law we live under. The right of all adults to participate in the government must be given operational reality, at least in terms of regular elections, at stated intervals, and in a situation of real choice—that is, where the voter may choose from at least two candidates, and where there may be at least two opposing parties. "Majority rule" may indeed be subject to the charge of theoretical vagueness or literal inexactness in certain selected decisions of a democratic electorate, but in principle it has served, and can serve, as an impediment to élitist and despotic government, and as a positive directional standard to which progressives and reformers repair when government begins to cut free of a high degree of control or influence by "the people."

The third condition is related to the second, but broader. It is the freedom to explore all alternatives—which can only mean the freedom to inquire, to think, to speak, to write—so long as one does not seriously endanger the lives of others. This joining of republican or democratic theory with free inquiry is crystallized in a phrase that has more than historic interest—for it is a deliberate proposal to view the initial programs that might turn us in the direction of democratic society as "The American Experiment." The term "experiment" implies systematic investigation guided by an idea or hypothesis, rather than random activity. It suggests organized social inquiry in a setting which recognizes that everyone shares, in some degree, the supreme political power. It envisages the resolution of political problems in a social environment of intellectual freedom, criticism, trial and error, and a continuing process of self-correction. Moreover, the resort to an unusual term like "experiment" applied to political theory was, in its time, eloquent of the severe critical judgments these republican theorists made of nondemocratic governments and societies. They dared to advocate the hypothesis that democratic society would honor human freedom more, on the grounds that the monarchies, aristocracies, and dictatorships that they knew, or knew about, had blatantly and decisively employed power in the interest of an élite, a special class, or for aggressive wars, at the expense of "the most numerous class" in society, the people.

Their uncompromising rejection of the evil of concentrated power, and the easy transition from it to tyranny, provided all the stimulus they needed to try to formulate a political form that would promote human freedom. These conditions illuminate the political significance of "the right to liberty."

The fourth condition, the freedom to choose, envisages the manner of life of individuals. The range of choice can be wide in some contexts and relatively narrow in others, but there must be some real choice about the manner of the individual's life, his occupation, enjoyments, and so on, subject only to the other conditions. It is "the right to the pursuit of happiness."

It is obvious that all four conditions are interrelated. It should be equally obvious that no absolute freedom has been invoked. There are degrees of freedom, depending on the situation, resources, and overriding problems of the time; and also depending on the extent to which the above four conditions are realized. Thus, one other essential truth that is appropriately put in referring to democracy as an "experiment" is the obvious fact that an experiment can fail, and that the process of trial and error that it invokes is not one that calls for a perfected or rigid ideal. It is wholly consistent with a democratic experiment that there will be degrees of democratic realization and degrees of democratic failure. The development of a society organized by democratic political institutions can move in a democratic direction on some levels, or away from them in a more or less serious way. Difficult as it may be to demarcate, without a margin of theoretical dispute, what separates a "democratic" from a "nondemocratic" society, it cannot be sidestepped, and clearly relates to the defense of freedom as the end and standard of political action. In the characteristic language of his day, Jefferson was fond of putting the case for the moral superiority of democracy in this way: "The republican is the only form of government which is not eternally at open or secret war with the rights of mankind."

A final word on one of the most serious issues for contemporary democratic theory concerns the rule of the state in relation to welfare. The question here is worth posing, for it has been variously disguised and sometimes wrongly put. The question is: What must be done to give a positive content to freedom while maintaining sufficient limits on the state's power to secure the conditions for freedom? The empirical issue involved here embraces two sets of facts. The first set concerns nongovernmental power, which must be so controlled as to permit the larger range of freedom for ordinary people against any substantial nongovernmental restraints that might otherwise exist. The other set of facts has to do with the recognition that a danger always exists in providing more power to the government. Both sets of facts must be taken into account in specific issues about nationalization of industries or services, or about the extent of social security, or federal aid to education.

Since I have claimed that we have a vital democratic tradition in America in the thought and example of philosopher-statesmen like Jefferson and Madison, one might question what principles they afford in taming some of the most pressing issues of our time. For example, they did not deal in contemporary terms with the issues of big government in an industrial democracy; nor did they foresee the actual problems we face in the conflict between public interest and private interests associated with big business, big labor, and big agriculture. Most pointedly of all, how can they be appealed to for those momentous issues of foreign economic and political policy that today overshadow domestic problems and normal expectancies and may, if mishandled, obliterate the "experiment" along with the experimenters. All these questions are proper, and these are admittedly the areas where great eighteenth century philosopher-statesmen perforce left the labor and the defense of liberty to "those who come after us." But they did establish a basic framework for permitting the fuller use of organized intelligence on political matters; and they established the basic conditions for human freedom. These, in the light of new knowledge and new events, must be forever refreshed and deepened.

Some will say, mindful of a world stocked with hydrogen bombs and jeopardized by the continued testing of new nuclear weapons, that never was freedom more precarious, more difficult to maintain and extend, than it is in this critical age. This may be accepted or countered in various ways, but the issue is whether one must therefore consider that the ideals of "life, liberty, and the pursuit of happiness," the ideals of freedoom, reason, and science, have shown themselves bankrupt. Or have they proved themselves to be the continuing ideals of the non-Communist world—powerful enough to take root where they never did before? The philosophers who have been our spokesmen have a common faith, a faith that we can move forward to explore ways of life that would approach a life of freedom, of reason, and a world civilization.

INDEX

INDEX